Applied Ethics for Program Evaluation

This book is dedicated to our families
with a special note to
Gary Clure
Richard, Carl, and Autumn Clure
and
Ann Brown

We are glad you are here.

Applied Ethics for Program Evaluation

Dianna L. Newman
Robert D. Brown

SAGE Publications
International Educational and Professional Publisher
Thousand Oaks London New Delhi

For information address:

SAGE Publications, Inc.
2455 Teller Road
Thousand Oaks, California 91320
E-mail: order@sagepub.com

SAGE Publications Ltd.
6 Bonhill Street
London EC2A 4PU
United Kingdom

SAGE Publications India Pvt. Ltd.
M-32 Market
Greater Kailash I
New Delhi 110 048 India

Printed in the United States of America

Library of Congress Cataloging-in-Publication Data

Newman, Dianna L.
Applied ethics for program evaluation/Dianna L. Newman, Robert D. Brown.
p. cm.
Includes bibliographical references (p.) and index.
ISBN 0-8039-5185-X (cloth: alk. paper). — ISBN 0-8039-5186-8 (pbk.: alk. paper)
1. Evaluation research (Social action programs)—Moral and ethical aspects. I. Brown, Robert Donald, 1931- . II. Title.
H62.N587 1995
361.6′1′068—dc20 95-36416

96 97 98 99 10 9 8 7 6 5 4 3 2 1

Sage Production Editor: Gillian Dickens
Sage Copy Editor: Joyce Kuhn
Sage Typesetter: Janelle LeMaster

Contents in Brief

Detailed Contents

Preface

We have written this book out of a strong sense of need to address our own and our profession's sense of ethics. For the past several years, questions about the status of ethics in program evaluation have been part of the dialogue of professional evaluators. This dialogue has encompassed many forms—research studies, papers, debates, and, ultimately, multiple sets of guidelines for practice. As a result of these efforts, we needed to pause and reflect on the ethics of our practice. As we trained and supervised students, as we lectured and discussed the growth of evaluation methods, and as we conducted evaluations for diverse clients, we were struck continually by the variety and depth of ethical issues faced by evaluators on a day-to-day basis.

As part of our reflection on the ethical practice of evaluation, we examined multiple sources of information; each of these theoretical or practical sources gave us some guidance, but none provided us with a model that would aid us in ethical decision making, especially as it pertained to evaluation. As a result, we decided to develop a model of ethical thinking and decision making that would integrate components of models used by other service professions but that also would reflect the unique tasks, stresses, and risks of being a program evaluator. As we developed the model, we began to test various components of it with evaluators, stakeholders, and evaluation clients. The results of these research studies were used to modify and strengthen the model. This book presents the status of the model at the current time.

It is not our intention to present this work as the culminating guideline for ethical decision making in program evaluation. As we indicate throughout the text, questions of ethics are personal, corporate, and context specific. Our desire is to provide you with a framework for thinking about your practice and to assist you in your own ethical growth. We are continuing to test the model to find its strengths and weaknesses. We welcome your feedback on its applicability to your settings.

It is our hope that this book will be used in both formal and informal educational settings. We believe that it will prove useful in classes related to the training of evaluators and those who administer programs that others evaluate. In these settings, we suggest that the instructor use the material in the manner presented with special emphasis on discussion of the vignettes presented in Chapter 1 and throughout the book. The text also lends itself to use in workshops or specialty seminars for practitioners of evaluation or those who are only beginning the study of ethics. In these settings, we suggest that the materials in Chapters 2, 4, and 5 be emphasized and the material in Chapter 1 be used for group discussions or "hands on" work. The material in Chapters 3, 6, and 7 could be used for a second-level workshop or seminar of interest to those who train evaluators, conduct research on evaluation, or are interested in the delineation of theories in evaluation.

Many people are responsible for the final form of this book. We would like to acknowledge Karen Kitchner for her scholarly contributions in analysis and presentation of ethical principles and Harry Canon, who as a colleague, has stimulated our thinking about ethical issues, especially as they apply to professional practice. Special thanks also go to C. Deborah Laughton of Sage, who carried us through the writing and editing process and never lost faith in our vision. Michael Morris and Katherine Ryan made important substantive contributions, increasing the quality of the book with their insights. Thanks also go to Linda Papa for her faithful work on the manuscript and to the family of Maribel Gray for sharing her last months with us. We appreciate your time, effort, and faith.

1

Introduction

THE NEED FOR ETHICS IN PROGRAM EVALUATION

A Reader's Guide to Chapter 1

This chapter introduces the need to study ethics in relationship to program evaluation. It consists of two major components: an overview of the ethical debate in program evaluation and a series of examples derived from real practice. Specific topics covered are the following:

- The need for a model of ethical thinking
- Overview of a proposed model
- Overview of the debate presented in the following chapters
- Vignettes based on the model

Dilemma: a choice or a situation involving choice between equally unsatisfactory alternatives

Ethic(al): relating to or involving good and evil and moral duty, questions of right and wrong

Merriam Webster's Ninth
New Collegiate Dictionary (1988)

Newspaper headlines frequently describe alleged ethical misconduct by professionals in many fields. Psychotherapists are sanctioned for having sexual relationships with clients, dentists are accused of fondling young women, investors are caught using insider information, and politicians are charged with taking bribes. Every year at least one major athletic program is under fire for misbehavior in its recruiting procedures, and shock waves are felt when prestigious universities make headlines for allegedly misspending federal funds. Beginning with Watergate in the early 1970s, the increased reporting of ethical misconduct has stimulated commentators, practitioners, and users to suggest inclusion of, or greater attention to, ethical issues in training programs for professionals.

Among the good results emanating from this increased attention has been the growing discussion of ethical issues by professionals and also the increased emphasis on including ethical courses in professional training programs. A less positive outcome is that our interest is too often centered on "headline-making behavior," incidents and dilemmas that lead to attention-getting articles in newspapers or on television newscasts. Usually, these involve salacious acts or incidents of major fraud. This focus on the highly scandalous can lead to individual professionals ignoring the ways in which their own behavior is consistent or inconsistent with ethical principles. Also, small, everyday indiscretions seem dwarfed in relationship to the headlines about state and national scandals. "After all," many of us are tempted to think, "I'm not embezzling large sums of money, nor am I having a sexual liaison with my clients." Unethical behavior becomes identified too easily as having to do with the extraordinary and with others rather than our own ordinary, everyday behavior.

We believe strongly that professionals are confronted with ethical dilemmas and decisions every day of their professional lives and that this is true for professional evaluators as well. Rarely does the ethical misconduct of an evaluator appear in print, much less make the front-page headlines of the local newspaper. Nevertheless, the everyday decisions that an evaluator makes about what projects to accept, what information to collect, and how and when to report the information often have ethical implications and represent ethical dilemmas for the evaluator.

THE NEED FOR A MODEL OF ETHICAL THINKING

Few professionals have had much formal training in ethics. At best, a one-semester course, but more likely a chapter or two in a text or a seminar session or two in a professional course, represents the typical exposure of graduate or professional students to ethical issues in an formal manner. This is also true for professional evaluators. A recent analysis of 21 evaluation textbooks sampled from those published between 1972 and 1994 found that 80% did not mention ethics at all. In books that did make reference to ethics or professional standards, the coverage averaged about four pages per book.

Most professionals rely on four sources as guidelines for their ethical thinking:

- *Intuition.* Example: An evaluator may have an intuitive feeling that something is wrong when a client wants to look over the handwritten open-ended responses to an evaluation question.
- *Past experience.* Example: Past experience prompts the evaluator to have an explicit statement in the contract specifying that parts of the evaluation report are not to be extracted without the evaluator's permission.
- *Observations of conventional behavior among colleagues.* Example: A new professional may discuss with and replicate colleagues' behavior when working with clients who want to change the wording in reports.
- *Ethical rules as presented in ethical codes.* Example: The Joint Committee Standards and the American Psychological Association Code of Ethics provide relatively concrete guidelines for specific situations.

All of these sources are appropriate, but they are often applied haphazardly or inconsistently or, because they do not cover the specific situation, are ignored. Consequently, the concerned professional is too often on uncertain ground when confronting a new situation. Practice, experience, and benefiting from past mistakes are excellent ways to learn, but in the case of ethical issues, they may result in learning too little too late. Also, the resulting focus is on making sure the evaluator does nothing wrong through commission or omission. This limits attention to the negative and minimizes, if not eliminates, attention to any proactive behavior the evaluator might take to be ethical.

Over the past 20 years, we have jointly and separately served as evaluators on over 30 major projects, encountered hundreds of clients and users, and talked with numerous evaluators. We have also, through our university affiliations, supervised students on over 200 projects and directed multiple intern settings. Throughout all of these experiences, we have perceived the need for a more structured way of studying and discussing the role of ethics in program evaluation. Through our work with personnel evaluation, we became acquainted with several models of ethical decision making. After studying, discussing, and experimenting with several, we found one that could be modified to best meet the needs of program evaluators. Because of our methodological backgrounds, however, we were not content merely to propose a model; we also wanted to validate it. Consequently, since 1982, we have been conducting multiple studies related to ethics in program evaluation. In these studies, all or parts of the model have been presented to over 2,000 stakeholders in the evaluation process. We have also tested the model in applied settings on actual projects. Using the feedback from these studies and applications, we have built, tested, rebuilt, and retested the proposed model. As a result, although we do not consider the model complete nor that it will meet every need, we do believe that the model in its current form can both serve as a guideline for ethical discussions and be useful in ethical decision making.

OVERVIEW OF THE MODEL OF ETHICAL THINKING

The purpose of this book is to provide a theoretical model of ethical decision making for practitioners of program evaluation. The model, as presented, is based on Kitchener's (1984) five ethical principles: respecting autonomy, avoiding undue harm, doing good, being fair, and being faithful. These principles have served as the basis for development of ethical codes for several other professions, and a review of ethical codes indicates that they are typically found in the codes of most organizations. Underpinning these five principles is the belief that evaluators serve in different roles both within and across programs. The three most common roles are those of director/administrator, methodologist, and reporter. Our own experience and the literature indicate that our perceptions of membership in a profession and in society are both becoming increasingly common roles for evaluators and consequently have been included in our later writings. Our purpose in proposing this ethical framework is to generate discussion and research about the status of ethics in program evaluation. We acknowledge the fact that some readers may disagree with some or all of the principles and roles; however, the fact of disagreeing will generate dialogue and further the understanding of an important issue in evaluation.

BEGINNING THE DIALOGUE

To encourage discussion and research on ethics in program evaluation, we have provided a number of examples of ethical dilemmas experienced by evaluators or clients. Several of these examples are placed near the end of this chapter as a means of beginning the dialogue through the realization that different perceptions occur as to appropriate practice. Other examples appear throughout the book to stimulate continued examination of specific points. We encourage the reader to refer to these examples while progressing through the text.

Chapter 2 presents the proposed framework for ethical principles in program evaluation and provides the reader with a theoretical background in ethical reasoning. Chapter 3 summarizes our current research, providing evidence of the validity of the framework and showing its relationship to practice. Chapter 4 translates the proposed framework into a decision-making model and also presents a possible means of examining ethical dilemmas and suggested ways of sorting out the issues. Chapters 5 and 6 address special issues related to the application of ethical principles to program evaluation: Chapter 5 discusses the impact of various roles on evaluators' practice and how these roles change perceptions of acceptable practice, and Chapter 6 discusses the issue of acceptable practice in special contexts and provides information on their impact on ethical reasoning. Chapter 7 delineates a series of activities that we believe will facilitate the discussion of ethics in program evaluation and that will aid in the growth of the profession. In this final chapter, we also attempt to debunk a series of myths common to the field of applied ethics.

EXAMPLES OF ETHICAL DILEMMAS: VIGNETTES OF ETHICAL PRACTICE

The 10 vignettes that follow reflect a variety of settings, programs, and viewpoints. Both clients and evaluators perceive ethical issues as important but frequently for different reasons. It is important to note these differences. The vignettes are organized under headings representing different roles performed by evaluators. This does not mean that the ethical dilemma is caused or occurs only at that point. It is possible that, in reflecting on these vignettes, many readers will see the seeds and the fruits of the dilemma at different points.

Readers are encouraged to weigh each vignette against their own experiences and values. Some will perceive a particular vignette as representing a serious violation of their ethical standards, others may perceive the solution as obvious and will have already met and solved that dilemma several times, and still others may not perceive a particular vignette as portraying a dilemma at all. Our objective in presenting these vignettes is to provide the reader with a wide range of problems that will allow exploration of alternative solutions and aid in the development of ethical thinking.

All vignettes presented within this book are based on real-life experiences with alterations of name, agency, and site details. To obtain the vignettes, we interviewed professional evaluators, consumers of evaluation, and other stakeholders, asking them for examples of situations where they felt ethical violations had occurred. The respondents' experience level with evaluation ranged from beginning to 20-plus years of service; both evaluators and evaluation clients were interviewed, and in some situations, the respondent had served in both roles. We found in collecting, editing, and validating these vignettes that, indeed, "truth is stranger than fiction." Selecting the sample vignettes for inclusion proved to be a difficult process, for each was an ethical issue for that particular respondent. The vignettes have been numbered and provided with a mnemonic title for later reference and are presented under the evaluator roles of consultant/administrator, data collector/researcher, reporter, member of profession, and member of society. These roles are discussed further in Chapter 5.

The Evaluator as Consultant/Administrator

One of the initial areas of evaluator-client contact is as an expert/consultant or administrator representing a unit that conducts evaluations. In this role, the evaluator is responsible for obtaining contracts, establishing the boundaries of the evaluation, maintaining formal records, and directing staff members in the process of evaluation. It is in this role that the evaluator is an entrepreneur, politician, salesperson, staff manager, budget analyst, and public relations director. Of major importance at the initiation of a project, this role recurs at frequent intervals throughout the project.

Vignette 1.1 Abuse of Expertise?

George Harlan is contacted by a major state agency about responding to their Request for Proposal. George sends for the material and agrees that he and his staff have the credentials to conduct the evaluation. He spends several days preparing a proposal and bid. Two weeks after the deadline, he is called by the agency, informed that his bid is the only one under serious consideration, and asked to attend a meeting the next week to clarify the evaluation proposal. At this meeting, 3 hours are spent explaining, modifying, and documenting a valid sample selection procedure that will meet the grant's needs. The next day, he receives a phone call that the agency has decided not to hire anyone to conduct the evaluation at this time. Two months later, George is talking to colleagues and finds out that the agency is conducting the evaluation with its own staff "and has a fantastic sampling plan." After taking a day to think about the process, George is very unhappy and feels used.

- Did the agency have the right to use George's plan?
- What can or should George do now? Should he call the agency director and risk bad feelings, or let the issue go and hope for future contracts?
- Does the agency owe George anything?
- How could George stop this from happening in the future?
- Who owned the plan? George or the agency?

Vignette 1.2 Middle Management Crunch?

As a middle manager, Joe Blank heads up a small evaluation staff in a large agency. His team is usually in great demand and has more projects than it can handle. In fact, Joe has just submitted his yearly budget request and is asking for more staff. On this day, Joe gets to the office and finds a message requesting that he attend an immediate meeting with the Bureau Director. At this meeting, Joe is welcomed warmly, thanked for the budget update, and invited to give his staff the opportunity to conduct a major research project. Joe points out that they are already understaffed on the current projects, have their focus on evaluation rather than research, and additionally have no staff member with content expertise or interest in the proposed study. The Bureau Director responds that the project is an area in which he, the director, has a personal stake and that it would be for the good of the agency. Joe responds that he will have to speak to his direct supervisor before he makes a commitment. Early the next day, Joe gets a phone call from the Bureau Director stating that Joe's team must either take on the project or lose staff for reassignment to it. Consequently, Joe pulls two evaluators off current projects, delays the completion date of three reports by 6 months, and leads the Director's project.

- Did Joe make the right decision?
- How much of this should he report to other clients when explaining late reports?
- Did the Bureau Director have the right to make this demand?
- Were there other alternatives?
- If this happens again, what should Joe do?

The Evaluator as Data Collector/Researcher

This is the role of the evaluator seen most frequently by program staff at the project site level. In this role, the evaluator becomes an expert technician who can use a multitude of tools to aid in the collection and interpretation of information. He or she is carrying out the process agreed on between the client and the consultant/administrator and is responsible for collecting, analyzing, and interpreting the information called for by the evaluation plan. In this role, the evaluator will have contact with a wide range of program stakeholders and will be working directly with program personnel.

Vignette 1.3 Confidentiality of Sources Versus Good of the Program

Sally Miles, Director of Science Education for a local district, is evaluating a newly proposed middle school curriculum by obtaining teachers' perceptions. After several meetings with the teachers, it becomes obvious that a significant core is opposed to the new curriculum. Without revealing who is opposed, Ms. Miles informs the principal that there may be implementation problems if the curriculum is selected. The principal wants the names of the teachers who are opposed to the curriculum, stating that perhaps a little individual assurance will be enough to change their opinions. Ms. Miles believes the new curriculum is better than the current one and wonders if maybe the problem is just "fear of the unknown." The principal assures Ms. Miles that the teachers will never know that their names were given out because the principal will speak to all teachers. Ms. Miles gives the principal the names.

- Has Ms. Miles made the right choice?
- Which is more important—teacher confidentiality or the students' right to a good program?
- Did the principal have a right to the information?
- Was there an alternate solution?

Vignette 1.4 The Need to Intervene

Tom Smith is serving, and has been serving, as a consulting evaluator for several years. He has recently acquired a contract with an out-of-town school district to evaluate the effectiveness of using manipulatives in their elementary math curriculum. Part of his evaluation includes observing teachers while they present the material in the classroom. After 2 days of regular observations, Tom sits in on Ms. Brown's third-grade class where she is teaching multiplication. To Tom's amazement, Ms. Brown is using the method correctly but is teaching the wrong fact (i.e., $6 \times 8 = 54$). After 15 minutes, he observes that the students are getting very frustrated because their answers do not match Ms. Brown's. Ms. Brown is getting frustrated because the students are not understanding the concept. The situation is rapidly deteriorating into chaos. Tom steps to the front of the room, corrects the facts written on the board, points this out to the students, and reiterates the concept. He then returns to his seat and resumes his observations.

- Did Tom intervene in the program?
- Should he have corrected the material then, later, or never?
- Is the evaluation now valid?
- Which is more important—the role of objectivity, nonintervention in the classroom, students' rights/needs, or teachers' feelings of adequacy?
- Was there an alternate way of handling the situation that would have not raised questions of validity and intervention?

The Evaluator as Reporter

In this role, the evaluator puts a major emphasis on communicating results to various clients, audiences, and stakeholders. At this point, the evaluator may, once again, become a salesperson, a motivator, an objective mediator, or a catalyst between opposing sides. The importance of utilization, although present in the two previous roles, becomes paramount in this role. Traditionally, this role occurs at the end of the evaluation and is still seen by some clients as the final stage of the evaluation process. A growing number of clients and evaluators, however, are incorporating this role throughout the evaluation process and are adding a creative component to the method of reporting.

Vignette 1.5 Report Ownership

Harry Levin has completed an evaluation on an innovative mathematics project funded by the State Department of Education. John Newley is the agency contact, program developer, and direct recipient of the evaluation report. Both Harry and Joe are pleased with the program and the report. Six months after completion of the project, Harry receives a package from a publisher. Enclosed are three copies of the newest issue of *Math Teacher Today*. Puzzled, Harry flips the pages until he finds an article entitled "An Innovative Math Program for Today's Schools" by John Newley and Harry Levin. Harry begins to read the article; halfway through he quits reading and gets his copy of the report he submitted to John Newley. After double-checking the entire article, Harry's perception is confirmed; the entire article is a word-for-word copy of his report. Irate, Harry calls John, demanding to know why John would presume to coauthor something that Harry wrote. John calmly replies that Harry was paid for the report, that the report now belongs to John, and that John was actually doing Harry a favor by including Harry as coauthor. Harry hangs up, very upset.

- Was John right? Does the report now belong to him?
- Where does the line between authorship and paid-for copy begin?
- Is there anything Harry can do about this now?
- How can Harry avoid this problem in the future?

Vignette 1.6 The Helpful Reporter?

Dr. Art is a program developer for a small state agency whose major function is to serve as a catalyst for other state agencies providing human services. His current program brings together and coordinates services related to neonatal disability care. As part of the coordination effort, the other agencies request an evaluation that will examine all their services as a joint effort. Dr. Art agrees with the request, seeks funding from his director, and hires an external evaluator. The evaluator goes to work and begins to examine the various programs sponsored by the agencies. The evaluation is scheduled to take approximately 1 year. Three months later, Dr. Art goes to a meeting and is approached by one of the agency directors who says she is quite pleased with evaluation reports she has been getting. Puzzled, Dr. Art calls the evaluator and asks if interim reports are being issued. The evaluator's response is that "yes," she is issuing interim reports to the agency heads as she evaluates their services. Dr. Art reminds the evaluator that she has been hired by Dr. Art's agency and that the goal of the evaluation is to compare *joint* services. Consequently, Dr. Art requests that he receive copies of all reports, if not before, at least at the same time as all agency heads. The evaluator responds that the reports are only interim in nature, useful only to agency heads of the specific program under evaluation, and that the final report will combine and compare all information. Six months later, despite two more requests from Dr. Art, the agency heads still are receiving individual interim reports about their specific programs, and Dr. Art is still not getting any copies of any reports.

- In this situation, is the evaluator underreporting or overreporting?
- If the reports make the stakeholders happy, what are the evaluator's responsibilities to Dr. Art?
- Is there any way that Dr. Art could solve this problem at the 3-month point, at the 9-month point, at conclusion of the project, and on future projects?
- Is the evaluator just being insensitive to Dr. Art's request, or is she improving ultimate utilization by including other stakeholders?

The Evaluator as Member of a Profession

This role reflects the evaluator's membership in a growing peer group that is involved in a common task. There is an interactive relationship among members of a profession in terms of acceptable practice, training and experiences, development of theory, and commitment to further professional growth and development. Membership in a profession is a developmental role; one's perception of belonging and involvement may range from none to total commitment.

Vignette 1.7 Monitoring Peers

An independent team of evaluators has been hired to conduct a meta-evaluation of state-sponsored innovative evaluations. For the past 2 years, the contracting agency has been attempting to generate higher-quality evaluations by providing extra funds for evaluations using qualitative data. In reviewing the evaluations, the meta-evaluation team determines that one particular evaluation has an inflated budget when cost is compared to evaluation product. Further investigation reveals that the evaluator charged three times the normal amount for services rendered than did other evaluators with similar qualifications on similar projects. Examination of the report and follow-ups on utilization of information indicate that nothing useful came out of the report because there were no funds left for "disbursement of results."

- What should the meta-evaluators do? How much of this, if any, should be reported to the client?
- Are the evaluators obligated to report this information to anyone else? Should they discuss the issue with the project evaluator?
- Should they recommend that the agency set standard fees? What are the pros and cons of this recommendation?
- If the meta-evaluators do report this information, how do they phrase it? What, if anything, is wrong?

Vignette 1.8 The Roles of Internal and External Evaluators

As part of its grant for development of computer-assisted instruction, a local community college hires a half-time internal evaluator and a consulting external evaluator. The internal evaluator works closely with faculty and administration on the design, implementation, and restructuring of courses, and keeps in touch with local community needs. After a year, the internal evaluator has developed a lengthy, detailed list of recommendations she believes would improve the program and aid students and faculty. This memo is prepared for distribution to administrators at the quarterly board meeting, which occurs next month. In the meantime, the external evaluator is making a single 3-day trip to see the campus, meet project staff, and review documents. The internal evaluator is permitted to meet with the external evaluator for approximately 30 minutes over coffee. During that time, she provides him with a copy of the memo she will be presenting the next month. Three weeks later, and 2 days before the board meeting, the external evaluator submits a draft of his report, the major portion of which uses all of the internal evaluator's recommendations. No reference is made to the internal evaluator.

- Is the internal evaluator wrong to feel "used"? Should she not have shared her information with the external evaluator?
- What can she do in 2 days for her report?
- Who should monitor this situation? Anyone?
- Did the external evaluator fulfill his contract? Was he going behind the internal evaluator's back, or was he supporting the internal evaluator's findings?
- If something is wrong, how could an internal evaluator keep this from happening in the future?

The Evaluator as Member of Society

Overriding all of the other roles of the evaluator is the contextual background of both the evaluator and the program. An evaluator brings to the program a self-perception of what constitutes culturally and socially acceptable behavior. The role of the evaluator as a member of society reflects the evaluator's personal background and overlaps with his or her commitment to the profession and any other level of involvement in evaluation. The boundaries of this role are vague, frequently unrecognized by evaluators and clients alike, and only now beginning to be acknowledged. Phrases such as "good of the community," "greater good," and "overriding needs" are frequently used in discussion about this role.

Vignette 1.9 Benefiting the More Needy

Carla Rogers is director of a mid-size evaluation consulting agency. She has recently taken on two new projects. The first deals with providing formative information for a preschool program for at-risk youth in a low-socioeconomic-status community. The community is sponsoring the self-help project, and funding is limited. The second project is an evaluation of a weekend driver education program for a suburban community center. This program has been in existence for 5 years and needs its standard annual evaluation for continuation of funding. The project and evaluation are well funded. Carla is sitting at her desk, looking at the two projects and their budgets. The budget for the at-risk program is low and will not cover enough evaluator time and expenses to truly determine the worth of the program. The driver education program is well budgeted, evidence to satisfy grant needs is easily obtained, and in Carla's eyes, the results will have little obvious impact. Carla is wondering if she can juggle the two budgets and use some of the driver education funds to pay for extra evaluator time on the at-risk program.

- If Carla juggles the budgets, is she depriving the driver education client of its right to a full report?
- Is it ethical for her to do a lesser report on a "low impact" project so that she can do a better report on one that seems to have more impact?
- Is it Carla's money to juggle?
- Whose "good" is most important?
- What are Carla's options?

Vignette 1.10 The Good of the Individual

In the middle of evaluating a year-long medical technicians training program, Evaluator Harkins conducts several confidential interviews with students and faculty. During these interviews, several students and one faculty member indicate that sexual harassment is a frequent occurrence in classes taught by Professor X. Harkins takes this confidential information to the dean of the unit, who replies that she will deal with the problem immediately. A month later, it is announced that Professor X has decided to resign from the faculty and seek employment elsewhere. Several banquets and awards are announced in Professor X's honor. At this time, the interviews conducted by the evaluator indicate that students are very upset with the honors awarded Professor X and believe that "something should be done." The evaluator returns to the dean and suggests that some services should be made available for those who may have suffered harm by Professor X. The dean agrees in principle that this should be done but points out that (1) she has no evidence of actual harm nor of who might have been harmed—only Harkins has this information and was told in confidence—and (2) even if she knew the names she has no money for such services. Harkins responds with an inquiry as to where the funds were obtained for the banquets and awards. The dean responds that it is better for the institution as a whole if Professor X resigns with dignity, that counseling is available for any student who wants it through student services, and that the evaluator must remember that his information was obtained in confidence and was not part of the contracted evaluation. Two days later, Harkins receives a letter thanking him for his contribution to the program's evaluation and enclosing a check for full services rendered.

- Was Evaluator Harkins obligated to convey the information pertaining to sexual harassment to the dean when it was not part of the contracted work? Was he obligated to convey the feelings about the awards and to recommend counseling for those injured?
- Is this a situation in which Harkins should override confidentiality and contracts and make the information public? If he can do so without revealing names, should he?
- How should Harkins respond to the dean's termination of contract? Does this termination change his role as advocate for student aid?
- Would your responses have differed if the issue had been suspected misuse of funds instead of sexual harassment?

CONCLUSION

In this opening chapter, we introduced the need for the study of ethics in program evaluation and the need for a model to guide the discussion of ethics in program evaluation and in ethical decision making. We also presented a series of vignettes to illustrate the variety and complexity of ethical issues facing those involved in program evaluation. Some of these vignettes may appear to be trivial to the reader; to others, the vignette may appear to be serious either because of its consequences or because of the frequency of its occurrence. As the reader, you have no doubt noted that we did not provide an answer or a solution to any of the vignettes. That is because, for practicing evaluators and stakeholders, these were indeed dilemmas: situations where there were two or more conflicting options, each with its own positive and negative consequence.

The chapters that follow provide a proposed framework that can be used in weighing these options. The purpose of the framework is to facilitate thinking about and discussion of ethical issues pertaining to program evaluation. As in most decision making, there are no "right" answers; however, we do hope to give you tools that can be used to aid your decision making. The task of ethical decision making is not an easy one; it is not our purpose to make it any easier. Our purpose is only to make it a more informed decision.

2

Ethical Theories and Principles

A Reader's Guide to Chapter 2

This chapter provides background information on ethical theories and ethical principles that will help you as an evaluator be an ethical practitioner. The three primary sections of this chapter include the following:

- Provide definitions of key terms used when discussing ethics
- Describe how ethical theories provide criteria and questions to help guide ethical decision making
- Present ethical principles that can guide practice

Vignette 2.1 Following Codes and Rules

"I am a trained __________ (fill in—e.g., educational researcher, psychologist, sociologist). My profession has an ethical code and I am knowledgeable about the Joint Committee Standards. This is sufficient for me. I will abide by the codes and rules. I believe this is enough to permit me to be a competent and ethical practitioner in evaluation."

- Do you agree? Is abiding by the codes or standards sufficient?
- How frequently do you refer to the codes and standards? Are they useful?

The evaluator in Vignette 2.1 has access to ethical codes available to educational researchers (American Educational Research Association, 1992), psychological researchers (American Psychological Association, 1992), and those of other professional associations. These codes are useful for evaluators, as many of the ethical issues they confront overlap with similar issues in educational or psychological research. The lack of direct applicability of codes from these professional associations, however, served as the impetus for the development of standards by the Joint Committee on Standards (1981, 1994) (hereafter simplified to Joint Committee Standards) and the Evaluation Research Society (ERS) (Rossi, 1982).

Besides the ethical codes themselves, accompanying or supplementary case studies serve as valuable resources for comparing the specific situation we are confronting with the code, rule, or standard. For example, Joint Committee Standard P7 (Conflict of Interest) says, "Conflict of interest should be dealt with openly and honestly, so that it does not compromise the evaluation processes and results" (1994, p. 115). This standard suggests that the evaluator needs to be sensitive to and alert for potential conflicts of interest. Follow-up guidelines (e.g., "When appropriate, release evaluation procedures, data, and reports publicly, so they can be judged by other independent evaluators," p. 116) and examples of pitfalls (e.g., "Assuming that following well-established evaluation procedures will eliminate all conflicts of interest," p. 116) provide the evaluator with more specific criteria. Codes and rules can be helpful to the practitioner. No doubt, a solid grounding in the codes and working through case examples serves to sharpen our ethical thinking.

Adhering to professional codes, however, is insufficient. Codes, unfortunately, are too often designed to protect professionals from outside regulation and are often conservative. They are more likely to focus on what should not be done and on the minimal behavior rather than on what should be done and on ideal behavior. Kitchener (1984) criticizes the code for psychologists as not being explicit enough regarding issues of autonomy, justice, and truthfulness. Codes from different professional associations also can conflict with each other or give greater emphasis to some issues than to others. Another reason why ethical codes and rules for professionals may lack comprehensiveness is that they usually represent a consensus of opinions. For example, numerous professional groups were involved in the development of Joint Committee Standards, but, although appropriate, consensus agreements seldom fully represent ideals. Special interest groups or specific critical historical incidents are more likely to cause professional organizations to attend conscientiously to their own specific issues and concerns.

Despite these limitations, statements of ethical codes and rules are a hallmark of maturity for a profession, serving as useful guidelines for both experienced and new professionals. They are insufficient, however, unless the practitioner also has experience in relating these codes and rules to broader ethical theories and principles when thinking through ethical dilemmas.

DEFINITIONS

Box 2.1 Terminology

"I'm confused. I cannot figure out the difference between ethics and morality. How does all this differ from religious guidelines? Also, what is the difference between codes, rules, and standards? The American Psychological Association refers to a 'code,' but the Evaluation Research Society and the Joint Committee's guidelines are referred to as 'standards.' "

- How do you distinguish ethics from morality? From religion?
- Are ethics just a set of rules we follow? What if our practice is not that clear-cut? Are there higher levels of ethical thinking?

Ethics and Morality

There are three primary definitions of the term **ethics:** as the principles of morality, particularly those dealing with the right or wrong of an action; as the rules of conduct for members of a particular profession; and as the science of the study of ideal human behavior, the concepts of good behavior (Barnhart, 1966; Neilsen, 1936; Stein & Su, 1978). All three definitions come to mind for most of us when we consider professional ethics, but improper emphasis on any of the three to the exclusion of the other meanings leads to misunderstanding and potentially to misapplication.

When considering professional ethics, for example, we are prone to think that ethics defines what is wrong behavior—we think in terms of "ought not" more often than "ought to." This prompts us to emphasize behavior that we hope helps us avoid being unethical, but this focus leads us to neglect putting equal emphasis on proactive ethical behavior, or doing good. We confuse morality and ethics with religious prescriptions. We get caught up in the concept of rules, thinking of them as prescriptions that tell us specifically what we are to do in a particular situation. Also, we too often portray ethical behavior as ideal behavior as contrasted to pragmatic behavior that is necessary for our situation. As a result, we help perpetuate an ethos where ethical practice is characterized as an impractical ideal rather than as an achievable goal.

One way to characterize what constitutes an ethical statement is to define it by the terms used. Brandt (1959) defines a statement as ethical if it contains or implies the concepts of "is a desirable thing," "is morally obligatory," "is one's moral duty," "is reprehensible," or "is morally admirable" (p. 2). Among the individual words that, depending on their usage, may be considered as ethical terms are *immoral, wrong, right, shameful, discreditable, shocking, excellent, good, bad, wicked, sinful,* and *unjustifiable.* The word **moral** is often used synonymously with the word **ethical.** If a distinction is made, **ethics** is used to refer to the science of rules and standards of conduct and practice (Neilson, 1936), whereas **morals** refers to right practice. In many instances, the terms are interchangeable. For our purpose, we choose to use the terms ethics and ethical rather than morals and moral, with ethics referring to the study of right and wrong behavior and ethical referring to right practice.

Distinction Between Rules, Codes, Standards, Principles, and Theory

Ethical **rules** are specific statements about ethical behavior, in our situation related to a professional setting or professional practices. These rules prescribe behavior in a relatively detailed fashion. Rules about obtaining informed consent from evaluation or research participants, for example, are frequently specific, although they may vary in the amount of detail. The Joint Committee on Standards' (1994) statement regarding informed consent is relatively brief: "Standard P3: Evaluations should be designed and conducted to respect and protect the rights and welfare of human subjects" (p. 93). The guidelines that follow this statement discuss obtaining permission from authorities and the participants themselves and also issues related to anonymity and confidentiality. The American Psychological Association's (1992) and the American Educational Research Association's (1992) statements on the same matter are more detailed, presenting specific issues related to deception, filming subjects, minimizing invasiveness, permitting withdrawal, and informing participants of the results.

Ethical **codes** are compilations of ethical rules. The code of conduct for psychologists contains eight sections that focus on general standards, client evaluation, advertising, therapy, privacy and confidentiality, teaching and publishing, forensic activities, and resolving ethical issues (American Psychological Association, 1992). The ethical code for educational researchers has six sections: responsibilities to the field, research populations, intellectual ownership, editing and reviewing research, users of research, and students and student researchers (American Educational Research Association, 1992).

Writers and editors of guidelines specific to program evaluation have chosen to publish **standards** rather than codes or rules. In general usage, a standard is considered synonymous with a rule but also can suggest model behavior. The evaluation standards focus on overall quality of evaluations (Joint Committee on Standards, 1981, 1994; Rossi, 1982), not on specific rules. Use of the word ethics is assiduously avoided in these standards, but embedded within them are guidelines that might be considered ethical in nature. For instance, one section of the Joint Committee Standards is labeled "Propriety," which in everyday usage refers to what is proper or correct etiquette but can also refer to what is right or just (Barnhart, 1966). The Propriety section has eight subsections dealing with a service orientation, formal agreements, rights of human subjects, human interactions, fair assessment, disclosure of findings, conflict of interest, and fiscal responsibility (Joint Committee on Standards, 1981, 1994).

Ethical **principles** are broader than rules or codes and often serve as the foundation on which rules and codes are built. Principles such as "do no harm" and the Golden Rule provide guidance for many ethical decisions and are helpful when the rules or codes conflict or do not provide specific guidelines for our ethical concerns. The American Evaluation Association (1995) has recently approved a set of Guiding Principles for Evaluators. These principles are not rules, nor are they standards that must be met on every occasion. Rather, they offer guidance for ethical decision making and may, in the future, serve as the foundation for rules or codes when consensus is reached on a particular point of evaluation practice.

Finally, ethical **theory** refers to efforts to explain how people go about making ethical decisions. Ethical theory is the science of ethical decision making. Ethical theories are general ways of determining what behavior is considered right or wrong. Although they are more abstract than principles, theories also provide questions useful for ethical decision making.

In summary, ethical rules are specific statements about ethical behavior; ethical codes are compilations of ethical rules. Ethical standards can be synonomous with ethical rules and codes but may go beyond that definition to suggest model behavior. Ethical principles are broader than rules, serving as the foundation for codes. Principles stand as models of behavior and practice, providing and encompassing not only situational rules but also serving as guides for unspecified practice. Ethical theories provide a justification for how we make ethical decisions and aid us in resolving conflicts among principles or rules. (A succinct summary of these distinctions is provided in Table 2–1.) The next two sections of this chapter discuss ethical theories and ethical principles and how they can help us think about ethical issues.

TABLE 2–1 Summary Distinctions Between Ethical Rules, Codes, Standards, Principles, and Theories

Rules	Statements of specific dos and, most often, don'ts *Example:* Provide mean and median scores on all standardized tests used in an evaluation
Codes	Compilations of rules, usually adopted and endorsed by a professional organization *Example:* Ethical codes of American Educational Research Association and American Psychological Association
Standards	Similar to rules but often suggest ideal behavior *Example:* Make sure that all stakeholders understand the technical terms used in an evaluation report
Principles	Broader than rules or codes; provide guidance when rules conflict or when rules are not specific to the context *Example:* Evaluate programs as you would want your program to be evaluated
Theories	Justification or criteria for ethical decisions; the science and rationale for making ethical decisions *Example:* The consequences of an action are the determinants of what constitutes ethical or unethical behavior

ETHICAL THEORY AND CRITERIA

Vignette 2.2 Changing the Diet

The state agency on aging has sponsored a program on nutrition. Its intent is to improve the dietary eating habits of the elderly through reducing fat and cholesterol intake and improving intake of essential minerals and vitamins. The program is delivered through several methods including pamphlets delivered with meals on wheels and monthly brief workshops at senior centers. As the evaluator for the project, you find the workshops are well attended and the pamphlets well received. Participants are interested, and pre- and post-surveys indicate that they are making changes in their eating habits. You have some concern about the accuracy of the self-report data, however, and would like to validate it by some unobtrusive measures of the eating habits. The program staff is somewhat resistant to this idea; they are satisfied with the positive findings you report. You also note that those participating in the program tend to be those who already have good nutritional habits; those with poor habits seem not to be participating.

- What are the possible ethical concerns in this situation?
- What criteria would you use to decide what to do?

Numerous philosophers and ethical theorists describe and delineate their unique beliefs about what constitutes ethical behavior, and analysts place similar theories into categories in an effort to provide an overarching framework within which to compare the theories. Our purpose in this chapter is to use the theories to derive helpful guidelines for thinking about ethical behavior rather than to provide an in-depth comparative analysis. We find it helpful to classify ethical theories into five categories based on criteria used to decide whether the behavior is right or wrong: consequences, duty, rights, social justice, and ethics of care. Like other classifications proposed by ethical theorists, these categories are not necessarily mutually exclusive, nor do they necessarily lead to different decisions. Nevertheless, they are useful organizers when we consider our rationale for making ethical choices. In the following sections, we discuss the theoretical perspectives behind each of these criteria and comment on their strengths and weaknesses.

Consequences

In deciding what to recommend regarding the nutrition program for the elderly (see Vignette 2.2), the evaluator might consider the consequences of different recommendations. What is likely to happen if the recommendation is supportive of the current program? Will the program be able to shift directions and work with the elderly not participating and who have poor nutritional habits? Will a less than enthusiastic response result in the entire program being cut? Theories that propose that the rightness or wrongness of an action is determined by the consequences of that action are referred to as teleological theories. Utilitarianism, which is the most prominent of teleological theories, views actions as right when they result in the greatest possible good for the greatest number of people. To take the right action, you must estimate the effect of each action you are considering on all the parties involved and select the one that optimizes the satisfaction of the greatest number. From this perspective, lying is bad in some circumstances, but in other circumstances, it is good, depending on its consequences. As with most philosophical theories, utilitarianism's roots can be traced to the ancient Greeks and early philosophers, but its modern roots lie in late 18th- and early 19th-century writings of Bentham (1789/1970), Hume (1751/1983), and Mill (1863/1962).

Utilitarian theories are categorized as either act or rule utilitarian. If we use the act utilitarian approach, we emphasize making decisions solely on the outcomes or consequences of an act. An evaluator of the nutritional program using this rationale would choose the act that produces the greatest social good and make recommendations accordingly. An evaluator using the rule utilitarian rationale would follow a set of rules. This latter evaluator would find the rule relating to the situation and follow it. If the rule said a program accomplishing its stated objectives should be recommended for continuation, this rule would guide the evaluator to recommend continuation of the nutrition program. This may not lead to the greatest good in every specific situation, but over the long term, the rule utilitarians believe that this approach will result in the greatest societal benefit compared to all alternatives. Rules, according to this perspective, must be adhered to consistently and must not be bent to fit particular situations. We have a rule for automobile drivers that says they must stop for red lights. This rule is to be followed even on a Sunday morning with no other traffic in sight. Religious ideologies (e.g., the Ten Commandments), general society (e.g., the Golden Rule), and ethical codes (e.g., "Do not plagiarize") provide rules.

The act utilitarians, however, believe that in all situations, persons ought to act in a way that leads to the greatest good for the greatest number. The act utilitarians would be more likely to make a decision based on the particulars of the specific situation rather than search for a rule applying to all similar situations.

When using utilitarian ethics and the criteria of consequences as a guide for ethical decision making, the determination of what is good is essential. Utilitarians seek to maximize the good for the greatest number of people. But what is good? How is it defined and determined? Is it money, satisfaction, self-esteem, or some combination of these or other "goods"? Another key question is whose good is being considered. Is it the welfare of the decision maker? What if those receiving a service benefit from it but at the expense of those providing the service? These questions are particularly salient for the program evaluator.

Utilitarianism by itself does not tell us what is good. Hedonistic utilitarians believe that only pleasure and happiness are good in and of themselves. Pluralistic utilitarians broaden their definition of pleasure to include health, knowledge, and beauty. In their view, these are intrinsic goods, that is, goods without reference to possible future consequences; they are not means to another end but are good in themselves.

Much debate among utilitarian philosophers centers on the question of *whose* good, that is, whether the individual considers the consequences of an action for him- or herself (psychological egoism) and/or the consequences of an action for others or society in general. Some argue that a restrained egoist (one bounded by restrictions, such as legal regulations) with a long-term view, which considers the larger public good, is the most functional perspective for society. This debate is common within the business and human services sectors where there are frequent discussions about the long-term financial benefits of providing quality services and products versus practices that often seem to be aimed at making a quick profit or containing financial outlay at the expense of perceived quality.

Measuring and comparing goods is an essential feature of utilitarianism. If decisions are based on determinations of what produces the greatest net good, then some quantitative indicator of "goodness" is necessary so that comparisons can be made. Bentham (1789/1970), a 19th-century philosopher, developed a hedonic calculus that determined total happiness by adding quantitative units of individual happiness and subtracting units of individual unhappiness. Among his indicators were intensity, duration, degree of certainty and closeness, fecundity, and purity. With quantitative indicators of happiness, it would be possible to compare the value of similar goods from individual to individual or from group to group.

Although obtaining quantitative measurements of happiness and values may seem extremely difficult or even impossible, social scientists—and evaluators—have been doing so for decades. Likert-type scales asking individuals how satisfied they are with programs, whether or not they would come back again, and to what extent they would recommend the program to a friend have remained mainstays in the evaluator's assessment tool kit. Evaluators often summarize these data and use them to compare programs and make reports about the relative worth of the programs to the participants and stakeholders.

The utilitarian perspective of what the consequences of an action are has immediate appeal for many persons conducting evaluations. It is congruent with evaluation's long history of looking at program outcomes and products. It is at the center of what many evaluators see as their mission. It is natural to ask questions about the consequences of the nutritional program for the elderly and to seek answers with pre- and post-indicators. Many evaluators, however, currently recognize that broader consequences to others beyond the target population must be considered.

When investigating the consequences of an educational program, the evaluator must consider the educational attainment of students, the goals of parents, and the activities of teachers and school officials. Perhaps students learn a lot but end up disliking the subject matter. Students might benefit from a longer instructional day, but the teachers suffer burnout. What place does the good of the program staff have when considering the welfare of the program's participants? What about the good of the taxpayers who are funding the program through bond issues and property taxes? An educational program clearly may be having a positive impact on students' learning, and parents and teachers might be pleased with the program, but a decision to fund the program means the city bus system will have to go another year with curtailed services, causing numerous inconveniences for persons in the city who are disabled. Whose good serves as the determination of how the funds are spent in this situation?

Similar questions confront evaluators of health service programs and agencies, such as the nutritional program described in Vignette 2.2. Those receiving services may clearly benefit—but at what cost to the staff or to other persons whose differing needs are not being met because of insufficient funds or staff to provide both services? A hospital's intensive care program, for example, may provide excellent service from the perspective of the patient but be highly stressful for the nurses who eventually seek transfers and even leave the profession, resulting in dwindling numbers of available staff. In this situation, whose good is determined, and how?

Cost analysis, particularly cost-benefit analysis, can be a useful evaluation tool to assist stakeholders in sorting out the relative impact of different consequences. Cost-benefit analysis will seldom yield a final or definitive conclusion equally satisfying to all, however, and new issues often emerge throughout the process. The process can be helpful in identifying indirect program impacts, but the decisions about what is ultimately the ethical course of action must rely on other criteria.

Finally, and critical for the evaluator, is the question of who determines the answers to these questions. Is it the evaluator? Is it the program's funder? Is it a consensus of all stakeholders?

Duty

Ethicists who are strong supporters of duty and obligation as the essential criteria for making ethical choices assert that duty takes precedence over the production of good as a determination of ethical behavior. They are referred to as deontologicalists. Right actions are not determined by their consequences but, rather, by our sense of duty based on relationships that exist and other criteria such as personal commitment, the existence of a rule or law regarding behavior, or perhaps a religious command. Kant, an 18th-century philosopher, is most associated with this theory in modern times through what we refer to as his categorical imperative. According to Kant (1788/1956), all persons should act as if their actions were to become universal. When making a decision about how to act, I must ask what would happen if everyone acted in similar circumstances in the same manner. One side of this formulation is the familiar Golden Rule—"Do unto others as you would have them do unto you"—but the other side is not treating others in ways you would not want to be treated if you were they.

Many lapses in ethical behavior result from a failure to consider Kant's imperative and to consider ourselves and our specific dilemma to be an exception. It is easy to rationalize, to believe our situation is different, unique, and merits a different response. I might rationalize that it is OK for me to cheat on my income taxes because of my personal circumstances and assert that my cheating affects no one else. But what would happen if everyone in my same circumstance cheated? Would I condone this behavior? An evaluator might be tempted to soften a report of a negative finding because the program administrator is hard-working and under unusual stress. No apparent harm will result. But what if every evaluator did the same? What would be the result for the programs being evaluated and the trust and faith in evaluation efforts?

Others have expanded the concept of duty to consider the special obligations that professionals have because of our unique roles in society. Teachers have special obligations to their students, pastors to their church members, physicians to their patients, and parents to their children. What expectations does society and specific clients have of evaluators? Are there greater expectations for candor, honesty, and objectivity?

Another aspect of duty or obligation, going beyond fulfilling a requirement or responding to the rights of an individual, is living up to an ideal, that is, surpassing normal expectations. This is behavior we might expect of heroes risking their lives. We do not expect ordinary citizens to risk their lives by entering a burning building to save another person, but we do expect that from a firefighter. This aspect of evaluation duty is not well defined. For example, what duty does the formative evaluator have to save a floundering program? Typically, we restrict ethical considerations to behaviors related to expected obligations and exclude ideals. As we noted earlier, however, we believe that this too often limits our consideration only to the "ought nots." We prefer to think of obligations as a continuum, with no sharp distinction between what is expected and what is heroic.

It should be noted that duties, expectations, and ideals might be different for an internal or external evaluator or for a person commissioned to conduct a formative as opposed to a summative evaluation. An internal evaluator for the nutritional program who sees the evaluator's role and obligation as primarily directed to the people being served and to the program's delivery staff may see no need to comment on people not being served. An external evaluator who believes that his or her obligation is to the legislative funding committee or the broader community might consider it essential to note the populations not being served. When making decisions that might have ethical implications, the evaluator needs to ask, "What are the expectations and obligations in this setting based on my relationship with the client and the client's resulting expectations?"

Rights

Another criterion, closely associated with duty, is consideration of the rights of persons. Kant, among other philosophers, suggests that human beings have unconditional value as humans and must never be treated as means to an end but as ends in themselves. From this perspective, we must have respect for persons and recognize their rights. Unlike a strict utilitarian who might justify an infringement on individual rights for the betterment of the total society, a supporter of individual freedom would find this behavior inappropriate. Statements about fundamental rights are not universally accepted across all societies. In fact, ancient Hebrew and Greek do not have equivalent expressions for our terms "a right" and "rights" (Beauchamp & Childress, 1983). Rights language, however, has been particularly important in the Anglo-American heritage. The U.S. Bill of Rights protects the right to free speech, religious freedom, due process, and privacy, to name a few.

Evaluators need to consider issues relating to privacy, confidentiality, and the rights of individuals not to participate in evaluations. Because evaluations do not always involve experiments, and programs being evaluated are not typically seen as having potentially negative side effects, evaluators may overlook important rights of persons regarding participation or privacy. Also important in evaluations is the right of stakeholders to have access to the evaluation information and subsequent reports. There are two obligations associated with this right: the obligation of the evaluator to respond to inquiries regarding evaluation results and have them available for significant stakeholders, and the obligation to report evaluation results to others proactively without waiting to be asked.

Most ethicists discuss rights as claims that individuals and groups can make on others. A right may be viewed as property that one possesses and over which one has control. To have an ethical or moral right is something completely different from having a legal right. Legal rights are claims that we justify on the basis of legal principles or rules, whereas ethical rights are justified by moral principles and rules. Even though ethical and legal rights are often similar or even identical, it is important to note the distinction.

Most philosophers would not consider rights as absolute. Conflicts may arise between rights, and decisions must be made about which right takes precedence. A "violation" of a right refers to an unjustified action against a right. An "infringement" of a right refers to a justified action overriding a right (Beauchamp & Childress, 1983). When a right is infringed, it does not disappear and, indeed, may still have implications for actions taken. The right to free speech may be restricted, for example, regarding documents the government classifies as related to the national defense, but these restrictions are carefully delineated, and the Freedom of Information Act allows private citizens access to information the government has restricted for a period of time. Evaluators need to respect, as much as possible, a person's right to privacy regarding information revealed, but if an illegal act is revealed or if significant harm is a possible outcome, this respect for the right to privacy must be infringed upon. Decisions about when and how certain rights take precedence over others is not always straightforward. At this point, the evaluator might wish to examine the question from the perspective of the consequences of the action and look at the relative balance between infringement of one right or the other.

Rights are closely related to duties and obligations in what philosophers refer to as the doctrine of logical correlativity (Braybrooke, 1972). A positive right suggests that someone else has an obligation to act in a certain way (Feinberg, 1973, 1984). A negative right suggests someone else has an obligation to refrain from acting in a certain manner. If persons being interviewed have a right to privacy, the person interviewing them has an obligation to take the necessary actions to ensure that privacy is guaranteed by shutting the door, locking up any records, and removing identification from files. Evaluators also have an obligation to refrain from discussing a client's private matters in a public hallway or with others not involved in the evaluation. If we say that a person or group has a right to certain evaluation information or the entire evaluation report, we imply that someone else has an obligation to make that information or report available and, in some cases, is responsible for seeing that those with that right receive copies.

Social Justice

Another important ethical criterion in determining whether behavior is right or wrong is social justice. Rawls (1971) is one of the most prominent theorists espousing an egalitarian, social justice perspective. He emphasizes equity but adds conditions that are in opposition to the utilitarian perspective. Rawls proposed two principles: The first recognizes that each person has an equal right to basic liberties, and the second states that efforts to combat social and economic inequalities should be arranged to benefit the least advantaged. He supports equal access but also supports an unequal distribution if it assists the least well off in society, which then will benefit all of society. This approach uses a different way of determining indicators of what has benefited everyone and has direct application to evaluation.

When evaluators use the aggregated mean of an outcome indicator to determine benefits of an economic program, for example, an overall higher mean usually suggests that the economic program was successful, but a close examination of disaggregated data might reveal that the rich have become so much richer that the overall higher mean masks the fact that there was no improvement or perhaps even a downward trend for the poor. This may apply to educational and health programs as well as to economic programs. The overall mean academic achievement scores on a math test for high school students might increase significantly compared to the performance of comparable students 5 years earlier, but this could be the result of students from well-financed school systems performing substantially higher while at the same time those from poorer school systems perform the same or lower than they did 5 years ago. (An excellent illustration of how economic status of the school district is particularly relevant to assessing outcomes is found in Jonathan Kozol's 1991 book, *Savage Inequalities.*)

Gender or ethnicity characteristics are also important attributes traditionally related to equity and justice. If the overall math achievement score averages rise but a closer examination of the scores indicates that the rise occurred for males but not females, using the social justice criterion, this is important information. If overall college retention rates rise but an increase is not evident for ethnic minority groups, questions of program effectiveness arise. Similar considerations apply to health programs. The overall infant mortality rate could go up or down for certain segments of the population, masking a dramatic opposite movement for particular segments of the population.

Rawls (1971) suggests that resources must be distributed to the least advantaged, even if, at times, this is at the expense of the total aggregated good. This distribution pattern must continue until the point when the disadvantaged would receive a greater benefit if the distribution pattern favored the advantaged.

House (1976, 1980, 1990, 1991, 1993) has been the most persistent voice in evaluation suggesting the need for evaluators to consider social justice issues and to consider Rawls's (1971) approach. He notes that leaders in the United States often give more attention to overall increases in the gross national product than its distribution, even if this means spending disproportionate sums on the already advantaged. Some suggest that a descriptive approach to values and ethics is the appropriate neutral stance for evaluators (Cook & Shadish, 1986), but House holds a different opinion: Evaluators need to become advocates for the disadvantaged and powerless. Even when a stakeholder approach to evaluation is used, the powerless are seldom involved and, too often, the critical issues are not discussed. As early as 1976, House noted, "Evaluation should not only be true; it should be just . . . justice provides an important standard by which evaluation should be judged" (p. 75). Later, he stated, "Evaluators cannot be value neutral in these matters. Our conceptions and even our methodologies are value laden. Evaluators do not live in a state of methodological grace" (House, 1991, p. 245). More recently, House (1993) suggests that evaluation should be a method for democratizing public decisions in society. His voice has recently been joined by Ericson (1990) and Sirotnik (1990), who focus on educational concerns and suggest that evaluators must acknowledge their positions on social justice issues and must be active in pursuing justice.

The evaluator in our nutritional program example might take two actions if the social justice perspective were a prime criterion. First, the results of the data could be disaggregated to see if the program is having a differential impact on subgroups among the participants. That is, are there different results associated with socioeconomic status? Do women respond differently from men? Another variable might be marital status. Examination of these relationships could provide clues as to whether the program is differentially effective with different subgroups. Second, the evaluator could assume the role of an advocate for those who are not participating. A case could be made for looking at the possible variables related to lack of participation and making recommendations that funds be expended to support a study of other delivery systems for the program.

Ethics of Care

The ethical theories and their resulting criteria described so far focus extensively on logic and reasoning. This is not surprising, as the dominant paradigm for discussing and studying ethics focuses on thinking and reasoning. The goal seems to be to resolve a concrete dilemma by analyzing it objectively and abstractly through general theory and principles. Feminine perspectives on ethics, however, give greater attention to relationships and to the specific context of the ethical dilemma. These perspectives have yet to receive full attention in the mainstream discussions of ethical theory. We believe, however, that because of the nature of our profession—and their growing inclusion in evaluation literature (e.g., Farley & Mertens, 1993; Mertens, 1994; Ryan, 1994; Ryan & Ory, 1993)—these perspectives warrant attention when evaluators discuss ethics.

Gilligan (1982) believes that the masculine approach to ethics emphasizes individual rights and the development of general rules, which is characteristic of the utilitarians and deontologicalists. Women, however, from her perspective, are more likely than men to consider how an ethical decision will affect human relationships and to seek a resolution that fits the specific situation rather than to search for a general rule that fits all situations. An ethics of care, which she proposes, would be more concerned with relationships and with context than with universal laws or principles.

Noddings (1984) also proposes an ethics of care. She suggests that an ethics of care is not a rejection of rational thinking, but rather that rational thinking must serve something higher. That something is caring for others. Objectivity and analysis remain important to Noddings, but how relationships are affected also enters into her decision equation. Being ethical and rational has traditionally meant being aloof and impersonal but also has meant neglecting the personal life circumstances and relationships of the people affected by the decisions. Noddings and other proponents of an ethics of care emphasize the importance of considering how particular individuals and institutions would be affected by the available alternative choices.

We find many of the tenets of an ethics of care highly congruent with House's (1993) and Sirotnik's (1990) views on social justice. Also, the Fourth Generation social constructivist perspective of Lincoln and Guba (1989), which seeks to empower the typically disenfranchised, is compatible with an ethics of care. Evaluators who see the formative evaluator's role as one of assisting program developers in a supportive or nurturing manner would also find the ethics of care consistent with that role.

Schwandt (1989, 1992) has been encouraging a moral discourse in evaluation and has begun to explore the implications of an ethics of care for the practice of evaluation. He notes that if evaluators are to be "morally engaged practitioners," they must do the following:

- Give attention to, be receptive to, and be mindful of what meaning the specific context has for individuals and organizations (this being one aspect of caring).
- Keep the ethical-moral issue concrete, even when seeking guidance in abstract principles.
- Engage in social criticism.

Schwandt (1992) sees the evaluator as a reflective practitioner who helps stakeholders determine the meaning of their programs through exploring and probing rather than as an expert who promotes a specific moral perspective.

From an ethics-of-care perspective, the evaluator of the nutritional program in Vignette 2.2 would focus on the specific program and how the relationships among people would be affected by different evaluation strategies and reporting styles. This would necessitate knowing the program firsthand and not depending on data that just summarize outcomes. More attention would be paid to the specific context in which the program is offered, and comparisons with other alternatives would be considered.

It is too early to determine where further thinking about an ethics of care may lead. We acknowledge that an ethics of care will be considered by some as antithetical to the logic and universality that many consider essential for ethical reasoning. Others will argue that its perspectives may be easily integrated with the consequences or the social justice criterion. We believe, however, that because the ethics-of-care perspective provides a unique view of the ethical choices we must confront, it warrants its own lens to provide a viewpoint not necessarily attainable by looking at the same situation using the lens of the other criteria.

We hope by presenting the concept of an ethics of care in this text that further debates about ethics and evaluation will include discussions of the ethics-of-care perspective. Does an ethics of care mean the evaluator would assume a different role (e.g., more nurturing, less aloof)? Should it be the ultimate criterion for making a decision or only one of the criteria? Does being guided by an ethics of care encourage evaluators to become more intensely aware of what is happening to their clients and stakeholders? These and similar questions merit extensive discussion.

TABLE 2–2 Strengths and Weaknesses of Criteria Relevant to Judging Evaluation Behavior Decisions

Criterion	*Strengths*	*Weaknesses*
Consequences	Facilitates calculating outcomes and making comparisons Focuses on outcomes Congruent with traditional outcomes-oriented evaluation	Difficult to assess effects on all those affected Can result in abridging some persons' rights Difficult to define what is good and whose good takes priority
Duty	Can provide a clear picture of expectations Considers contractual and professional relationships	Can overemphasize managerial perspectives Might neglect needs of stake-holders
Rights	Provides minimal protection of individuals Sets behavior standards independent of outcomes	Might fail to consider social justice issues Rights are not absolute and may conflict
Social justice	Ensures that allocations of goods are distributed fairly	Can emphasize entitlement at the expense of effort/creativity Could abridge some stakeholder rights Changes traditional role of evalu-ator from neutrality to advocate
Ethics of care	Considers specific context Examines effect on relationships	May appear relativistic Difficult to determine whose cares are most pertinent

Critique of the Criteria

Each of the theories supporting the five suggested criteria and the criteria themselves have their strong and weak points. The strong points of one may be the weakness of another, or the weakness of one criterion may be counteracted by the strength of another. Cavanaugh, Moberg, and Velasquez (1981) analyzed the strengths and weaknesses of several ethical theories as they relate to the business community. We expanded and adapted their analysis and summarize it in Table 2–2. The consequence criterion, if used exclusively, might exclude consideration of individual rights or of justice issues. A rights perspective might be inadequate for recognizing social justice issues. A focus on duty may place too much emphasis on the managerial perspective and not the needs of the stakeholders. A focus on social justice might lead to a lessened consideration for individual rights. Finally, an ethics of care perspective has the advantage of considering specific contextual factors but may be too relativistic for persons seeking universal rules.

ETHICAL PRINCIPLES

Ethical theories lead to the development or statement of ethical principles. Believing that I should conduct an evaluation of a program as I would want *my* program evaluated would be a guiding principle consistent with theories related to the consequences of an action. Whatever the consequences of my evaluation, they should be similar to what I would hope is for all evaluations. Based on this principle, I could develop specific rules about completing reports on time or ensuring statistical findings are clear and understandable to the reader. Principles, in turn, can serve as a foundation for establishing the ethical rules and serve as an organizational framework for an ethical code. The process of developing ethical codes may or may not be linear (i.e., from theories to principles to rules), but it is helpful to understand the possible relationships when trying to make ethical decisions, which is discussed in Chapter 4.

Numerous principles and ethical models could be used as a framework for guidelines for the evaluation profession. For example, Perloff and Perloff (1980) classified ethical rules under four concerns:

- Not informing participants of the nature of the research or involving them without their knowledge
- Exposing participants to physical stress or situations that would diminish their self-respect
- Invading participants' privacy
- Withholding benefits

House (1993) suggested three principles: "mutual respect, noncoercion and nonmanipulation, and support for democratic values and institutions" (p. 167). Kitchener (1984), drawing heavily on the work of Beauchamp and Childress (1983) and Drane (1982), presented five ethical principles as specifically applicable to the helping professions:

autonomy, nonmaleficence (doing no harm), beneficence (doing good), justice, and fidelity.

Several authors examined the applicability of Kitchener's formulation of the principles for other professions. Brown and Krager (1985) successfully adapted these principles for delineation of the responsibilities of graduate faculty and graduate students. Krager (1985) looked at the relevance of these same principles for student affairs administrators in higher education, as did Upcraft and Poole (1991). Kitchener's (1984) five principles served as the basis for several of the studies on ethical evaluation practice reported in Chapter 3, and they serve here as the framework for our discussion of ethical principles. Each principle is described in the following section along with examples of its applications to evaluation practice.

Respecting Autonomy

Autonomy includes the right to act freely, make free choices, and think as you wish. Philosophers from several schools of thought support the principle of autonomy. On one hand, Kant (1788/1956), who believed that ethical choices should be determined by what is considered a duty or obligation, argued that persons must be treated as autonomous ends and never as means to others' ends. All persons have unconditional worth as ends in themselves. Mill (1863/1962), a 19th-century utilitarian (what is ethical is determined by an act's consequences), on the other hand, saw the consequence of free autonomous expression to be maximization of benefits of all because conformity reduces creativity and eventually productivity that would benefit all (Beauchamp & Childress, 1983). Individual freedom and independence are considered to be basic human rights, and the right to liberty is one of the "inalienable rights" in the U.S. Declaration of Independence.

The principle of autonomy, however, is not just a right but also an obligation. As individual persons, we have the right to autonomy, but at the same time we have the obligation to respect the autonomous rights of others. Our autonomy is bounded by the need to respect the autonomy of others. Individuals cannot, by their actions, restrict the freedom or rights of other persons, who must be able to express their own autonomy. Trespassing on another person's property or reading another person's confidential papers is not permitted as I exercise my freedom to go where

I want or read what I want. Autonomy is not only a right but also a limitation. I am bound to respect the rights of others to autonomy. How can I expect others to respect my autonomy unless I respect the similar rights of others?

Another boundary to autonomy is the relationship of competency to behavior and free choice. The principle of autonomy does not apply equally to persons who are immature, ignorant, or coerced. Parents do not permit their 2-year-olds to roam freely in the streets because the toddlers do not fully comprehend the dangers. Chemistry students are not permitted to conduct laboratory experiments until they can demonstrate competence in using lab equipment. None of us is allowed to drive an automobile until we have passed a driver's test attesting to our knowledge of the rules of the road and competence in driving a car. These are just a few examples where our freedom of action or autonomy is limited unless or until competence is demonstrated (see Collopy, 1988; Miller, 1981).

The impact of the relationship between autonomy and competency is the delineation of what constitutes competency. In a bureaucratic society, restrictions on behavior because of lack of competence are not left to the judgment or whim of individuals. Indeed, we have many licensing and certification procedures designed to protect the public from incompetent practice in fields as divergent as plumbing and medicine. Restrictions on autonomy due to lack of competence are usually skill specific. The person with no competence in plumbing may be an excellent carpenter. The physician competent to remove an appendix may not be competent to perform brain surgery. Decisions about competence are not as easy in matters where certification or legal permits offer no definitive guidelines.

Questions of competence of the participants and of the evaluator have ethical implications. Two important considerations are informed consent and disclosure of information. Although their discussion focuses on biomedical contexts, Beauchamp and Childress (1983) provide a useful standard that may be applied to evaluation: A person is competent if, and only if, that person can make decisions based on rational reasons (p. 72). In an evaluation context in which we are considering informed consent of participants, this means that participants must be able to (a) understand what will be required, (b) weigh the risks and benefits, and (c) make decisions in light of this knowledge. The Joint Committee on Standards' (1994) Standard P3 (Rights of Human Subjects) includes issues of informed consent, but there is no discussion of autonomy and competence. As another example, although the Joint Committee Standards have a section entitled "Disclosure of Findings" (Standard P6), most of the guidelines in the section refer to the content of the report and determination of to whom it should be distributed. No discussion of autonomy or competency requirements are included.

Within the medical profession (Beauchamp & Childress, 1983), three standards for disclosure are considered: professional practice, reasonable person, and subjective. If applied to evaluation, these standards would indicate that the way professional evaluators customarily disclose is sufficient. The professional practice standard suggests that traditional disclosure practices serve as the criteria for adequacy. This standard has weaknesses; it assumes that a customary standard exists when it may not, or that if a customary standard does exist, it is always in the best interests of all participants. This may not be true in evaluation. What is in the best interests of clients may not be in the best interests of stakeholders.

The reasonable person standard suggests that the guidelines be determined by what significance a hypothetical reasonable person would attach to information. We are still plagued, however, with not knowing whether or not a jury of participants, for example, would arrive at the same decision as would each individual participant. Because in evaluation most decisions are made in an organizational context, the dynamics of group interactions is important.

The subjective standard recognizes individual differences in needs when applying the reasonable person standard. This standard is reflective of more current evaluation approaches. Because of a particular history within an organization, the reasonable person standard would adapt disclosure to meet that individual organization's needs. Perhaps several previous evaluations conducted at the site were highly intrusive and the evaluators never fully informed participants of their purposes and activities. It would be understandable under these circumstances for the staff to be paranoid, and so the evaluator might suggest more full and open disclosure than one would ordinarily provide.

A combination of the reasonable person standard and the subjective standard would work well in most evaluation situations. First, use the reasonable person standard to determine what information should be disclosed and to whom, and then add to this what other information is desired or needed by those involved at the particular site.

Nonmaleficence (Doing No Harm)

According to many ethicists, this principle takes precedence over all other principles: Above all else, do no harm. The principle of nonmaleficence is congruent with those who support using the consequence criterion (i.e., do no harm) and those who support using duty and obligation as criteria for making ethical choices. Although not all philosophers distinguish between nonmaleficence and beneficence (doing good), when a risk-benefit analysis is necessary, it is helpful to consider them as distinct prima facie principles. Like Beauchamp and Childress (1983) and Kitchener (1984), we find it useful to consider these principles as distinct. Nonmaleficence is the duty to not inflict evil or undue harm. This means that we sometimes limit our actions or take no action. Beneficence, discussed in the next section, is the duty to prevent or remove harm by taking action and/or by doing and promoting good.

Harm can refer to physical injury or to psychological injury, such as damage to reputation, property, self-esteem, or liberty. For example, psychological injury resulting from evaluation could be undue aggravation and stress. Evaluations frequently are highly stressful for program staff members being evaluated. How the evaluator reacts to this stress can influence not only the degree of stress but also its seriousness. As another example, how the evaluator writes reports has the potential for affecting people's reputation and self-esteem. What we say—or don't say—and how we say it have repercussions for all stakeholders.

The duty to avoid harm, or any rule derived from this principle, is not absolute. It is sometimes advisable, and even necessary, to inflict harm to avoid a greater harm. The physician may cause pain with an inoculation to prevent a person from becoming infected with a disease. A therapist may decide that a client needs to confront painful memories before current problems can be discussed. A program evaluator may suggest that program staff members spend extra time in their current schedule to review program implementation so that weaknesses can be spotted early. Avoiding harm in evaluation does not mean ignoring negative findings. The emphasis is on "undue" harm. Negative findings should be presented in a way that does not damage unduly the program, staff, or clients.

The principle of nonmaleficence also means avoiding placing others at risk of harm. Conducting evaluations of health programs involving experimental treatments with drugs or specific medical applications can easily involve placing participants at risk through either commission (e.g., treatment groups suffering negative side effects) or omission (e.g., control or placebo groups not receiving sufficient treatment). Evaluators have long had concerns about unintentional negative side effects as a source of invalidation of otherwise positive evaluation results (Scriven, 1972). The principle of nonmaleficence places the responsibility on the evaluator to be concerned up front about the potential harm that may arise directly or indirectly from the program being evaluated.

It is important in all situations where harm is inflicted to avoid a greater harm by carefully weighing the consequences. What are the tradeoffs? There must be an appropriate balance between the probability of the harm, the extent of potential harm, and the expected or hoped-for benefit. Health officials must weigh the risks and benefits associated with a massive vaccination program. What are the potential side effects? How injurious might they be? What is the probability of their occurring? An evaluator must think through with the appropriate stakeholders the risk-benefit analysis of using potentially psychologically upsetting instruments as an outcome measure. What is the risk of someone becoming upset through the act of completing the instruments? Do the potential benefits outweigh the potential risks?

Some risks or harms are unintentional and unexpected. In emergency medical care and in psychological therapy, the harm or pain that the practitioner inflicts is usually apparent and expected. This is generally not the case in the practice of evaluation, where it is more likely that harm is unintentionally caused by an act of commission or of omission. The evaluator can violate the principle of nonmaleficence without even being aware of the harm or risk. To practice "due care," evaluators should first acquire the proper knowledge and skills and then diligently monitor their practice. Although the title does not directly imply concern about the evaluator's level of competence, the description of Joint Committee Standard U2 (Evaluator Credibility) mentions the competency of the evaluator as an important consideration. The evaluator is expected to be alert to social and political forces and possess the competencies needed to conduct an evaluation. As the Joint Committee on Standards (1994) further describes this standard, it notes the importance of the evaluator seeking appropriate consultation when necessary. Research presented in Chapter 3 indicates that evaluators and stakeholders perceive lack of competence as a major ethical violation in program evaluation.

Although the principle of doing no harm is often cited as the first principle, our discussion suggests that it is not absolute, nor is it always straightforward. There are times when doing harm or risking harm may be appropriate to achieve a greater good. However, it is essential that persons making these decisions in an evaluation context exercise great caution. One way to do this is to adhere to the principle of autonomy as well. Ideally, persons at risk should be fully informed and fully involved in the decision making.

Beneficence (Benefiting Others)

This principle has a tradition going back to Socrates (Baumgarten, 1982; Kitchener, 1985) and the Hippocratic oath but is one that needs to be revisited and reaffirmed in today's society if it is to have credibility outside the rhetoric of mission statements of professional associations. Professions by their nature are grounded on the principle of helping individuals, organizations, and society as a whole. At one time, a profession was considered a vocation or a calling to provide a service to others. Ideally, professionals seek to benefit both those they serve directly and society as a whole. In general, it is agreed that serving others is often also in the ultimate best interests of the individual professional.

Benefiting others, or doing good, is a neglected principle. Because, in most situations, the principle of nonmaleficence or avoiding harm is given precedence over all other principles, discussions about ethics usually center on avoiding violations of others' rights rather than on what good can or must be done. Some philosophers perceive the principle of beneficence as a duty, but others view it as a virtue and therefore not an ethical obligation. For them, beneficence means providing mercy, kindness, and charity—behavior beyond normal expectations. According to their viewpoint, we are not always obliged to benefit persons.

The arguments supporting beneficence as a duty take a variety of forms, and the distinction is not always clear. One argument is that if we see something bad happening (e.g., somebody dying from starvation), we have a duty to prevent it (Singer, 1993). Singer (1993) suggests that the duty to prevent harm always applies unless some other prima facie duty conflicts. Other ethicists suggest that it is not morally wrong to refrain from an act of doing good (e.g., devoting one's life to aiding the sick and the poor) if this would involve interfering with one's lifestyle and life plan.

Some ethicists justify beneficence on grounds of the reciprocal responsibility we have, in a contractual society, to do good for others and they to do good for us. This fair-play argument makes sense, but it does not help us determine when we must take action. Beauchamp and Childress (1983) suggest five conditions requiring a duty of beneficence. We describe them here as they might apply to the relationship between an evaluator and the client or significant stakeholders:

- There is a risk of significant loss or damage to the client, participants, staff, or relevant stakeholders.
- The evaluator is the person who needs to act to prevent the loss.
- The evaluator's action would probably prevent the loss.
- The evaluator's action would present no significant risk to the evaluator.
- The benefit that the client, participants, staff, or significant stakeholders receive will outweigh any harm the evaluator might suffer.

Ethicists supporting the importance of duty and obligation criteria are interested in the role relationships between the individuals involved. The duties of a parent, a teacher, or an evaluator differ because of that person's role and relevant responsibilities. An evaluator who is an external consultant may have less responsibility to be beneficent than an internal evaluator who is a regular staff member. This is an example of another difference between the principle of nonmaleficence and beneficence. The duty to avoid harm is relatively independent of roles and must be observed in all situations, but one's duty to benefit others by taking extreme measures may depend on our specific role in a situation.

Consider, for example, an evaluator whose data analysis yields no significant differences on short-term outcome measures but whose knowledge of the research literature suggests that significant differences are more likely after a longer exposure to the program. Reporting the short-term results without this additional information could result in the program being cut or significantly curtailed. If the evaluator spends a bit more time in summarizing the related research literature, the decision makers will have a fuller contextual basis for making program decisions. This example is far from dramatic, but it illustrates how pervasive ethical principles can be in affecting everyday professional practice. Some ethicists add other considerations to deciding when being beneficent is a duty or not by using a utilitarian approach focusing on the likely outcomes rather than the process. Will a good actually occur, and what is its probability?

The principle of doing good must be balanced with the need to consider other principles. This is the case when issues arise regarding the potential for doing harm as well as doing good and when doing good may conflict with the principle of autonomy. When these conflicts occur, Kitchener (1984, 1985) and others suggest that the responsible action to take is to apply the balancing concept. When the potential good has been noted, it must be balanced against the likely harm. Several illustrations help clarify these dilemmas.

Physical punishment is frequently seen as harmful. Parents who have difficulty using spanking or some other physical reprimand as a form of punishment may decide that the balance between doing good—preventing a toddler from wandering into the street unprotected or potentially being burned by a hot pan—prompts them to employ a physical signal that inflicts momentary pain (harm) rather than solely a verbal warning or reprimand. The evaluator may decide to recommend a more expensive test battery, which is going to hurt the client's pocketbook, because the quality of the information obtained will be superior and serve the best interests of the client.

The principle of benefiting others must also be balanced with the principle of autonomy. When you provide help to others in ways that affect their autonomy, you risk becoming overly paternalistic or maternalistic; you are acting as a parent who "knows best." Parents who limit the use of the family car by an adolescent family member (restricting autonomy) do so for the overall protection and good of the adolescent. The assumption is that the person in authority, the parent, knows what is good for the individual, the adolescent. The use of authority restricts the freedom of the individual against that individual's will. The balancing act between these two principles is reasonably straightforward when considering parent and toddler relationships, gets fuzzy when considering parent and adolescent relationships, and becomes more complex when considering parent and adult child relationships. When considering relationships between adults in authority or professional relationships with each other, the balancing act becomes even trickier.

Several ethicists discuss issues related to balancing the principles of helping others and at the same time respecting their independence (Beauchamp & Childress, 1983; Kitchener, 1984; Powell, 1984) and suggest guidelines for deciding when it is permissible for the principle of doing good to take precedence over the principle of respecting autonomy. Powell (1984) suggests two guidelines: The potential outcomes of the decision are quite serious, and there is doubt regarding the competence of the individual making the decision. These criteria would clearly be met when a parent restricts the street-crossing liberties of a toddler.

Evaluators also risk being maternalistic or paternalistic with their clients, program staff, or others. Evaluators may be in an authoritative position because of their expertise in design, measurement, statistics, data gathering, and data analysis. When and how should the evaluator assert a course of action that is appropriate because it is for the good of the program, staff, or the participants? What technical decisions should be left in the hands of the client? How much effort should the evaluator spend to educate clients so they can make decisions autonomously and with sufficient competence?

The balancing act between risks, harms, and benefits leads to attempts to quantify the variables and arrive at a numerical "solution" through formal cost-benefit or risk-benefit analysis. These analyses can be helpful in making ethical choices, especially for decisions that affect many people, but the choices always remain complex, and it is doubtful that a formula will lead to a clear solution. Particularly difficult is determining whose values or weights are to be considered when the decision affects numerous people.

Justice

Being just is being fair, equitable, and impartial, and it means responding to, reacting to, and making decisions about people independent of their race, gender, socioeconomic status, or other inappropriate attributes. Being just also implies responding to people in a way they deserve. We speak of giving people their "just deserts" (Beauchamp & Bowie, 1979). This expression, from a justice perspective, has both a positive connotation (e.g., reward) and a negative connotation (e.g., punishment). The person who wins a race deserves the best prize; the person who commits a crime deserves to be punished. These uses of the term and concept of justice are important when making decisions about ethical behavior in general and specifically in an evaluation context. Is true worth being recognized or true needs being met?

Distributive justice is a particularly important dimension for program evaluators. Distributive justice refers to the appropriate distribution or nondistribution of social benefits and burdens. Food stamps and social security benefits are examples of distributed benefits; property taxes and military service are examples of distributed burdens. According to economists, distributive justice applies only to the distribution of scarce benefits for which there is competition. Distribution should not be based on the arbitrary characteristics of individuals. People who are similar on the relevant attributes should be treated similarly, whereas those who differ on a related characteristic should be treated proportionally differently. Students who have identical financial circumstances should be eligible for the same loan program; students in varying financial situations should be eligible for loans compensative with their financial status.

Attributes relevant to distributive justice include the following:

- Simply being a person and thus each receiving an equal share
- Individual need
- Individual effort
- Extent of societal contribution
- Individual merit

Egalitarian theorists support equal access to the goods in life that every rational person desires. In its purist form, everyone would get an equal share of what is being distributed; in its more practical form, egalitarianism supports equal access, which might not in itself result in equal distribution. Thus, we might seek to provide each person with equal access to a college education, but not everyone would take advantage of the opportunity. Marxist theorists base their distribution system on individual need. Definitions of need, however, are seldom clear-cut. Utilitarian theorists recognize the value of several of the criteria, but the ultimate consideration is that the public and private utility must be maximized.

Libertarian theorists consider the contribution and merit of individuals and their behavior as the primary basis for distribution. Their emphasis is on the rights to social and economic liberty. Generally, libertarians reject utilitarianism and egalitarianism. According to the libertarians, the very best world possible is one in which people seek to make the best of their own individual worlds (i.e., looking out for themselves). Any or all of these characteristics are considered when decisions have to be made about who will serve in the military draft or who is eligible for a heart transplant. Beliefs about the relative importance of these and other attributes have differing levels of support among ethical theorists identified with different schools of thought.

Distributive justice is less of a problem when there are plenty of the material goods in question than when there are scarcities or when priorities must be established. Political debates about resources allocated to health care, making higher education accessible, and funding medical research programs (e.g., AIDS research) have been issues in the United States for decades.

Distributive justice can be viewed from the macro and the micro level (Beauchamp & Childress, 1983), and each of these views has relevance for evaluation practice. At the macro level, decisions are made by the makers of public policy (federal and state legislatures) and by private foundations. The complexity and difficulty of decisions about distributive justice are often most dramatic in health care situations. Just a few questions illustrate the complexity of the issues: Should the federal government make more funds available for heart transplants or for AIDS or cancer research? Should the emphasis be on prevention or on remediation? Should the government even be involved, or should decisions be made by what happens in the marketplace? Similar questions could be framed about educational issues (e.g., voucher systems, loans for higher education). These are questions that must be resolved by policymakers at the macro level. They do so, as politicians or as political appointees, within an environment shaped also by the attitudes, opinions, and, eventually, voting support of their constituents.

Evaluators frequently assist or serve as consultants to persons and groups who make policy decisions that have an impact on equity and other justice issues. Needs assessment data may influence decisions about which programs are funded and which populations are targeted. Decisions about what outcome measures are used and how data are aggregated, analyzed, and reported may have a dramatic effect on program continuation recommendations. These are examples of where principles of justice have a direct bearing on the everyday behavior and decisions made by an evaluator.

Kirkhart (1995) uses the term *consequential validity* to refer to "the soundness of change exerted on systems by evaluation and the extent to which those changes are just" (p. 4). Thus, she is tying together consequences and justice. As we noted earlier, House (1990, 1991) and Sirotnik (1990) have commented frequently on the importance of justice issues as they relate to program evaluation. More recently, Schwandt (1992) also has suggested that evaluators need to be "morally engaged." All three writers encourage evaluators to examine carefully the social purposes and outcomes along with the effectiveness of programs they are evaluating.

Fidelity

Fidelity means being faithful, which implies keeping promises, being loyal, and being honest. Veracity could be discussed as a separate principle, but we find it helpful to include it within the principle of fidelity. The principle of fidelity follows directly from ethicists who believe that consideration needs to be given to relationships when considering duties. A few philosophers consider fidelity as the fundamental principle from which all others follow, but most recognize it as one of the important prima facie principles. Beauchamp and Childress (1983) believe that fidelity is best understood when it is related to other principles like autonomy and justice, but we concur with Kitchener (1984) and Ross (1930) that it merits consideration as a separate principle. It is especially important in professional relationships in evaluation, in which explicit promises are made through contractual agreements, and implicit expectations are present because of the expertise of the evaluator.

Making promises can turn ethically neutral acts into obligations and duties. Whether or not an evaluation report contains cost-benefit analysis information may have an impact on its usefulness, but by itself may not be an obligation of the evaluator. However, if the evaluator has promised verbally or in a written contract that cost-benefit information will be provided, then clearly this becomes an obligation.

Among the duties of fidelity is not to neglect the client, patient, or contractee. The physician is expected, once he or she has taken on a patient, to not withdraw from the case without sufficient notice. The same holds true for an evaluator. Regardless of other obligations or demands, the evaluator needs to follow through on explicit promises and implicit expectations.

A bit more needs to be said about implicit expectations. These expectations are frequently tied to perceived role expectations. Not every expectation is spelled out in detail, not even in the most formal contracts. The evaluator, by the nature of the professional role, is expected to possess certain expertise and to accomplish certain tasks. The general public is undoubtedly less aware of what these are for evaluators than what they are for doctors or dentists. This makes it essential that the evaluator determine what the implicit expectations are besides those delineated clearly in a contractual agreement. Body gestures, and even silence, can lead to expectations that then take on the form of promises. What was initially a neutral act may now become an obligation. When an evaluation client says, "I'm sure the data you collect will help us obtain refunding for our grant," and the evaluator responds with a smile or silence, is it unreasonable for the client to interpret this as agreement?

Fidelity is not an absolute principle. Promises to do something wrong are not binding. Contracts are binding for evaluators, but they can be in conflict with other duties or principles. An important question for evaluators is, To whom do they owe their fidelity? Is it to the client who hires them? Is it to the board of directors for the program being evaluated? Is it to the program participants, to the taxpayers, to the field of evaluation, or to society at large?

Benefits of Using Principles

In numerous ethical dilemmas, applying the principles will be extremely useful for guiding the resolution process. In many situations, examination of the principles will make the decision more complex, and occasionally, the principles will conflict with each other. We noted earlier Kitchener's (1984) discussion of the need to balance one against the other. This can still be quite complex. It is clear, however, that consideration of the principles tends to broaden our perspectives.

An Example To Tell or Not To Tell

Vignette 2.3

I am writing the final report of an evaluation of a new coed residence living arrangement on campus. The college board of directors has designated it as an "experiment." I was commissioned by the Director of Residence Life to conduct the evaluation. Positive findings indicated fewer vandalism incidents and lower damage repairs in the coed residence hall and better psychosocial development among the students. Students in the coed residence halls reported no greater degree of sexual behavior than did students in other residence halls, but more sexual activity took place within the coed residence hall than it did in other residence halls. The board of directors had requested information on the amount of sexual activity but had not explicitly asked for information about where the sexual activity took place. Should I report this "extra" piece of information or not? Some board members are looking for any excuse to cancel the experiment.

- How would you handle this situation?
- Did the evaluator go wrong? If so, where?

Look at the scenario in Vignette 2.3. What questions would the five principles prompt us to ask? Using the autonomy principle as a guide, the evaluator might ask whether or not to report where the sexual activity took place is really the evaluator's decision. Should this information be reported to the Director of Residence Life and let that person decide whether or not to report it to the board of directors? Is the evaluator restricting the director's autonomy by making this "extra" information part of the formal report? Next, what harm might the evaluator be causing (nonmaleficence) by reporting or not reporting the information? A good program might be dropped if this bit of information becomes available to certain board members.

Conversely, can this information or how the evaluator treats it lead to some good (beneficence) for key stakeholders? A discussion of where sexual activity takes place might be healthy for all staff and students. Perhaps by dealing with this issue now, future problems and issues (again, nonmaleficence) might be avoided. Are there any issues of fairness (justice) involved especially related to collection of data? Finally, would revealing this information in the official report to the board be breaking an implicit promise (fidelity), a contractual expectation?

These are examples of how the principles can be used to generate questions. What further questions can you generate?

CONCLUSION

In this chapter, we described ethical theories as they relate to five criteria for making ethical choices and are rephrased here as questions:

1. What are the consequences of my choice? What would happen, for example, if every evaluator made the same decision?
2. What duties and obligations do I have as an evaluator?
3. What rights do my clients have? What rights do I have?
4. What would be just or fair in this situation?
5. What would be the caring response or course of action?

Each of these questions can be asked as a way to help us respond to ethical choices.

The framework for ethical principles that we have found useful for thinking about ethical choices is provided by Kitchener (1984), who presented five principles as guidelines for ethical conduct: autonomy, nonmaleficence, beneficence, fidelity, and justice. These principles, in turn, can serve as the basis for developing rules and codes of ethical conduct. The Guiding Principles for Evaluators, adopted by the American Evaluation Association (1995), implicitly include Kitchener's principles as we have applied them to evaluation contexts. The AEA statement provides five guiding principles (see Appendix C) that focus on the evaluator: conducting a systematic inquiry, providing competent service, being honest throughout the evaluation process, respecting people, and being responsible for the general and public welfare. Although the AEA statement makes no explicit mention of broader ethical principles, Table 2–3 summarizes how we see the AEA principles relating to Kitchener's formulation of ethical principles.

We hope the discussion throughout this book of the broader ethical principles will assist evaluators in implementing the AEA statement and other professional codes that evaluators use for the guidance. Table 2–4 provides a succinct summary of how the theories, or criteria as we presented them, relate to Kitchener's principles.

TABLE 2–3 Relationship of the American Evaluation Association's (AEA) Guiding Principles for Evaluators and Kitchener's (1984) Ethical Principles

AEA Guiding Principle	*Kitchener's Principle*
Systematic inquiry Evaluators conduct systematic, data-based inquiries about whatever is being evaluated.	Beneficence Nonmaleficence
Competence Evaluators provide competent performance to stakeholders.	Nonmaleficence
Integrity/honesty Evaluators ensure the honesty and integrity of the entire evaluation process.	Fidelity
Respect for people Evaluators respect the security, dignity, and self-worth of the respondents, program participants, clients, and other stakeholders with whom they interact.	Autonomy Beneficence
Responsibilities for general and public welfare Evaluators articulate and take into account the diversity of interests and values that may be related to the general and public welfare.	Justice

As we have noted, use of the theories, principles, and codes for thinking about ethical decisions can move from the abstract (theories) to the general (principles) to the specific (codes) or in the reverse direction. When making a decision about a specific ethical dilemma, we suggest (as we discuss in Chapter 4) that it is most helpful to move from specific codes to the principles and then to the theories.

Ethicists and philosophers will continue to debate which principles and which criteria are most logical, consistent, universal, and useful. These debates can be frustrating to the individual practitioner who simply wants to know what course of action is right and thus may lead the practitioner to using only the codes or rules as guides, as the evaluator in Vignette 2.1 wants to do. From our perspective, this is insufficient. A solid grounding in the ethical principles and keen awareness of ethical theory can be highly useful in

TABLE 2–4 Relationship Between Ethical Theories and Principles

Theory/Criteria	*Related Principles*
Consequences (utilitarianism)	Autonomy Beneficence Nonmaleficence
Duty (deontological)	Autonomy Beneficence Fidelity Nonmaleficence
Rights	Autonomy Justice Nonmaleficence
Social justice	Justice Beneficence Nonmaleficence
Caring (ethics of care)	Beneficence Nonmaleficence

assisting evaluators in thinking about ethical issues and becoming ethical practitioners. The principles and the theory, which we presented as criteria, are highly interactive. Like rules, they cannot always be applied straightforwardly, sometimes they conflict. When rules conflict, we look at the ethical principles for guidance. When ethical principles conflict or do not provide clear answers, we use the criteria derived from ethical theory as more abstract guides. As we have stated throughout this chapter, these principles and criteria do not lead to the resolution of ethical dilemmas through application of a formula, but they serve as the foundation for the development of codes and as guides when codes and experience are insufficient. They help us think about ethical issues; they do not resolve the issues for us.

In Chapter 3, we look at what existing research says about evaluation practice and ethical dilemmas and particularly how the ethical principles relate to practice and standards. In Chapter 4, we present a decision-making process that can be used to apply these principles and criteria to ethical decision making about evaluation practice.

3

Ethical Issues Related to Program Evaluation

RESEARCH ON PRACTICE

A Reader's Guide to Chapter 3

This chapter summarizes research studies pertaining to the five ethical principles. It explores the relationship between the principles and written standards and between the principles and major functional roles of evaluators and perceptions of violations of evaluators' actions and the principles. The chapter's purpose is twofold: first, to validate the relevance of the principles in evaluation ethics, and second, to encourage others to conduct research on ethical practice by providing examples of questions that can be raised. Questions addressed in this chapter include the following:

- Do the principles reflect what commonly is accepted as adequate evaluation practice?
- Are the varying roles assigned to evaluators, and the resulting expectations, related to the proposed principles?

- Using the principles as a framework, can we identify specific areas of evaluation practice that are considered violations of appropriate practice?

In Chapter 2, we presented a theoretical model that could be used to clarify the ethical dilemmas surrounding the practice of program evaluation. The method of incorporation is discussed in the following chapters. In this chapter, we present a review of the research used to develop the model. We begin with a brief synopsis of research on ethics in program evaluation, followed by summaries of research on the model.

RESEARCH ON ETHICS IN EVALUATION

Research on ethical concerns in the area of program evaluation has been limited. Many of the articles on ethical issues and reactions to the evaluation standards are thought pieces about ethics in general (e.g., Bunda, 1985; Lincoln, 1985; Smith, 1985) or describe dilemmas or issues through anecdotes as Kytle and Millman (1986) did when sharing their personal experiences as applied researchers in search of principles. They described several ethical dilemmas and, in particular, their difficulty in finding ready solutions and their resulting disillusionment. Referring to what they call the "value illiteracy" among social scientists in contrast to the scientists' technical competency, they recommend more dialogue about values and ethical issues.

In one of the first empirical studies of ethical issues among evaluators, Sheinfeld and Lord (1981) reported three broad areas of concern among evaluators:

- Protection of human rights, which includes issues related to confidentiality, informed consent, and participant's right to terminate
- Freedom from political interference, which includes pressures from interest groups and conflicts related to misuse of evaluation data
- Evaluator technical competency, which includes openness about evaluator's technical abilities and assurance of objectivity

They noted that evaluators seem dependent on and responsive to those who fund the evaluations, and when the evaluators acquire more resources and power, they may begin to express greater concern for such values as distributive justice.

McKillip and Garberg (1986) asked 22 evaluation experts to rate the compatibility of implementing pairs of standards from the Joint Committee on Educational Evaluation Standards. They arrived at five sets of standards that they referred to as "demands" on practicing evaluators:

- Attending to the contextual and political contexts
- Exhibiting professionalism
- Conducting an evaluation openly and consulting widely
- Meeting the canons of social science practice
- Attending to the specific needs of the evaluation setting

They found that the first demand, attending to the contextual and political context, presented the greatest possibility for conflict with the other standards.

Stockdill (1987) asked evaluators in both business and educational settings to sort out the relevance of the Joint Committee Standards and those of the Evaluation Research Society (ERS) for their fields. He used q-sort, small group discussions, and questionnaires with 42 evaluators (21 each from business and from education). Stockdill found no differences in appropriateness ratings between the business and education evaluators for either the Joint Committee Standards or the ERS Standards, but overall, the Joint Committee Standards were rated as more appropriate. Even after Stockdill had removed obvious overlapping standards, his participants reported considerable redundancy and overlap among the standards.

Honea (1990) interviewed 6 professional evaluators about their experiences, thoughts, and opinions regarding ethics in program evaluation. These evaluators cited what could be described as guidelines, or principles, that they followed: being faithful to obligations to clients, being honest, being professional, and going back to personal values. Fairness was another principle mentioned. The evaluators believed that maintaining the role of the objective scientist was an effective way of responding to ethical concerns.

Later, Honea (1991) interviewed 9 evaluators working in the public setting for the federal or state government and uncovered four reasons why evaluators found discussing ethical issues problematical:

- *Trying to be an objective scientist.* These evaluators believed if they were honest and objective scientists, they would not be confronted with ethical issues.
- *Being involved in a team.* They also believed that working as a team protected them from being unethical because they would informally monitor each other.
- *Making certain assumptions.* Ethical concerns were discussed more as methodological issues than as ethical ones. For instance, if the evaluator used the right sampling processes and correct measurement and analysis procedures, it was assumed that this would take care of any ethical concerns. The evaluators also operated on the assumption that everyone was trying to be ethical and that making ethical decisions was an implicit part of the process; therefore, it did not have to be discussed explicitly.
- *Having no time.* These evaluators believed that there simply was not enough time to think about ethical issues.

Morris and Cohn (1993) conducted a survey to assess evaluators' perceptions of ethical practice. Respondents were asked to describe ethical problems they encountered in their work and also to describe the most frequent and the most serious problems they had ever encountered. Nearly all of the respondents reported having faced an ethical problem, covering a wide range of ethical issues. Three of the four most frequently reported ethical concerns occurred during the post-data-analysis phase, and these revolved around presentation of the findings, disclosure agreements, and misinterpretation or misuse of the final report. The fourth issue, identifying and contracting with stakeholders, related to the entry stage of evaluation. Morris and Cohn concluded that many of the ethical issues for evaluators centered on role concerns, particularly the difficulty in maintaining their role as scientists.

Toms (1993) explored the relationship between professional and personal ethics and their influence on practice among 27 Canadian and U.S. evaluators. She found that U.S. evaluators placed more emphasis on protecting equality of access to program objectives, viewing this as an obligation to the stakeholder or the individual. Canadian evaluators emphasized an ethic involving self-determination and efficient use of programs and perceived this as an obligation to society.

There have been too few studies to warrant any generalization that might come close to reflecting the concerns among all evaluators in their many different work settings. Several themes seem to be emerging, however, and these center on the tension between being an objective, neutral scientist and at the same time providing useful information to the stakeholders and sorting out to whom the evaluator is responsible—the funder or a broad range of stakeholders.

RESEARCH ON THE MODEL OF ETHICAL THINKING

We conducted a series of studies that focused on the validity and utility of the ethical principles presented in Chapter 2 and the functional roles ascribed to evaluators. Our research to date has emphasized three main questions:

- Do the principles reflect what is commonly accepted as adequate evaluation practice?
- Are the varying roles assigned to evaluators, and the resulting expectations, related to the proposed principles?
- Using the principles as a framework, can we identify specific evaluation practices that are considered violations of appropriate practice?

Over a 10-year period, close to 3,000 respondents were involved in these studies representing evaluators, program administrators, clients, and other program stakeholders. Evaluators ranged from those with many years of experience to novices just entering the profession; stakeholders were program users, program staff, program administrators, clients who commission evaluations, clients who use others' reports, and program consumers. Because our areas of expertise lie in the education and psychology disciplines, these areas have a higher representation than may actually be found in the broader domain of evaluation. We have tested the model, however, in other disciplines, most notably health and social services, and would welcome further replication. To facilitate the reader's integration of this information, we summarize our findings for each of the three questions in Tables 3–1 through 3–7. An in-depth look at related studies is afforded by the boxed summaries throughout the chapter.

Question 1: Do the principles reflect what commonly is accepted as adequate evaluation practice?

To determine if the principles reflect current evaluation practice, we conducted several studies involving written evaluation standards and actions portraying those standards. Respondents were presented with information pertaining to standards of program evaluation practice (Joint Committee on Standards, 1981, 1994; Rossi, 1982) or actions representative of the standards and then asked to indicate which of the five principles these standards portrayed. (Note: Later research used only the Joint Committee Standards.) The purpose was to determine if a relationship existed between the principles and accepted practice, as exemplified by a written standard or by common actions.

Respondents were evaluators and stakeholders from multiple disciplines and backgrounds. Practicing evaluators were from the United States and Canada. Degree of experience ranged from novice to 20-plus years of practice. Stakeholders included program administrators, program staff, and program participants. The context of evaluation practice involved education, health, and mental health.

Perceptions of Written Standards

Results of studies investigating evaluators' perceptions of the principles and how well the principles reflect practice currently deemed acceptable indicated that among evaluators, the five principles not only represent current practice but illuminate some weaknesses in current guidelines and standards (see Table 3–1). Using the actual wording of both Joint Committee and ERS standards, evaluators matched standards with the principles of nonmaleficence, beneficence, and justice. Even greater congruence was found between written standards and the principles when evaluators were categorized according to programmatic area (see Box 3.1).

Stakeholders' perceptions of the principles were similar to those of practicing evaluators (Box 3.2). Consensus was reached on written standards that fell under the categories of beneficence, justice, and fidelity; however, stakeholders did not perceive any written standards as guidelines for protection of autonomy or nonmaleficence.

TABLE 3–1 Categorization of Standards,[a] by Principles

	Principle				
	Autonomy	*Nonmaleficence*	*Beneficence*	*Justice*	*Fidelity*
Evaluator	Political Viability F2*	Practical Procedures F1	Stakeholder Identification U1	Report Dissemination U6	Evaluator Credibility U2
	Disclosure of Findings P6*	Reliable Measurement A6 Valid Measurement A5 Conflict of Interest P7 Disclosure of Findings P6*	Information Scope and Selection U3 Report Clarity U5 Systematic Information A7 Analysis of Quantitative Information A8	Formal Obligations P2 Report Timeliness U6 Practical Procedures F1	
		Rights of Humans P3 Analysis of Qualitative Information A9 Human Interactions P4	Complete and Fair Assessment P5 Defensible Information Sources A4	Impartial Reporting A11	
		Justifiable Conclusions A10 Political Viability F2*			
Stakeholder			Information Scope and Selection U3 Report Timeliness and Dissemination U6 Balanced Reporting P6	Values Identification U4 Rights of Human Subjects P3	Evaluator Credibility U2 Formal Obligation P2

NOTE: Joint Committee Standard A = Accuracy; F = Feasibility; P = Propriety; U = Utility.
a. Titles used in this table; respondents were given actual standard.
*Tied.

Box 3.1 Written Standards Reflecting Principles: Evaluators' Perceptions

When asked to match specific professional standards with the principles, a majority of the evaluators reached consensus for nonmaleficence, beneficence, and justice. Nonmaleficence was characterized as providing valid and reliable measurement, reviewing and correcting data throughout the evaluation process, and correct analysis of both qualitative and quantitative data. Avoiding undue harm included keeping program disruptions to a minimum. Standards reflecting improved usefulness of the report were matched with beneficence, providing good to the client. These included selection and scope of pertinent information; clear, timely, and balanced reporting; and follow-through after the evaluation.

Standards matched with justice were those exemplifying justice to the client (meeting formal obligations), justice to program participants (rights of human subjects and rights of human interaction), and justice to the public (public's right to know). Standards guiding report dissemination to all right-to-know audiences and objective reporting also were matched with justice and could be considered part of the public right to know.

Only limited evidence for current practice was found for the principles of autonomy and fidelity. U. S. evaluators did not match consistently any standards with fidelity; however, Canadian evaluators did perceive standards reflecting evaluators' credentials and credibility, that is, competence, trustworthiness, and acceptance by clients as part of fidelity. Neither Canadian nor U.S. evaluators matched any written standards with the principle of autonomy.

Interviews with the evaluators indicated that they had ambivalent perceptions about their autonomy and the individual right of evaluators, clients, and other stakeholders and frequently experienced conflicts about this issue. Concerns about loyalty or fidelity were also viewed as stressful, particularly in situations where the evaluator was internal to the system. None of the evaluators interviewed was able to cite an example of a standard from any of the known guidelines that covered these issues.

Additional support for the principles encompassing existing practice was found when the classification of written standards with principles was reexamined by respondents' primary discipline. Evaluators in the mental health area classified 16 of the 30 Joint Committee Standards with a principle. Of these, most were placed within beneficence and fidelity. Evaluators affiliated with health-related programs classified 13 standards across all five principles. Private consultants, who served primarily as external evaluators, also matched 13 standards with the principles of nonmaleficence, beneficence, and fidelity but saw limited matches for autonomy and justice. Evaluators in education saw most of the standards reflecting nonmaleficence, beneficence, and justice, with few matches for fidelity and no matches for autonomy.

Box 3.2 Written Standards Reflecting Principles: Stakeholders' Perceptions

When matching written standards with the five principles, program administrators saw reflections of beneficence, justice, and fidelity. Standards matched with beneficence were reflected in requirements related to information source and the report. These included selection and scope of material and broad dissemination of a timely, balanced report. Justice was typified by standards pertaining to rights of human subjects and values interpretation. Providing the rationale for value judgments and protecting the rights of participants at all levels were perceived by program stakeholders as guidelines for equity and fairness. Administrators perceived written standards concerning evaluator credibility and credentials as guidelines representative of the principle of fidelity. For program directors and administrators, competency and trustworthiness of the evaluator, resulting in acceptance by the client, were indications of evaluator fidelity and loyalty. Stakeholders did not reach any agreement on the relationship of any written standards to the principles of autonomy and nonmaleficence.

Perceptions of Evaluator Actions

When statements portraying actions were used to represent Joint Committee and ERS standards, evaluators matched adherence and/or violations of the standards to all five principles (see Box 3.3). The majority of the matches between actions and principles represented negative actions, that is, violations of the standards. Many of these were methodology violations and were identified by evaluators as lack of nonmaleficence, that is, failure to avoid undue harm. Examples are incorrect analysis of data, failure to determine quality of data, and failure to provide methodological information. Other examples of negative actions are violations of proper reporting techniques, seen as a negative representation of fidelity, and misrepresentation of fiscal issues, perceived as a violation of autonomy. Less consensus was reached on adherence to standards, and where agreement was reached, most of it reflected beneficence. For example, providing a balanced report was seen as an act of beneficence. Overall, it appears that it was easier for evaluators to identify and discuss principles through actions portraying violations than through actions portraying adherence.

Stakeholders (Box 3.4) were able to identify evaluator actions as examples of ethical practices more readily than they were able to identify written standards. When responding to positive and negative statements of evaluator practice, as represented by actions, stakeholders matched actions with four of the five principles: autonomy, beneficence, justice, and fidelity. Autonomy, or lack of autonomy, generally was represented by violations, such as excluding the client and overemphasizing the evaluators' role. Beneficence and justice were more reflective of adherence to positive actions, such as inclusion of multiple stakeholder groups. Presence or absence of evaluator credibility was seen as a reflection of fidelity.

Overall, for stakeholders, positive actions matched with principles tended to reflect inclusion in the process, whereas negative actions reflected exclusion. Nonmaleficence was not perceived as a principle of evaluation in word or deed by stakeholders.

Box 3.3 Actions Reflecting the Principles: Evaluators' Perceptions

When investigating the relationship of the principles to actions reflective of current practice, evaluators frequently debated the meaning of written statements with the investigators; it was much easier for them to identify both positive and negative actions that would exemplify the principles. Practicing evaluators were able to match actions representative of standards with all five principles. For instance, declining to conduct an evaluation when they have insufficient skills, an action associated with standards of competence, was selected as an indicator of the evaluator's right to autonomy.

Another action representative of the client's right to autonomy was to request information that justified the evaluation's cost, associated with standards of cost-effectiveness and fiscal responsibility. Statements representative of evaluator loyalty, or fidelity, included positive and negative actions related to report timeliness and to fulfillment of formal obligations. Violations of the rights of human subjects by promising confidentiality when it could not be guaranteed was seen as a violation of client loyalty. The principle of justice was matched with actions portraying adherence to, and violations of, standards pertaining to the political viability of the evaluation and the rights of human subjects. These include such actions as determining the political context of the program, avoiding conflicts of interest, and having regard for the human worth and dignity of all stakeholders.

Two positive actions were consistently seen as representing "doing good" (beneficence): encouraging key audiences to use the evaluation information and adhering to balanced reporting. Balanced reporting was perceived as incorporating both program strengths and program weaknesses.

The principle of nonmaleficence was most frequently evidenced in actions portraying violations of practice, that is, matched with actions evaluators ought not do. Most of these actions reflected methodological issues. Actions included failure to provide reliability and validity information, incorrect analysis of data, and not documenting data collection.

Box 3.4 Actions Reflecting Principles: Stakeholders' Perceptions

When asked to relate actions to the principles, stakeholders saw a relationship between actions and the principles of autonomy, beneficence, justice, and fidelity.

Stakeholders matched the principles of autonomy with three negative evaluator actions: making decisions without consulting with clients, reflecting the evaluator's own self-interest, and not determining audience values. These actions were viewed as misuse or violations of evaluator independence to the exclusion of client rights.

Beneficence was reflected by the evaluator performing positive actions: identifying all stakeholders so that different needs can be addressed, describing and documenting the purpose of the evaluation, reporting information valuable enough to justify the evaluation, and encouraging key audiences to use the information. These positive actions reflect desire for inclusion on the part of the stakeholder, whereas the negative actions reflect perceptions of exclusion.

Justice was represented by positive and negative actions. Positive actions included using a broad scope of information such that all audiences were included, providing the reasons for using the instruments selected, respecting the worth of all participants, considering all viewpoints, and making the report available to all audiences. Negative actions included nonperformance or poor performance of these actions: being more concerned with the interests of one key audience, and assuming that all information sources are providing equivalent information. These actions indicate that, for consumers, an important aspect of justice is the inclusion of all audiences and a sense that the evaluator recognizes all stakeholders' worth and dignity.

Fidelity was reflected by stakeholders' perception that the evaluator was credible. This included competence and trustworthiness. Knowledge and skills pertaining to evaluation methodology and to the program under evaluation, as well as actions reflecting this knowledge, are necessary for trust and feelings of loyalty.

No actions, negative or positive, were identified with the principle of nonmaleficence. Interviews with stakeholders indicated that this may be the result of generally negative perceptions of evaluation. Because many stakeholders perceive evaluation itself as negative, they do not see evaluators as concerned with harm or lessening harm to those associated with the program.

Comparing Evaluators and Stakeholders

Evaluators and stakeholders perceived the proposed principles as reflecting portions of accepted professional practice (see Tables 3–2 and 3–3). For evaluators, most of the matched standards were identified with the ethical principles of nonmaleficence, beneficence, and justice.

TABLE 3–2 Categorization of Actions, by Principles: Evaluators

Ethical Principle	*Action*	*Standard*
Autonomy	Evaluator conducts an evaluation when he or she lacks sufficient skills or experience. (–)[a]	Utility
	Evaluation report provides information of sufficient value and use to justify its expense. (+)[b]	Feasibility
Nonmaleficence	Evaluation plan necessitates major disruptions and significant changes in staff activities. (–)	Feasibility
	Evaluator assumes that all information sources are equally adequate. (–)	Accuracy
	Evaluator selects a test primarily because of his or her familiarity with it. (–)	Accuracy
	Evaluator uses one type of reliability (internal consistency) to support test-retest reliability. (–)	Accuracy
	Evaluator does not have keypunched data verified for accuracy. (–)	Accuracy
	Evaluator interprets interview data intuitively. (–)	Accuracy
	Limitations of the evaluation are not described in the report. (–)	Accuracy
	Evaluation procedures provide safeguards to protect findings against distortion. (+)	Accuracy
Beneficence	Evaluation is designed to encourage key audiences to use the information. (+)	Utility
	Evaluation report indicates program strengths and weaknesses. (+)	Propriety
Justice	Evaluation is planned so that it considers the different positions of various interest groups. (+)	Feasibility
	Evaluation seems to be responding to the concerns of one interest group more than another's. (–)	Feasibility
	Evaluator respects the dignity and worth of other persons associated with the evaluation. (+)	Propriety
	Evaluator is more respectful toward project management than toward the staff. (–)	Propriety
	Evaluation report is written so that partisan interest groups can delete embarrassing weaknesses. (–)	Propriety
Fidelity	Evaluation report is timely. (+)	Utility
	Evaluation report is not available until well past its due date. (–)	Propriety
	What is to be done, how, by whom, and when is agreed to in writing. (+)	Propriety
	Evaluator makes decisions without consulting the client when consultation has been agreed to. (+)	Propriety
	Evaluator promises confidentiality when it cannot be guaranteed. (–)	Propriety

a. (–) indicates that statement exemplifies violation.
b. (+) indicates that statement exemplifies adherence.

TABLE 3–3 Categorization of Actions, by Principles: Stakeholders

Ethical Principle	*Action*	*Standard*
Autonomy	Evaluator makes decisions without consulting the client when consultation had been agreed to. (–)[a]	Propriety
	Evaluation report reflects the self-interest of the evaluator. (–)	Propriety
	Evaluator fails to find out what values are important to right-to-know audience. (–)	Utility
Nonmaleficence	(None stated)	
Beneficence	Evaluation is designed to encourage key audiences to use the information. (+)[b]	Utility
	Persons involved in or affected by the evaluation are identified so that their needs can be addressed. (+)	Utility
	Evaluation report provides information of sufficient value and use to justify its cost. (+)	Feasibility
	Purposes of the evaluation are described in enough detail so they can be assessed. (+)	Accuracy
Justice	Evaluation report is available to all right-to-know audiences. (+)	Utility
	Scope of the information collected is broad enough to address different audience needs. (+)	Utility
	Evaluation is planned so that it considers the different positions of various interest groups. (+)	Feasibility
	Evaluation seems to be responding to the concerns of one interest group more than another's. (–)	Feasibility
	Evaluator respects the dignity and worth of other persons associated with the evaluation. (+)	Propriety
	Evaluator selects a test primarily because of his or her familiarity with it. (+)	Accuracy
	Evaluator assumes that all information sources are equally adequate. (–)	Accuracy
Fidelity	Evaluator is competent and trustworthy. (+)	Utility

a. (–) indicates that statement exemplifies violation.
b. (+) indicates that statement exemplifies adherence.

Stakeholders matched fewer standards; most of their matches were with beneficence and justice. Canadian evaluators and stakeholders perceived the principle of fidelity as reflective of evaluator competence and trustworthiness; U.S. evaluators did not reach agreement on what constitutes fidelity. Evaluators matched both standards and actions with the nonmaleficence principle, and most of these matches reflected methodological issues. Stakeholders did not match any standards or actions with avoiding undue harm. In general, stakeholders were able to match more positive actions with the principles than were evaluators; the latter tended to reach consensus on what constitutes a violation of practice but not on what constitutes good practice.

Question 2: Are the varying roles assigned to evaluators, and the resulting expectations, related to the proposed principles?

We conducted a series of studies investigating the relationship between the principles and three major functional evaluator roles. (Chapter 5 discusses these roles.) Our intent was to determine if responsibilities or expectations for the principles rested with a particular functional role or if adherence to some principles was seen as an expectation of all roles.

Studies investigating the relationship between roles and principles began with an attempt to validate consensus on the presence of roles reflected in current practice, especially practice that was considered ethical in nature. Consequently, the first question to be addressed was whether or not evaluators and stakeholders matched current written standards, representing ethical practice, as belonging to a particular functional evaluator role. Standards examined were those advocated by the Evaluation Research Society and the Joint Committee on Standards. (Again, later research used only the Joint Committee Standards.) Standards matched with roles were then cross-matched with principles to determine if a particular standard by principle relationship was found within roles. Study participants were U.S. and Canadian evaluators representing the disciplines of education, mental health, public health, and private consultation. Stakeholders were program administrators, program staff, and program users.

The Role of Evaluator as Administrator

The role of evaluator as administrator is one of the three most common functional roles for program evaluators. In this role, the evaluator is in charge of soliciting and managing evaluation projects, monitoring evaluation personnel, and responding to program stakeholder needs. Additional duties of an evaluator as administrator may vary depending on the evaluator's status within the organization and with the program under review. For example, administrative functions of internal and external evaluators may differ from those of directors of large evaluation units and from those of private consultants.

Evaluators identified several common expectations for administrative roles. These included providing for evaluation impact, managing contractual functions, monitoring political aspects of evaluation, and overseeing the rights of human subjects. Evaluators from all disciplines indicated that evaluation impact and financial considerations were the domain of the administrative role. When matched with principles, the evaluator as administrator was seen as primarily responsible for standards and actions related to beneficence and justice. Special emphasis was placed on the expectation that the evaluator as administrator was responsible for providing for evaluation impact as a function of doing good and maintaining the rights of human subjects as a matter of justice. Variations in additional responsibilities were present on a discipline-by-discipline basis (see Box 3.5). Evaluators perceived no administrative function as representative of autonomy or nonmaleficence.

Stakeholders (Box 3.6) agreed on two expected responsibilities for the evaluator as administrator. The first was monitoring the politics of the program, especially politics related to special interest groups, and countering any attempts to bias the evaluation. The second involved obtaining and documenting a true understanding of what the program was supposed to be, what it actually was, and why the two differed. These responses are similar to evaluators' expectations regarding program politics and impact but differ in that they exclude financial and human rights considerations. Stakeholders did not perceive monetary finances and human rights as part of the administrative role. No matches were found when stakeholders' perceptions of administrators were sorted with principles.

Box 3.5 Role of Evaluator as Administrator: Evaluators' Perceptions

Results of studies investigating U.S. and Canadian evaluators' perceptions indicate that evaluators as administrators are responsible for evaluation impact and the rights of political aspects of the evaluation (e.g., avoiding conflicts of interest and determining the political viability of the evaluation).

Evaluators in the mental health area saw evaluation impact, fiscal impact, and cost-effectiveness as responsibilities of the administrator role. Evaluators, as private consultants, agreed with the responsibilities of human rights, evaluation impact, fiscal responsibility, and cost-effectiveness but also saw determination of information scope and objective reporting as responsibilities of the evaluation administrator. Evaluators in health-related areas emphasized the administrative functions of evaluation impact, cost-effectiveness, and the public's right to know. Educational evaluators emphasized political aspects, clarification of formal obligations, determination of context of program, rights of human subjects, and evaluation impact.

Consistency also was found among evaluators' responses when examining the relationship between the administrator role in evaluation and the five principles. The evaluator as administrator was responsible primarily for standards related to beneficence and justice. The principle of justice, as expected of administrators, included maintaining formal obligations, providing a cost-effective evaluation, avoiding conflict of interest, and maintaining the rights of human subjects. Monitoring and improving evaluation impact was perceived as fulfilling the principle of beneficence. Education evaluators perceived cost-effectiveness as reflective of justice or fair play; mental health, private consultant, and health evaluators matched cost-effectiveness with fidelity or loyalty to the client. No matches were found for the administrator role with the principles of autonomy or nonmaleficence.

Box 3.6 Role of Evaluator as Administrator: Stakeholders' Perceptions

Stakeholders matched two standards with administrative responsibilities: program documentation and political viability. Program documentation included obtaining and confirming information on what the program should be as well as what it is and making the information accessible. Political viability included anticipating special interest group reactions and needs and countering any attempts to curtail, mislead, or bias the evaluation.

When asked to match standards with the five principles, no consistent matches occurred. Some clients saw these expectations as outcomes of justice and fidelity; others saw them as nonmaleficence or beneficence. Consequently, although stakeholders agreed that evaluators as administrators are responsible for two important functions, there was no consensus on what type of ethical behavior the expectations reflected.

The Role of Evaluator as Data Collector/Researcher

The role of the evaluator as data collector/researcher is one of the most traditional, yet most varied functional roles of the evaluator. Derived from the social sciences, this role carries with it all of the expectations of the objective scientist but borrows heavily from the humanities in terms of selecting and valuing information. Most of the discipline-based ethical codes of professionals conducting program evaluation address aspects of the data collector/researcher role. In some instances, these codes are very specific; in others, expectations are more general. Overall, the functions and expectations of the evaluator as data collector/researcher are most well known.

The role of the data collector is seen as an important one by both evaluators (Box 3.7) and stakeholders (Box 3.8). Both groups matched similar guidelines or tasks as expectations of this role: providing reliable and valid measurement, balancing reporting, efforts, documenting information, and protecting the rights of human subjects. Evaluators and stakeholders differed, however, on the principles that this role typified. Evaluators saw the data collection role, especially activities related to data measurement, collection, and documentation, as representative of nonmaleficence, whereas clients and program staff perceived these tasks as beneficence. Both groups perceived maintaining human rights as exemplifying justice. Evaluators saw balanced reporting as a function of justice. Private consultants and mental health evaluators agreed on the perception of evaluator credibility as a function of fidelity, but education and health evaluators did not. Neither evaluators nor stakeholders perceived the principle of autonomy as part of the data collector role.

Box 3.7 Role of Evaluator as Data Collector: Evaluators' Perceptions

For evaluators, the role of data collector/researcher encompasses responsibilities associated with methodological issues related to instrumentation, sampling, and procedures. Responsibilities related to instrumentation included documentation of data sources, selection of valid and reliable measures, and control of access to data; sampling issues were typified by the selection of subjects, measures, and information sources. Procedural functions included human interactions and objective reporting. Canadian and U.S. evaluators did not differ markedly on the key functions of the evaluators as data collector/researcher. Evaluators serving mental health areas and private consultants, however, differed from evaluators in education and health-related disciplines on the expectations of this role. The former perceived practice and functions related to evaluator credibility to be a component of the evaluator as data collector; respondents from health and education did not.

Evaluators placed more emphasis on the principle of nonmaleficence than on any other principle. This included guidelines associated with validity and reliability, control of data, and documentation of data sources. Beneficence and justice also were considered responsibilities of the data collector/researcher but to a lesser degree. Standards reflecting human interactions and balanced reporting were considered acts of justice for data collectors, whereas information scope and following appropriate procedures were seen as beneficence. Evaluators as data collectors were not viewed as responsible for autonomy. Mental health evaluators and private consultant evaluators saw evaluation credibility as a function of justice.

In summary, evaluators perceived themselves, when in the role of data collector, as being primarily responsible for avoiding undue harm. Guidelines related to this principle included sound measurement practice, unobtrusive behavior, and consideration of stakeholders' status in the program. The latter included the rights to balanced reporting and respect of individual rights.

Box 3.8 Role of Evaluator as Data Collector: Stakeholders' Perceptions

Of the tasks assigned by stakeholders to the three roles, over half were matched with the evaluator as data collector. Tasks included responsibility for evaluator credibility, information selection, valid and reliable measurement, guarding against violations of human rights and human interactions, and objective reporting of information.

Stakeholders matched data collector functions with the principles of beneficence, justice, and fidelity. Information scope and selection and the use of practical procedures were viewed as beneficence on the part of the data collector. Justice was exemplified by maintaining the rights of human subjects and fidelity by being trustworthy, competent, and credible. No data collector functions were matched with the principles of autonomy and nonmaleficence.

The Role of Evaluator as Reporter

The role of evaluator as reporter is one of the least codified when examined in light of evaluation training, evaluation textbooks, and evaluator practice. Although most professional evaluators are well trained and experienced in the aspects of data collection, analysis, and interpretation, less emphasis is spent on how to report the resulting information. Concepts of what constitutes good reporting vary from discipline to discipline in the training literature and among practicing evaluators. Acceptable formats range from presentation of statistical tables to multiple documents and oral presentations. Acceptable modes are formal written reports, creative media presentations, and group meetings.

Both evaluators (Box 3.9) and stakeholders (Box 3.10) perceive the role of reporter as exemplifying certain functions and principles. Both groups have expectations of timely, clear reports available to multiple audiences. Evaluators also had expectations related to type and amount of information to be reported and variations of disclosure. These expectations varied by discipline of practice.

Both evaluators and stakeholders viewed report timeliness and clarity as a function of doing good, not as a right of clients nor as an act of fidelity. Evaluators perceived full and frank disclosure as an autonomous right, justified conclusions as avoiding undue harm, and provision of accurate information as fidelity to the client. Stakeholders did not perceive current practice, as exemplified by reporting, as reflecting any principle but beneficence.

Box 3.9 Role of Evaluator as Reporter: Evaluators' Perceptions

Evaluators placed equal weight on the role of evaluator as reporter with those of evaluator as administrator and as data collector. Expectations assigned to the role included balanced reporting and adequate dissemination of results. Dissemination of results encompassed functions associated with full and frank disclosure, the public's right to know, and availability of information to all concerned stakeholders. Balanced reporting included justified conclusions, report clarity, report timeliness, and inclusion of multiple viewpoints. Both U.S. and Canadian evaluators selected report timeliness as the most important function. Evaluators whose primary association was with health or education programs stressed balanced reporting and full and frank disclosure of results as key expectations. Educational evaluators also included expectations related to proper analysis of qualitative and quantitative data under this role. Mental health evaluators placed more emphasis on determining and documenting valid and reliable measures than on the process of reporting results. Private consultants perceived report timeliness as the key action for practicing evaluators.

Expectations of the evaluator as reporter represented all five principles for practicing evaluators. Full and frank disclosure of results was associated with the right of all clients and viewed as an indicator of autonomy. Report timeliness and clarity represented doing good or beneficence. Justified conclusions and accurate analysis of data typified nonmaleficence; providing information that is accurate and available was seen as fidelity.

Although some differences were found on the basis of discipline of practice, balanced reporting, timeliness, and clarity were seen as important along with balanced dissemination. All groups of evaluators, except those who primarily served as private consultants, viewed dissemination of results as an important issue. For private consultants, timeliness was the main and most important issue.

Box 3.10 Role of Evaluator as Reporter: Stakeholders' Perceptions

For stakeholders, the evaluator as reporter was responsible for balanced reporting as well as report dissemination. Balanced reporting, for administrators and program staff alike, included clarity, timeliness, and balanced viewpoints.

Report dissemination included presenting the report to appropriate audiences and making the information available to all right-to-know groups. When these expectations were matched with principles, stakeholders uniformly viewed them as acts of doing good. Reports distributed in a timely manner to all participants were not perceived as a right of stakeholders nor as an act of fidelity but as beneficence.

Functional Roles, Expectations, and the Principles

In general (as seen in Table 3–4), the expectations assigned to evaluation roles appear to be encompassed by the five principles. Not surprising, evaluators had a broader range of expectations than did stakeholders for all three roles and saw all five principles exemplified in current practice. Evaluators perceived the role of the evaluator as administrator to reflect evaluation impact, financial concerns, political viability, and regard for human rights. These were primarily seen as issues of justice and beneficence. For evaluators, the role of data collector/researcher included responsibilities associated with methodology and design, such as instrumentation, sampling, and procedures. These functions were seen primarily as reflections of avoiding undue harm, or nonmaleficence. The role of reporter, for evaluators, included expectations of balanced reporting and adequate dissemination of results, such as full and frank disclosure, the public's right to know, availability of information to all concerned stakeholders, justified conclusions, report clarity, and report timeliness. All five principles were perceived as part of the domain of evaluator as reporter.

Stakeholders had fewer expectations of the evaluator as administrator, delegating most functions to the data collector or reporter roles. For stakeholders, the evaluator as administrator was perceived as responsible for program documentation and monitoring of the political aspects of the evaluation; however, there was no consensus on the ethical domain of these actions. The evaluator as data collector/researcher was responsible for evaluator credibility, data selection, data collection, maintaining human rights, and balanced reporting. These functions were perceived as products of beneficence, justice, and fidelity. For stakeholders, reporter responsibilities encompassed duties associated with well-balanced and adequately disseminated reports. This included information that is understandable and available to all right-to-know groups. These actions represented beneficence, or doing good. In general, stakeholders did not perceive any ethical guidelines for evaluators that monitor avoiding undue harm, nor did they perceive any standards that safeguard their autonomy.

TABLE 3–4 Categorization of Standards,[a] by Principle, for Three Roles

	Role	Principle: Autonomy	Nonmaleficence	Beneficence	Justice	Fidelity
Evaluator	Administrator	Political Viability F2	Practical Procedures F1 Context Analysis A2	Stakeholder Identification U1 Evaluation Impact U7	Cost-Effectiveness F3 Formal Obligation P2 Rights of Human Subjects P3 Human Interactions P4 Conflict of Interest P7	
	Data Collector/ Researcher		Defensible Information Sources A4 Valid Measurement A5 Reliable Measurement A6 Systematic Information A7	Information Scope and Selection U3		Objective Reporting A11
	Reporter	Full and Frank Disclosure P6	Analysis of Quantitative Information A9 Analysis of Qualitative Information A9 Justified Conclusions A10	Report Clarity U5 Report Timeliness U7 Complete and Fair Assessment P5	Report Dissemination U6 Disclosure of Findings P6	
Stakeholder	Administrator					
	Data Collector/ Researcher			Information Scope and Selection U3 Practical Procedures F1	Rights of Human Subjects P3	Evaluator Credibility U2
	Reporter			Report Clarity U5	Report Timeliness and Dissemination U6	

NOTE: Joint Committee Standard A = Accuracy; F = Feasibility; P = Propriety; U = Utility.

Question 3: Do ethical violations occur in evaluation practice, and if so, do they reflect violations of specific principles?

Examination of literature pertaining to evaluation practice indicates that several attempts have been made to identify and clarify violations of ethical practice (e.g., Amen, 1990; Bunda & Halderson, 1985; Honea, 1990, 1991; McKillip & Garberg, 1986; Morris & Cohn, 1993; Sheinfeld & Lord, 1981; Stockdill, 1987; Toms, 1993). The majority of these studies asked evaluators for examples of poor practice. Although this has the advantage of obtaining evaluators' firsthand perceptions of what they perceive as wrong practice, it has the disadvantage of respondent bias. Using this method, even though clients, society, or other evaluators may view an action as wrong, if the evaluator does not perceive the action as incorrect, it never gets reported as a violation. We chose to use a different approach; we used examples of poor practice, as identified in the standards issued by the Joint Committee on Standards (1981, 1994), as statements representative of possible evaluation actions and asked evaluators and stakeholders to provide their opinions of how frequently these actions occurred in the practice of evaluation.

After obtaining information on frequency of occurrence, we then asked evaluators and stakeholders for perceptions of the seriousness of these errors. This method permitted us to identify frequency and seriousness of areas of unethical practice in the field of program evaluation that we might not have been able to obtain in any other way. Later studies further validated these perceptions by asking various stakeholder groups to confirm perceptions of these actions as serious and common occurrences in program evaluation and then elicited case study examples.

The purpose of these studies was twofold: first, to determine if practicing evaluators and stakeholders perceived violations of ethical practice in their work setting as a common occurrence and their perceptions of the seriousness of such violations, and second, to determine the relationship of these occurrences to the proposed framework of evaluation principles. When examining responses to violations, we found it helpful to provide a further delineation of respondents than was used in earlier studies and subsequently categorized information for three groups.

Group 1 represented practicing evaluators, similar to those in the previous sections. Group 2 consisted of stakeholders who had experience with evaluation; these respondents were self-identified as having either commissioned evaluations or participated in multiple programs that were evaluated and where they perceived themselves as part of the evaluation effort. Respondents in this group were, in general, administrators, upper-level program staff, and special services personnel. We designated this group "Program Administrators." Those in Group 3 were stakeholders with less experience in evaluations. These respondents indicated that, even though their program may have been evaluated, they had little involvement in the evaluation. This group was usually composed of program staff or program implementors, so we called this group "Program Staff." Tables 3–5 through 3–7 provide a summary of the three groups' responses; additional information is provided in Boxes 3.11 through 3.14.

Frequent Violations of Practice

Examination of Table 3–5 indicates that all three groups ranked "Evaluator selects a test primarily because of his or her familiarity with it" as the most frequent evaluator violation. Also identified as a frequent violation by all three groups was the statement "The evaluation report responds to the concerns of one interest group more than another." Both program administrators and program staff indicated a perception of lack of credibility on the part of the evaluation process through the high frequency given to the item "Evaluation is conducted because it is 'required' when it obviously cannot yield useful results." Lack of credibility of the evaluator also was indicated by these two groups in their high ranking for frequency of occurrence of "The evaluation report reflects the self-interest of the evaluator" (program staff) and "the evaluator conducts an evaluation when he or she lacks sufficient skills or experience" (program administrators and program staff). Administrators perceived frequent violations related to evaluators' lack of knowledge of the audience and overuse of highly technical reports.

When examining responses for least frequent violations of evaluation practice, several commonalities were found among evaluator, administrator, and program staff responses. All three groups indicated that the evaluator's practice of changing the question or making decisions without consulting with the client were infrequent violations. Program staff appeared to see few violations related to accuracy of information, whereas evaluators saw few violations related to the product.

Support for perceptions of the frequency of the occurrence of these violations was found in additional studies of educational administrators and teachers (Boxes 3.13 and 3.14). Teachers perceived a high degree of failure to check accuracy of classroom information, believed that evaluators lacked knowledge about the content of the program, and felt that evaluators did not investigate the program context adequately. Teachers also indicated a perception that evaluators frequently disrupted classroom procedures, safeguarded their own (evaluators') self-interests, and were more respectful of administrators' special concerns. Administrators did not perceive evaluation as disruptive of classroom procedure, nor did they perceive evaluators as being more respectful of administration needs than those of teachers. Administrators perceived frequent failure on the part of the evaluator to check on accuracy of information, particularly program context, and believed that the evaluator was frequently not adequately skilled.

In summary, although responses from evaluators and both groups of stakeholders reflect some consensus on frequency of type of violation, there was disagreement on significant points, especially when stakeholders were stratified into program administrators and program staff. All three groups perceived selection of instrumentation and response to concerns of selected special interest groups as frequently occurring violations. Both program administrators and program staff frequently perceived that evaluations were being conducted because they were "required," not because they were "useful." Staff frequently perceived evaluations as too general and reflective of evaluators' own self-interests; program administrators were more concerned about lack of knowledge of limitations of the evaluation and the competency of evaluators.

Serious Violations of Practice

Responses from evaluators, program administrators, and program staff (see Table 3–6) indicated that the three groups were similar in their selections of serious violations of appropriate evaluator practice. Evaluators and program staff selected the same five violations as most serious, and administrators selected four of the five. All three groups indicated that promising confidentiality when it could not be guaranteed and conducting an evaluation when one is not competent are serious

(text continues on page 86)

TABLE 3–5 Items Ranked Most and Least Frequent,[a] by Degree of Experience

Most Frequent	*Least Frequent*
Program Staff	
1. Evaluator selects a test primarily because of his or her familiarity with it. (A5)	26. Evaluator does not have keypunched data verified for accuracy. (A7)
2. Evaluation is so general that it does not address differing audience needs. (U1)	27. Evaluator makes decisions without consulting with the client when consultation has been agreed to. (P1)
3. Evaluation responds to the concerns of one interest group more than another's. (F2)	28. Evaluation plan necessitates major disruptions and significant changes in staff activities. (F1)
4. Evaluation report reflects the self-interest of the evaluator. (P3)	29. Evaluator lets client make the final edit. (A11)
5. Evaluation is conducted because it is "required" when it obviously cannot yield useful results. (F3)	30. Evaluator changes the evaluation questions to match the data analysis. (A8)
Program Administrators	
1. Evaluator selects a test primarily because of his or her familiarity with it. (A5)	26. Evaluator promises confidentiality when it cannot be guaranteed. (P5)
2. Evaluator responds to the concerns of one interest group more than another's. (F2)	27. Evaluator makes decisions without consulting with the client when consultation has been agreed to. (P1)
3. Evaluation is conducted because it is "required" when it obviously cannot yield useful results. (F3)	28. Evaluator does not have keypunched data verified for accuracy. (A7)
4. Limitations of the report are not described in the report evaluation. (A10)	29. Evaluator changes the evaluation questions to match the data analysis. (A8)
5. Evaluator conducts an evaluation when he or she lacks sufficient skills or experience. (U2)	30. Evaluator lets client make the final edit. (A11)

Evaluators	
1. Evaluator selects a test primarily because of his or her familiarity with it. (A5)	26. Evaluator promises confidentiality when it cannot be guaranteed. (P5)
2. Evaluator loses interest in the evaluation when the final report is delivered. (U8)	27. Evaluation report is written so that partisan interest groups can delete embarrassing weaknesses. (P7)
3. Evaluation responds to the concerns of one interest group more than another's. (F2)	28. Evaluator assumes that all information sources are equally adequate. (A4)
4. Evaluator fails to find out what the values are of right-to-know audiences. (U4)	29. Evaluator makes decisions without consulting with the client when consultation has been agreed to. (P1)
5. Evaluator writes a highly technical report for a technically unsophisticated audience. (U5)	30. Evaluator changes the evaluation questions to match the data analysis. (A8)

SOURCE: An earlier version of this table appeared in Newman and Brown (1992).
NOTE: Joint Committee Standard A = Accuracy; F = Feasibility; P = Propriety; U = Utility.
a. Rank of 30 items.

Box 3.11 Violations of Practice: Evaluators' Perceptions

Evaluators indicated an inverse relationship between frequency of negative practice and seriousness of actions. When presented with statements portrayed as pitfalls or nonadherence to Joint Committee Standards, actions that were perceived as serious violations were not perceived as frequent occurrences. Four of the five most serious violations were included in the five least frequent violations. Three of the five most serious violations reflected propriety issues; three of the five most frequent occurrences were concerned with usefulness of information. The item "Evaluator changes the evaluation questions to match the data analysis" had the highest rating when ranked by seriousness but was the lowest-ranked item for frequency of occurrence. The item "Evaluator loses interest in the evaluation as soon as the final report is delivered" was the second highest item when ranked by frequency of violation but was the 29th item (out of 30) when ranked by seriousness of violation.

Box 3.12 Violations of Practice: Stakeholders' Perceptions

When assessing perceptions of violations of ethics, two groups of stakeholders were represented. Experienced consumers included administrators and special service personnel who had commissioned evaluations and/or participated in multiple programs for which an evaluation had been commissioned. Novice consumers consisted of teachers, program staff, and providers who worked for programs that had been evaluated by others but who indicated they had little or no direct experience with the process. Both groups ranked "Evaluator selects a test primarily because of his or her familiarity with it" as the most frequent violation. Both groups also indicated a perception of lack of credibility on the part of the evaluation processes through the ranking given to the item "Evaluation is conducted because it is 'required' when it obviously cannot yield useful results" and "The evaluation responds to the concerns of one interest group more than another's." Lack of credibility of the evaluator was indicated by both groups in their high ranking of "The evaluation report reflects the self-interest of the evaluator" (novice) and "The evaluator conducts an evaluation when he or she lacks sufficient skills or experience" (experienced consumers). Experienced consumers also tended to see frequent violations related to evaluators' lack of knowledge of the audience—for example, "The evaluator fails to find out what the values are of the right-to-know audiences" and "Evaluator writes a highly technical report for a technically unsophisticated audience."

When examining responses among stakeholders for seriousness of violations, lesser homogeneity was found. Both groups indicated that providing confidentiality when it cannot be guaranteed and conducting an evaluation when one is not competent are serious violations and that the evaluators' practice of changing the question or making decisions without consulting with the client were infrequent violations.

Box 3.13 Validation of Violations: Teachers' Perceptions

Actions described by consumers as either serious or frequent violations of evaluation were presented as part of a larger survey assessing educators' perceptions of evaluation. Respondents consisted of educators who were currently teaching in the state of New York. Six of the 14 items reflecting actions identified as violations were perceived by teachers to be common occurrences in the public school setting. Examination of the items indicated that most reflect teacher perceptions of disenfranchisement from the process of evaluation. The perceptions that evaluators fail to check the accuracy of information, do not discuss the context, do not present program context, and lack content knowledge indicate a lack of credibility of the process. These violations were categorized as failure to avoid undue harm, or nonmaleficence, in earlier studies. The perception that evaluators are more respectful to certain interest groups or are safeguarding self-interests indicates teachers' perceptions that their rights are not being monitored. These violations were viewed as nonadherence to justice and autonomy. Response to the item "Program evaluation necessitates major disruptions and significant changes in classroom activities" is of special note. Educators agreed that this was a very frequent occurrence in the classroom.

Box 3.14 Validation of Violations: Need for Inclusion

Teachers and administrators were asked to respond to a series of questions probing teachers' opportunities and willingness to be involved in the process of program evaluation. Using shared decision-making theory, three functional levels of involvement were identified that parallel the three functional roles of evaluators: evaluation design (administrator/consultant role), evaluation implementation (data collector/researcher role), and evaluation utilization (reporter). Respondents included teachers and administrators in public K-12 education in the state of New York. Results indicated differences between teachers and administrators on opportunities and willingness to be involved in evaluation. Overall, teachers indicated that they currently had limited involvement in program evaluation, that they were either not involved or were asked only to supply information for others to use. They indicated, however, that they would like to be more involved in program evaluation, especially in decisions related to design and use of information. In these areas, teachers indicated that they would like to provide not only information but would also like to be part of the team. Administrators indicated a greater perception of teachers' opportunities for involvement but perceived less willingness to be involved. In general, administrators perceived a disinclination toward and a distrust of evaluation on the part of teachers.

TABLE 3–6 Items Ranked Most and Least Serious,[a] by Degree of Experience

Most Serious	*Least Serious*
Program Staff	
1. Evaluator promises confidentiality when it cannot be guaranteed. (P5)	26. Evaluator assumes that the initial purpose of the evaluation will not be changed throughout the process. (A3)
2. Evaluator changes the evaluation questions to match the data analysis. (A8)	27. Evaluator fails to find out what the values are of right-to-know audiences. (U4)
3. Evaluator conducts an evaluation when he or she lacks sufficient skills or experience. (U2)	28. Evaluator interprets interview data intuitively. (A9)
4. Evaluator makes decisions without consulting with the client when consultation has been agreed to. (P1)	29. Evaluation plan necessitates major disruptions and significant changes in staff activities. (F1)
5. Evaluation report is written so that partisan interest groups can delete embarrassing weaknesses. (P7)	30. Evaluator loses interest in the evaluation when the final report is written. (U8)
Program Administrators	
1. Evaluator changes the evaluation questions to match the data analysis. (A8)	26. Evaluation report is available only to the hiring client, with no provision for other audiences. (U6)
2. Evaluator makes decisions without consulting with the client when consultation has been agreed to. (P1)	27. Evaluation is designed without consideration of the political context. (A2)
3. Evaluator conducts an evaluation when he or she lacks sufficient skills or experience. (U2)	28. Evaluator fails to find out what the values are of right-to-know audiences. (U4)
4. Evaluator promises confidentiality when it cannot be guaranteed. (P5)	29. Evaluator collects information that is relatively easy to collect but not necessary for the evaluation. (U3)
5. Evaluator fails to check the accuracy of the program description. (A1)	30. Evaluator interprets interview data intuitively. (A9)

Evaluators	
1. Evaluator changes the evaluation questions to match the data analysis. (A8)	26. Report is distributed on the basis of who it is convenient to send it to. (P4)
2. Evaluator promises confidentiality when it cannot be guaranteed. (P5)	27. Evaluator collects information that is relatively easy to collect but not necessary for the evaluation. (U3)
3. Evaluator makes decisions without consulting with the client when consultation has been agreed to. (P1)	28. Evaluator uses one type of reliability (internal consistency) to support another (test-retest reliability). (A6)
4. Evaluator conducts an evaluation when he or she lacks sufficient skills or experience. (U2)	29. Evaluator loses interest in the evaluation when the final report is written. (U8)
5. Evaluation report is written so that partisan interest groups can delete embarrassing weaknesses. (P7)	30. Evaluator interprets interview data intuitively. (A9)

SOURCE: An earlier version of this table appeared in Newman and Brown (1992).
NOTE: Joint Committee Standard A = Accuracy; F = Feasibility; P = Propriety; U = Utility.
a. Rank of 30 items.

violations. Changing the evaluation questions to match data analysis techniques that the evaluator favors and making decisions without consulting with the client also were identified as serious negative actions by all three groups.

Similarities among the three groups were not evident when least serious violations were considered. The only commonality was that "intuitive interpretation of interview data," indicative of incorrect analysis of qualitative data, was not a serious violation when it occurred. Program staff and program administrators also agreed that lack of attention to the values of different audiences was not a serious violation.

Comparing Frequency and Seriousness of Violations

When responses to seriousness of violations were compared to perceptions of frequency of violations, several inverse patterns were noted. For evaluators, the item "Evaluator changes the evaluation questions to match the data analysis" had the highest rating when ranked by seriousness but was the lowest-ranked item for frequency of occurrence. The item "Evaluator loses interest in the evaluation as soon as the final report is delivered" was the second highest item when ranked by frequency of violation but was the 29th (of 30) when ranked by seriousness of violation.

Administrators perceived the act of conducting an evaluation without the necessary skills or experience as not only a frequent violation but also a serious one. Three acts were considered serious but infrequent events by administrators:

- Promising confidentiality when it cannot be guaranteed
- The evaluator making decisions without consulting with clients
- Changing questions to match data analyses

Program staff agreed with program administrators on the latter two events; both perceived lack of consultation on question changes and evaluation process as a serious but not necessarily frequent event.

Evaluation Violations Reflective of Principles of Evaluation

When comparing responses of seriousness and frequency of violations of evaluation practice to perceptions of principles, it becomes apparent that evaluation principles are violated both frequently and seriously. For program staff, two frequent violations and three serious violations were indicative of evaluation principles (see Table 3–7). Conducting an evaluation because it is required was perceived as a frequent violation of beneficence, and presenting reports that reflect the self-interest of the evaluator was seen as a frequent violation of justice. Serious violations included the evaluator making decisions without consulting with the client, seen as a breach of autonomy; conducting an evaluation when lacking the skills or experience, seen as failure to avoid undue harm; and reporting to partisan interest groups, perceived as a serious violation of justice.

Program administrators also matched several violations identified with the principles. Administrators perceived responding to the concerns of one interest group over another and not providing the limitations of the evaluation in the report as frequent violations of nonmaleficence. Failing to check the accuracy of the program description was perceived as a serious violation of nonmaleficence, whereas making decisions without consulting with the client was seen as a serious violation of autonomy. For administrators, conducting an evaluation without sufficient skills was seen as both a frequent and a serious violation of nonmaleficence.

Evaluators' perceptions of violations could also be identified with the five principles. Statements reflecting frequency of violation included selecting a test primarily because of familiarity, seen as a violation of nonmaleficence, and responding to the concerns of one interest group more than another, identified as a misuse of justice. Making decisions without consulting with clients was viewed as a serious violation of fidelity, conducting an evaluation when lacking sufficient skills was seen as a serious violation of nonmaleficence, allowing partisan interest groups the right to edit the report was a serious breach of justice, and promising confidentiality when it cannot be guaranteed was a violation of autonomy.

TABLE 3–7 Comparison of Perceptions of Common Violations

Violation	*Respondent*	*Perception*	*Principle*
Evaluators fail to check the accuracy of the program evaluation.	Administrators	Serious	Nonmaleficence
Evaluation plan necessitates major disruptions and significant changes in the classroom.	Administrators	Not serious	Nonmaleficence
	Teachers	Serious	
Limitations of the evaluation are not described in the report.	Administrators	Frequent	Nonmaleficence
Program evaluators frequently lack adequate content knowledge of the program being evaluated.	Administrators	Serious	Nonmaleficence
	Program staff	Serious	Nonmaleficence
	Evaluators	Serious	Nonmaleficence
Evaluators frequently do evaluation for their own self-interest, not for the benefit of the client.	Program staff	Frequent	Justice
Evaluators are more respectful toward the project management (or special interest group) than toward the staff.	Administrators	Frequent	Nonmaleficence
	Program staff	Frequent	Justice
	Evaluators	Frequent	Justice
	Teachers	Frequent	Justice
Evaluation is conducted because it is "required" when it obviously cannot yield useful results.	Program staff	Frequent	Beneficence
Evaluators make decisions without consulting with the client.	Administrators	Serious	Autonomy
	Program staff	Serious	Autonomy
	Evaluators	Serious	Fidelity
Evaluators conduct an evaluation without the necessary skills and experience.	Administrators	Serious	Nonmaleficence
	Program staff	Serious	Nonmaleficence
	Evaluators	Serious	Nonmaleficence
Selecting a test primarily because of familiarity	Evaluator	Serious	Justice
Allowing partisan interest group to edit the report	Evaluator	Serious	Justice
Promising confidentiality when it cannot be guaranteed	Evaluator	Serious	Autonomy

Overall, it appears that actions representing evaluation practice can be classified according to principles and that evaluators and stakeholders perceive some of these actions as violations of practice.

CONCLUSION

These studies represent only the beginning stage of development and modification of an ethical framework that is applicable to program evaluation. Each study has its share of strengths and weaknesses; it is in their entirety that we begin to see a portrait of ethical practice. It appears that the principles reflect some aspects of evaluation as seen by evaluators and stakeholders. Current practice does not appear to address the principle of autonomy nor the principle of fidelity from the evaluators' point of view nor the principle of avoiding undue harm from the stakeholders' point of view. When examining actual practice, actions spoke louder than words. Evaluators and clients were able to cross-match more actions with principles and roles than they were able to cross-match written standards. Further evidence of this was found in the studies concerning violations of ethical practice. Evaluators and stakeholders rated a series of negative actions as frequent occurrences in the practice of evaluation and matched those actions with principles.

Before ending our discussion of the findings of our research, we want to share with you a common response found across all studies, no matter what setting, method, role, or discipline of respondent. We consistently found people whose generalized response was "What? Ethics? What does ethics have to do with evaluation?" This came from experienced evaluators, long-term users of evaluation, evaluation interns, and faculty members teaching program evaluation. (Others have subsequently received similar reactions—e.g., Honea, 1991; Morris & Cohn, 1993.) Clearly, the development of ethical reasoning in the profession of evaluation has begun but still has far to go.

4

A Framework for Making Ethical Decisions

A Reader's Guide to Chapter 4

This chapter provides a framework for reflecting on and making ethical decisions about evaluation practice. The first section of this chapter focuses on factors that affect ethical decision making:

- Levels of ethical decision making and analysis
- Stress associated with decision making
- Organizational context

The second section presents an ethical decision-making framework in the form of a flowchart that can be used to analyze and think through ethical dilemmas.

Vignette 4.1 Intuitive Misgivings

Jonathan is conducting an evaluation of a social agency and has an uneasy feeling about the process. His client suggests that the assistant manager of the agency should accompany him during the observations and interview. Jonathan is not sure if he should allow this, but he is not sure that there is really anything wrong with it.

- Should Jonathan feel uneasy?
- Could someone be harmed by the process?
- What actions could he take at this point?

After signing an evaluation contract with the Department of Education, Susan discovers that a reasonably close friend holds an important position in the program she has already begun to evaluate. She had not thought about conflict of interest as a problem when she signed the contract, but now she is not sure.

- Does Susan have a potential problem?
- Could the situation develop into an ethical conflict?
- What steps can Susan take at this point to avoid or stop future problems?

FACTORS INFLUENCING ETHICAL DECISION MAKING

Levels of Ethical Thinking

We believe that there are five levels of ethical thinking. The first three are based on Kitchener's (1984) work on ethical thinking: intuition, rules and codes, and principles and theories. The fourth is supported by the work of Drane (1982): beliefs, values, and philosophy. We have added the fifth level: taking action. Following is a brief description of these five levels and how they relate to ethical decision making in evaluation.

Intuition

The intuitive level occurs as our first reaction to a situation prior to being reflective. We say to ourselves, "Something doesn't feel right about this." Ethical decision making is not an entirely logical and rational process. The feelings we experience include stress, self-doubt, and a heightened emotional sensitivity (Haddad & Kapp, 1991). Being alert to these feelings is particularly important when there is no time for reflection or consultation. These feelings should prompt a mental caution sign to appear, suggesting that we need to proceed slowly through the evaluation intersections. We must be alert to our own sense that something in a situation warrants additional thought.

Evaluators frequently are confronted with decisions that must be made on the spur of the moment. For instance, you may be asked by a program administrator for a summary of the interview you just had with a staff member who was promised confidentiality. What is your first response? Or you could be asked pointedly at a board meeting what the mean performance level was when you know this masks extensive variability within the group related to important demographic characteristics. In these situations, you have to respond on the basis of your intuition.

We believe that it is possible to have an educated intuition. An evaluator who has thought through conflicts before either in simulations or in real life will, like the wine connoisseur who has an educated palate, be more sensitive and alert to the nuances of potential ethical conflicts. It is important to garner as much practice as possible in thinking through ethical matters. Also, it is important to feel comfortable enough to say "I need time to think this over" or "Let me talk this over with one of my colleagues and get back to you." Kitchener (1984) suggests that to act against our moral intuition is more likely to lead to error than to act consistent with our intuition. So, if our intuition makes us uncomfortable, we should see this as a prompt to reflect or to confer with a trusted colleague. If there is no time to reflect and an immediate response is needed, we must hope that our past reading, experience, and reflection provide an intuitive response that will satisfy as well our goal of being ethical.

Rules and Codes

As helpful as an educated or practiced intuition might be, it is insufficient. It may not cover all situations we face, and we cannot assume everyone's intuition is equally educated. This brings us to the next level of ethical thinking: reflecting and considering resources that we can employ to help our thinking. Ethical rules and codes are available for members of most professions. Evaluators who are trained in educational or psychological research programs have access to the ethical codes of the American Educational Research Association (1992) and the American Psychological Association (1992), the propriety standards of the Joint Committee on Standards (1981, 1994), and the Guiding Principles for Evaluators (American Evaluation Association, 1995).

Principles and Theory

Ethical principles are more abstract than rules and codes. They will not tell us specifically what to do in a particular situation, but they provide helpful guidelines when the rules do not fit our particular concern. They help us examine conflicts among rules and provide balance across situations. Theories are even more abstract than principles. They also can be used as general guidelines and can sometimes help when two principles apparently conflict when applied to our concern. As we noted earlier, we find Kitchener's (1984, 1985) exposition of ethical principles most useful and believe them comprehensive enough in their application to evaluation situations. We also believe that evaluators need to spend time becoming knowledgeable about ethical theory.

Personal Values and Beliefs

The fourth level of ethical decision making, suggested by Drane's (1982) work, emphasizes the use of our personal values, visions, and beliefs. This level involves knowledge of who we are and why we value actions on a personal level. Drane suggests that the intuitive, or first level of ethical decision making, and the fourth level, using knowledge of personal values and beliefs, are closely interrelated because they represent the core of who we are and who we strive to be as human beings. They represent what it is we truly believe, what it is we value, and what kind of person or professional we want to be. Decisions based on this level make our abstract visions concrete and also connect with our immediate feelings. At the principles and theory level of ethical reasoning, our ability to reason and think logically is an important element of the process. But logic alone is not going to resolve all ethical questions. At this level, our values ultimately play a major role in the process of ethical decision making. This is particularly true when principles conflict. At this level, we recognize our personal values and act accordingly.

Action

At this fifth level, which we have added to those of Kitchener and Drane, we move from thinking and feeling to acting on our ethical belief. At earlier levels, we explore the presence of an ethical dilemma, deciding if we should acknowledge the presence of an ethical issue. At the action level, we explore actions to be taken based on Levels 1 through 4—we have acknowledged the dilemma, now we must act. So, what do we do once it is decided that there truly is an ethical issue? What courses of action are open to us? Whom should we consult? What should happen next? Discussions of what to do once we find a rule or standard violated or in danger of being violated are sparse.

Stress, Time, and Decision Making

Ethical decision making often occurs in a context where there is a conflict and a confrontation is necessary. The conflict may be internal as we try to determine what is the right course of action, or the conflict may be between our views and those of others. Choices are usually between not taking action and confronting a colleague, a client, or a supervisor. Making ethical decisions under these circumstances can be highly stressful.

Janis and Mann (1977) proposed the conflict model of decision making, which suggests that our stress level is affected by (a) how strongly we believe a correct solution is available, (b) how much risk is involved, and (c) the amount of time we have to make a decision. These contextual factors influence how we process information and make decisions. Research, which we have conducted, indicates that these factors influence how information is processed in evaluation situations, and we believe that it is important to consider how stress and time pressures affect our decision making, particularly when an ethical choice must be made (Brown, Newman, & Rivers, 1984; Jatulis & Newman, 1991; Newman, Brown, & Rivers, 1987; Pflum & Brown, 1984).

The Janis-Mann (1977) conflict model has five contexts that vary in the degree of risk involved in the decision choice, whether or not you believe a better solution can be found, and the amount of time available to you to make a decision. Each context results in different information-processing behavior. When there is no serious risk involved in continuing the current course of action (unconflicted inertia), there is low stress and no vacillation when processing information. There is also low stress and no vacillation when there is a serious risk involved in continuing the current course of action but no risk from charting a new course of action (unconflicted change). When, however, there is a serious risk involved in either continuing the current course of action or taking a new course of action and little hope of finding a better solution (defensive avoidance), stress can be high, and the decision maker will often procrastinate.

The most stressful situation is when a serious risk holds for both the current course of action and the new course of action and there is hope for a better solution but limited time to search for it (hypervigilance). In this situation, the decision maker tries to either shift the decision-making responsibility to someone else or seek information in a biased way that will support a decision already made.

The ideal decision-making context (vigilance) is when there is a serious risk involved in both maintaining the current course of action and taking a new course of action, but there is hope for a better solution and sufficient time to search for and evaluate it. In this context, there is sufficient stress to be motivated to search for a solution, but having sufficient time makes the stress tolerable.

Our research suggests that Janis and Mann's (1977) conflict model of decision making holds true in many evaluation situations (Brown et al., 1984). Pflum and Brown (1984) reported that differing the amount of time to make a decision and altering the level of the importance of the decision influenced how small groups made decisions about evaluation information they received. Newman, Brown, Rivers, and Glock (1983) found that the relative importance the community gave to the decision influenced school administrators' evaluative decisions. Newman et al. (1987) reported that the amount of community support and the recommendations of the school superintendent influenced school board members' decisions. Krager and Brown (1991) found that higher education administrators' decisions were influenced by the amount of stress they reported experiencing, which affected their information use. Brown and Prentice (1987) measured the risk involved for nursing educators in an evaluation decision-making context and found that the greater the risk involved, the more time decision makers wanted to decide and the more likely they were to consult with others before making a decision. Jatulis and Newman (1991) found that the amount of time given to make deci- sions and the perceived risk of the consequences of decisions affected nurse managers' use of evaluation information, their willingness to take action, and their perceptions of control. Carpinello (1989) found that both the perceived consequences of decisions and the perceived power base of the evaluator are also an important part of the decision-making process.

Although these studies did not always involve ethical dilemmas, they provide evidence supporting the relevance of the Janis-Mann (1977) conflict model in evaluation contexts by suggesting that the amount of risk and the amount of time available for making a decision are related to the amount of stress experienced and how a person processes information.

The implications of this decision-making model and supporting research for ethical decision making are fourfold: First, it is important to assess the amount of personal risk you face in the ethical decision choice. Could you lose your job? Could you lose respect by making an incorrect choice or one not supported by others? Fear of loss of respect as someone who makes careful decisions can result in almost as much stress as fear of losing a job. Second, you need to allow yourself enough time to obtain the information you need to make a thoughtful decision. Third, you need to be aware that time pressures and level of risk affect how you process information and how you approach a decision. Finally, you need to be aware that these stress factors also can affect the decision makers with whom you are working in an evaluation context. Program directors and staff members may be at risk for losing their jobs and credibility as a possible outcome of the evaluation you are conducting. They must deal with time pressures and external critics. Thus, not only is the evaluator at risk in stressful evaluation situations but so are other persons involved in the program being evaluated.

Organizational Context: A Systems Approach to Ethical Decision Making

Most discussions of ethical decision making focus on the individual who is confronted with an ethical dilemma. Ultimately, each individual, no matter the context, must decide what constitutes the appropriate ethical behavior at that moment for him or her. This may mean either going along with what everyone else is doing or going against the grain of the group or organization. As important as this individual perspective is, consideration of ethical issues from a systems or organizational perspective is also essential, although frequently neglected. Program evaluation requires attention to interpersonal, organizational, community, and societal contexts of behavior, and this necessitates attention to the same variables when considering ethical behavior (Snow & Gersick, 1986).

A systems approach to ethical problems, in contrast to the more individually focused approach, looks at the context of the conflict by recognizing the possibilities of overlapping rights and responsibilities that require a systemic resolution (O'Neill & Hern, 1991). Three assumptions are customarily made when discussing ethical conflicts:

- The conflict is an ethical one.
- The conflict is internal, played out in one's individual conscience.
- The causes can be identified and blame assessed.

O'Neill and Hern suggest that these assumptions are seldom accurate. First, not everyone involved in a situation may see the problem as an ethical one. Some may see it as political or economic. Second, few solutions involve one individual taking unilateral, independent action. As a minimum, whatever action the individual takes is going to affect other persons and perhaps an entire organization. Although society recognizes the value and necessity of individual heroes, in many instances it is naive to expect one person's action to be effective or to lead to dramatic change in organizational behavior. Finally, there is limited value in attributing blame; assigning blame may, in fact, be counterproductive in bringing about change.

O'Neill and Hern (1991) suggest four factors to consider when taking a systemic approach to ethical decision making: boundaries, information, complexity, and goals.

Boundaries

Within formal organizations, **boundaries** are generally clear. Organizational charts tell us who handles what and who reports to whom. There is less potential risk when staying within the boundaries, so when it is necessary to cross them, this must be done cautiously. When facing an ethical dilemma within one school building or within one social service agency, the evaluator hopes the matter can be dealt with internally. If there is resistance to dealing with the issue, or if the dilemma involves persons at the top of the school or agency organizational chart, then the evaluator might have to go outside those boundaries and discuss the matter at another level. Establishing boundaries is sometimes difficult for evaluators because many times our programs and stakeholders cross boundaries. When ethical issues arise that cross boundaries, we may have to look for other factors to guide our decision making.

Information

How **information** is received, organized, and transmitted by and within a system is another important factor. For instance, how is information conveyed from the program's participants to the program's staff? How, in turn, does the staff convey information to the administrators, and what happens to the information when it is transmitted to program funders and advisory boards? O'Neill and Hern (1991) suggest that a system changes information either to make it consistent with information it already has or to make it less threatening. When an evaluator collects information from program participants that suggests services are not being delivered, the evaluator needs to be concerned about how this information will be transmitted through the system. How many transformations will the information undergo as it is transmitted in reports, in hallway conversations, and in board meetings? This is not to say that everyone in the system must have the same perspective on new information or particularly on negative feedback. Not everyone will place the same priority on the new information, but an evaluator must hope that the information is not distorted badly as it moves through the system.

Complexity

Complexity is another factor to consider in a systemic approach. The more complex the system, the less likely it is to respond quickly to a crisis. There may be barriers to sharing information across boundaries or among professional groups. Coordination of information is necessary in a complex system, and clear differentiation of roles is important. An evaluator who faces an ethical conflict within a complex organization needs to have a sense of how matters such as confidentiality and consultation are treated. Do teachers communicate comfortably with the school counselor? Does the school counselor share information with the principal? In an agency setting, how do professionals from different disciplines, such as psychology, psychiatry, social work, and medicine, communicate? Do they share information across their disciplines? Are their priorities the same? Answers to these questions provide clues as to what issues the evaluator must attend to and what courses of actions may be most effective.

Goals

Systems have **goals**, and ethical conflicts often center on conflicts among goals. Different persons in the organization may have different goals or different priorities. Teachers have different priorities than principals, who in turn have different priorities than superintendents and school boards. Social case workers have different relationships and goals than agency administrators. For some, the protection of privacy or respecting autonomy is highly important; for others, concern for the welfare of other staff members or the institution is primary. A systems approach to looking at ethical dilemmas does not eliminate these conflicting goals, but it does help by bringing them out into the open where they can be examined for their legitimacy.

Taking a systems or organizational perspective does not remove or lessen the responsibility of the individual. Instead, the systems perspective acknowledges individual responsibilities while recognizing that we seldom operate independently. The systems perspective actually places a greater burden on us as we confront ethical matters and formulate plans of action. It is incumbent on us to consider the total context within which the dilemma or conflict is occurring. Not only must we consider these multiple perspectives as they relate to the dilemma, but we must also consider the multiple courses of action necessary to resolve the problem. Different courses of action might reach the same or different ends.

We now weave levels of ethical decision making, stress, and individual and organizational contexts and values with the principles and ethical theory perspectives discussed in Chapter 2 into a decision-making flowchart.

ETHICAL DECISION-MAKING FLOWCHART

The flowchart shown in Figure 4–1 (see end of chapter) represents an integration of those developed by Cavanaugh et al. (1981), Winston and McCaffrey (1983), and Van Hoose and Kottler (1977). Integrated into the decision flowchart are Kitchener's (1984) analyses of ethical principles and levels of ethical reasoning and concerns about other factors affecting our ethical decision making, such as the stress involved (Brown et al., 1984; Janis & Mann, 1977) and the need to be concerned about the organizational context (O'Neill & Hern, 1991). We acknowledge that no decision-making flowchart can be used to answer every dilemma or question an evaluator may have about an ethical situation, but this chart, we believe, has heuristic value and can assist us in thinking about ethical situations.

The decision-making flowchart we propose is divided into five levels. The first four levels are based on those described by Drane (1982) and Kitchener (1984): intuition, rules, principles and theory, and personal values. The fifth level is taking action. Background information for each level appeared in Chapter 2 and earlier in this chapter; therefore, only brief descriptions are given here. Table 4–1 provides a brief overview of the model.

Level 1: Intuition

Hare (1981) and Kitchener (1984) refer to the intuitive response as the immediate, prereflective response to an ethical situation. We react on the basis of our prior ethical knowledge and experience, which can be rich and deep or limited and shallow. At this stage, you sense that something is awry. Your basic decision here is whether or not to take time to pursue the concerns further. Your decision can be aided by asking yourself two questions: Do I respond to my intuitive concerns? Do I have time for further analysis?

Do I respond to my intuitive concerns? Perhaps you have an uncomfortable feeling because your client seems to be insisting that the assistant manager of the program being evaluated must accompany you during your observations and interviews. Is this primarily a methodological issue, or are you concerned that the client wants everyone to be on their best behavior for purposes of biasing the evaluation? In another evalu-

TABLE 4–1 Decision-Making Flowchart (Outline)

Level 1: Intuition

Questions:

- Do I respond to my intuitive concerns?
- Do I have time for further analysis?

Decision 1: Stop, or pursue concern analysis?

Level 2: Rules

Question:

- What rule, standard, or code applies?

Decision 2: Does a rule, standard, or code apply?
If no, stop, or go to Level 3?

Decision 3: If yes, stop, go to Level 3, or take action (Level 5)?

Level 3: Principles and Theory

Questions:

- What is the relevance of each principle (autonomy, nonmaleficence, beneficence, justice, and fidelity)?
- How do the criteria (consequences, duty, rights, social justice, and ethics of care) apply?

Decision 4: To stop, consider values (Level 4), or take action (Level 5)?

Level 4: Personal Values

Questions:

- How do my personal values, visions, and beliefs affect my thinking?
- What kind of a person do I want to be?

Decision 5: To stop, or take action (Level 5)?

Level 5: Action

Questions:

- How much stress is involved?
- What are the risks to me?
- What are the risks to others?
- What do my colleagues think?
- What is my plan of action?
- How will the organization react to this plan?
- What cultural perspectives are important to consider?
- Has my action resolved the issue?

Decision 6: To stop, or implement an action plan?

Decision 7: Has the plan worked, or must I start again?

ation context, you may be concerned when you discover that a close friend and former colleague is a staff member of the program you are evaluating. You may have a faint recollection of having read about or discussed a similar situation in the past, or you may have a nagging doubt or concern that will not go away.

Do I have time for further analysis? Time constraints and pressures are present in every evaluation effort. Can you restructure the situation to provide more time to consider your concerns and the dilemma? Do you believe that you could make a right decision if only you had more time?

If there is not sufficient time, your alternatives are limited and depend on the stage of the evaluation project. If you are in the negotiating stage, you could decide to refuse to conduct the evaluation. If you are already in the midst of the evaluation, the alternative could be affected by how deep your concern is and how serious the ethical dilemma is. The more serious the matter, the more you need to consider withdrawing from the evaluation if the issue cannot be resolved. If you cannot negotiate or resolve the issue, the safest decision is to bail out. Often, more damage is done by carrying on with the evaluation and ignoring potential ethical concerns than by forcing a confrontation. Like every evaluator, you strive to anticipate and prevent these concerns in your initial negotiations, but even extensive efforts by experienced evaluators do not eliminate unanticipated events and dilemmas.

If you decide to stop, there is no need to consider other levels of decision making. If you have time, or if organizational pressures conflict and you decide to pursue the issue further, you move to Level 2 (rules).

Level 2: Rules

At this level, you have two decisions to make. First, you have to decide whether or not a code or rule fits your situation. If you do not find a fit, you move to Level 3, the principles and theory level. Second, if you find a fit, you have to decide whether to (a) take immediate action (Level 5) or (b) move to the principles and theory level (Level 3) for further analysis or (c) stop.

Using the ethical codes and guidelines provided by your professional association, those of the Joint Committee on Standards (1981, 1994) or the Guiding Principles for Evaluators (American Evaluation Association,

1995), you need to look for parallels to your situation. For instance, if you suspect a possible conflict of interest because of having had professional and personal ties with a staff member of the program you are being asked to evaluate, Joint Committee Standard P7 (Conflict of Interest) provides an example of a personal tie with a client as a potential conflict of interest. The guidelines suggest that the problem is not so much a matter of avoiding a conflict of interest as it is one of determining how to deal with it.

To use another example, suppose you are trying to write a balanced report that points out the strengths and weaknesses of a program. You find yourself stretching a bit to report positive findings. This makes you uncomfortable, so you search through the written standards for guidance. Joint Committee Standards P6 (Disclosure of Findings) and A11 (Impartial Reporting) seem to be appropriate. Examination of these guidelines suggest "full disclosure of pertinent findings and without omissions or other alterations" (1994, p. 110) and avoiding "wanting to please the client to the extent that it becomes difficult to report negative findings" (p. 182). On this basis, you decide there is a direct match between your situation and the Joint Committee Standards. You now have to decide whether or not to take immediate action or stop.

If the decision is to take immediate action, you proceed to Level 5 (Action). If no match is found or if, despite the match, you are still not ready for action, you should consider how the principles and criteria relate by going to Level 3 (principles and theory). When the action primarily involves only you and no one else, the choice between Level 3 and Level 5 is relatively straightforward. If you are writing the report and find yourself stretching to report positive results, you can read the guidelines in the Standards and change your writing outline and style. If, however, your concern now centers on how the report will be interpreted and used, you may decide to consider the relevant ethical principles and theories. If you find no parallel between your setting and any codes or rules, you need to consider a higher level of ethical thinking, such as principles and theories.

Level 3: Principles and Theory

At this level, you first analyze your situation from the perspective of the five ethical principles described and discussed at length in Chapter 2:

autonomy, nonmaleficence, beneficence, justice, and fidelity. The underlying principles are centuries old, but we owe much to the work of Beauchamp and associates (Beauchamp & Bowie, 1979; Beauchamp & Childress, 1983; Klaidman & Beauchamp, 1986), who illustrate their application to similar issues in business ethics, bioethics, and journalism, and to Kitchener (1984, 1985), whose framework we use throughout this book.

Next, you conduct a systematic examination of the relevance of these principles. Work through all five principles. Each is restated here in the form of questions you might ask yourself.

- *Autonomy.* Are anyone's rights affected—particularly, is there respect for your autonomy as the evaluator, and are you considering the autonomy of the client and the program participants? Is the client attempting to restrict your right to collect appropriate information or to write the report you believe is appropriate? Are you respecting the rights of the program participants to privacy?
- *Nonmaleficence (doing no harm).* What undue harm is likely to occur as a result of the decision and action? Harm must be considered from the perspective of psychological harm as well as physical harm. Is one's reputation or job at risk? Will program staff be exposed to excessive stress because of the evaluation process? Will program participants be exposed to undue harm through violation of privacy or through program ineffectiveness if improvements are not made in the program?
- *Beneficence (doing good).* What good can come to clients and participants through the evaluation? Is the maximum good being achieved? What good can be accomplished beyond the expectations of professional codes and rules?
- *Justice.* What issues are related to fairness and accuracy in this evaluation? Are multiple perspectives being gathered?
- *Fidelity.* What contractual arrangements have been made, and are they being fulfilled? Do you have unique obligations as an evaluator because of your role in the evaluation or within the evaluation context? Do the program participants expect you to be their advocate?

Then, ask yourself, what is the relevance of each principle, and if principles conflict with each other in your evaluation context, how might they be balanced? You should then move on to examine the relevance of the criteria derived from ethical theory.

Even if your examination of the principles provides persuasive arguments for you to stop or to take action, we suggest that you consider the criteria and questions that follow from ethical theory before making a final decision. This is particularly true when ethical principles do not provide sufficient guidance or when they conflict—questions derived from ethical theory can be helpful. Ask yourself these additional questions based on the ethical theories of utilitarianism, deontologicalism, and an ethics of care:

What are the possible consequences? You probably have already considered possible harm, but what are the possible consequences to relationships among the stakeholders? Most ethical codes and standards look at ethical dilemmas from the perspective of their impact on individuals. It is also essential to consider how the decision will affect others in the organization conducting the evaluation or others in the units or agencies being evaluated. How will the decision affect the client, program staff, program participants, and society at large?

Are there any special obligations or duties involved? How is your role perceived, and how do these expectations match up with your own perception of your role?

Are anyone's rights affected? Are participants' rights to privacy involved?

Is social justice being served? Are you, for example, considering the needs and interests of the less powerful or less influential?

What is unique about the context that may affect the consequences? How will a decision affect relationships among persons within this context?

You should be close now to making your decision about whether to take action or not. You can stop, decide to take action and proceed to Level 5, or proceed to Level 4 (personal values). We suspect that most people consider their personal values at this point, no matter what their decision is, and do so in an informal, if not formal, manner. We encourage you to consciously look at your personal values at this point, regardless of the direction your decision seems to be heading.

Level 4: Personal Values

It is possible, perhaps even likely, that at this point you have found two principles that conflict with each other, or you have raised questions with conflicting answers when based solely on the ethical principles. For example, if you wish to do good for the client and program participants by using the most sophisticated statistical analysis available, you may find that doing so conflicts with respecting their autonomy. Conflicts could be resolved readily if there was a clear hierarchy among the principles or rules, but there is none. A general guideline for many professions is the rule, "Above all else, do no harm." This places nonmaleficence as the primary principle. But not all ethical conflicts necessarily lend themselves so easily to this solution.

Drane (1982) suggests that at this juncture, the decision ultimately involves what kind of a person you want to be. What are your values, visions, and beliefs? These values will be influenced by your cultural background and your belief system. What principle you choose as paramount depends on your perceptions about human reality and your sense of self. Although this level is abstract and seems far removed from the concrete situation you may be facing, it spirals back to the intuitive level. Your notions of how you view human reality and yourself are intimately associated with your initial feelings about the apparent ethical conflict.

Drane (1982) notes that our response at this point is based on our core beliefs and our visions. He believes that being ethical is inevitably tied up with our philosophical or religious beliefs. Your intuition, your analysis of rules, principles, and theories, and your final ethical decisions will be influenced by your cultural beliefs and the rules and conventions of your society. At this level, your beliefs and values become explicit. This is when you say to yourself, "I know this is the rule, but a broader principle seems to be involved here, so I believe I need to respond in this way." At each point along the way, you can still stop, or you can move to Level 5 (action).

Level 5: Action

Before taking action, you need to examine all of the alternatives and take a close look at available resources. This may well demand courage. We suggest six action steps. Remember, at this stage you already have decided there is ethical dilemma—now you must decide what action to take.

Analyze how much stress this involves for you and for others. Ask yourself, Am I uncomfortable? Why do I have this feeling? Where is this feeling coming from? Also, ask yourself how you feel about dealing with a potential ethical conflict. Does this make you nervous? Do you fear a potential confrontation? Consider the risks for yourself and for others in this situation. Could your reputation or those of the clients or stakeholders be at risk by your decision to pursue the ethical concern further? Would asking the client, for example, to reconsider the program's goals be threatening to the client and not a customary role for you as the evaluator? What pressures is the client facing? Is the client, or are you, under a tight timeline? How do these pressures affect you?

Consult with colleagues. Feel free to consult with colleagues throughout the decision process. You might want to do this as early as the intuitive level. You might initiate your conversation with "I'm in this situation and I am a bit uncomfortable. I would like to describe it to you and see what your reactions are." We believe that evaluators confronting an ethical concern must consult with at least one colleague at some point. Ultimately, you must rely on your own judgment, but don't do so until you have consulted with a colleague. This will be risky and perhaps even uncomfortable, so it is helpful if you have established a trusting, confidential relationship with a professional colleague before an ethical issue arises. Ideally, you and the colleague have discussed ethical issues before. If a colleague is not available, you might wish to contact the ethical affairs committee of your professional association at the state or national level. It is always helpful to have the perspective of another professional.

Consider what impact the organizational climate and the cultural setting should have on your course of action. Like considerations of stress, you would be wise to consider organizational climate and the nature of your cultural setting throughout your analysis, but you must be especially attentive when you decide to take action. The questions we noted earlier are pertinent here. How are decisions made within this organization? What groups and individuals will be affected? If you are in a different country or in a multicultural setting, you need to consider how different actions will be implemented and interpreted.

Design a course of action. Let's assume that you have decided action should be taken. What do you do now? If it is only your behavior that is involved, you may be able to take unilateral action. Many times, however, the action will involve others. A suggested first step in many situations is to discuss the matter with the parties involved. This means going to the client and indicating that you do not think it proper for an administrator to accompany you during your observations and interviews. It may mean telling the client that you will have to issue a minority report if someone significantly tampers with your report. It may mean telling colleagues that you do not see their portions of the report as balanced. It is wise also to consider alternative courses of action. What happens if the client's mind is made up? What happens if your colleagues refuse to revise their portions of the report? It is unlikely that you will have much time for further analysis beyond this point, so you must be prepared to carry through with alternative actions.

Implement the plan. You proceed with the planned course of action.

Assess the impact of the plan. Now you must determine whether or not the action has had its intended impact. Has the client agreed with the analysis and agreed to let you proceed with your interviews of staff without an administrator present? Has the situation changed? Is the issue resolved?

If the issue is resolved to your satisfaction, you can stop, but don't forget about your initial concern. The experience should prompt you to reflect on the process you have been through and to explore future implications for you and the system or organization involved. You need to ask yourself the following questions: What have I learned about my own decision-making process and my familiarity with ethical rules, codes, and principles? What does the process and my actions say about who I am? Perhaps this might prompt the organization to consider its policy related to this and other ethical conflicts. Would a staff development workshop be appropriate? How can future conflicts be prevented? How can this experience serve as a learning experience for myself and for others involved? Ethical conflicts are seldom forgotten, but they are not always pursued as potential learning experiences.

At any point throughout these steps, you can still decide to stop or proceed ultimately to implementing your action plan. If, after you implement the plan, you decide the issue is not resolved, then go back to Level 1. Now you must ask yourself again, what are my feelings? Do I pursue it further?

Vignette 4.2 Using the Model: An Illustration

We suggest that you try out the decision process outlined and follow the flowchart for ethical concerns you have experienced. Let's take a look at how the process might work. Here is a brief illustration:

Mary is evaluating the staff development and staff evaluation program for a hospital. The hospital is divided into several functional units, and the director of each unit is responsible for coordinating the staff development programs and conducting the staff evaluations. Mary is gathering survey data from the staff members of all units and interviewing a random sample of staff members from each unit. As the data are being analyzed, it becomes apparent that staff members in one particular unit are the most dissatisfied, and the dissatisfaction seems focused on the personality and behavior of the unit's director. In ongoing update sessions with the hospital administrator, she discovers that this director was "fired" several years ago by a previous hospital administrator but was reinstated because of strong support from the hospital board of directors. Their rationale for reinstatement was the lack of sufficient concrete data to support the director's dismissal. Mary has an uncomfortable feeling about this. She is beginning to wonder if her current efforts are a cover for gathering evidence that will be used to dismiss the director. Throughout her discussions with all the directors, she has insisted that her role is to evaluate the programs and the processes, not the personnel.

Let's follow Mary as she uses Table 4–1 and Figure 4–1 to think about her concern. Mary starts out at the **intuitive level.** She has to make a decision whether to stop worrying about her concern at the moment or to conduct further analysis (Decision 1). By deciding to think about this more she has already responded to her intuitive concerns. She cannot nail it down, but the coincidences of the timing and focus of this evaluation coupled with comments by the hospital administrator are too great for her to ignore. Fortunately, she has a few more interviews to go and her report is not due for several weeks, so she has time to think about this and conduct a further analysis.

Mary moves on to the **rule level** and rereads the propriety and reporting sections of the Joint Committee on Standards (1981, 1994). She notes in the formal agreement section, which she used as a guide for drawing up the evaluation contract specifications, several sections that alleviate her concern somewhat. She has built in a process whereby each of the directors was involved in developing the evaluation plan and will also have an opportunity to rebut her report. Under the circumstances, she will want to make sure that opportunity exists for the director in question. Also, in the disclosure of findings and impartial reporting sections, she notes the importance of balanced reporting. Her contract seems to cover questions of editing the report that may come up, so she feels secure there. Her concern does focus on the section regarding rights of human subjects, however.

She has continually guaranteed staff members complete confidentiality but has never been explicit about identification of the directors of the hospital units. This came to her mind earlier, but because of the makeup and size of the units it would be difficult to mask their identities. She thinks this might be possible, but she wonders how the hospital administrator might react, and she also wonders about her responsibility to the hospital, if this director is incompetent. Right now, if the director is incompetent, it seems to be harming morale but nothing else.

Examination of the standards was helpful; they provide reminders of what she will add to future contracts. But she doesn't believe they provide a clear answer for her. She decides to proceed to the next level—**principles and theory.**

First, Mary looks at each principle's basic definition, and she sees particularly nonmaleficence, justice, and fidelity as critical principles pertinent to her concern. Her report could be used to cause harm to the director; the information could be used to support a rationale for his dismissal. She wonders about the fairness or justice of this if it happened. At this point, although the director's behavior and methods have had a detrimental impact on staff morale, she is not in a position to say the director is not open to change. The director will have the opportunity to rebut her report, but the information she gathered focused on only two dimensions of the director's job, not the full job description. She sees fidelity as a prime concern. Her repeated comments that she was there to evaluate the programs, not the personnel, was meant to apply to all personnel—directors as well as staff members. She believes that she would be breaking an implicit contract if she permitted her report to be used for different purposes.

When she examines the theoretical criteria, she finds several that apply: consequences, duty, rights, and ethics of care. There are conflicts that focus on the relative strengths of her obligations to the hospital administrator, the hospital, the director in question, and her profession of evaluation. Certainly, if every evaluation like this was later used to fire staff, this would not be good. Her obligation is to her profession as well as to her immediate client. The individual director has rights, which may be in jeopardy if her data are used in a backhanded way to release the director. The director is not without supporters among the staff, even some of those who disagree with the director's methods. The director has been with the hospital for 20 years in a variety of capacities. If Mary's hunch about how her data might be used is correct, this doesn't seem like a fair, just, or caring way to handle the matter.

Mary finds that the decision process thus far has illuminated the factors involved and what she needs to consider. She decides that she cannot sit still and let this happen; in her mind it violates her own perceptions of what she is about in her profession (her **personal values**). She has the feeling that she is being used almost as a spy. She concludes that this is not fair to her, to her profession, or to the director. Forgetting about it and hoping it will go away is not the behavior representing who she believes she wants to be. She decides that she must **take action,** which will not be easy. It will take some courage to confront the hospital director with her concern. She does not like to confront people. She doesn't know what stress this might provoke for the hospital administrator, particularly if releasing the director has been a high-priority goal. She decides to consult with a colleague both about her general concern and about procedural strategies.

Her colleague agrees with her concerns and her analysis. The colleague suggests several helpful alternative ways to proceed. She presents the hospital administrator with a plan whereby each director would have access to his or her program's findings but the overall report would not identify the directors.

She also suggests a workshop for the directors on ways they can use the information to improve their programs and staff morale. In the process, she underlines rather emphatically her expectations regarding the uses and possible abuses of her data.

The hospital administrator seems somewhat taken aback at first but then gets enthusiastic about the workshop and even wants to participate. Mary is guaranteed that the data will not be used against any individual staff member.

CONCLUSION

We see several uses for the decision flowchart as an aid to ethical decision making. It can be used in classes and workshops for students and participants to think through a variety of ethical dilemmas and decisions. Does everyone answer the questions the same way throughout the flowchart? Where do they diverge? What are the differing rationales for different responses? What additional information would they like to have? How good a fit is the flowchart for the situation? Would they have an opportunity to obtain the needed information and the time to use the flowchart reflectively to help them make a decision in a real situation? Organizations also could use the flowchart as a stimulus for discussions in workshops and staff development sessions. Thus, the chart can be a useful instructional tool to provide practice and stimulate discussion.

For new evaluation practitioners, the flowchart can provide a helpful reminder to double-check their thinking about ethical concerns. It is critical for persons in organizations to have a sense of support within their organization for thinking about ethical matters. Using the flowchart in staff meetings will provide opportunities for staff to obtain a sense of how their colleagues think about ethical issues and who they might turn to when they personally face an ethical dilemma.

Chalk, Frankel, and Chafer (1980) proposed six criteria for assessing the utility of ethical rules and principles. These same criteria can be applied to this ethical decision-making process:

- *Applicability.* Can the steps and decision points be applied to real-world problems?
- *Clarity.* Are the steps and decision points sufficiently clear to avoid confusion?
- *Consistency.* Are the steps internally consistent?
- *Ordering.* Are the steps and decision points in the correct order?
- *Coverage.* Are there any significant omissions on serious ethical issues?
- *Acceptability.* Should the decision points be accepted as ethically prescriptive?

Each evaluator and each organization must determine individually how well Kitchener's (1984) principles, questions raised by ethical theory, and the flowchart meet these criteria within a particular evaluation situation. We doubt that they fit each and every situation. Nevertheless, we hope that their use stimulates individual evaluators to be more reflective about ethical concerns and provokes discussions among colleagues and others involved in evaluations.

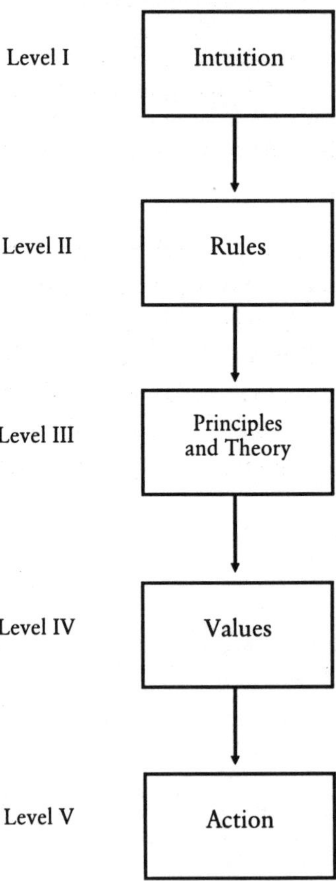

Figure 4-1. Ethical Decision Making Flowchart

Level 1: Introduction

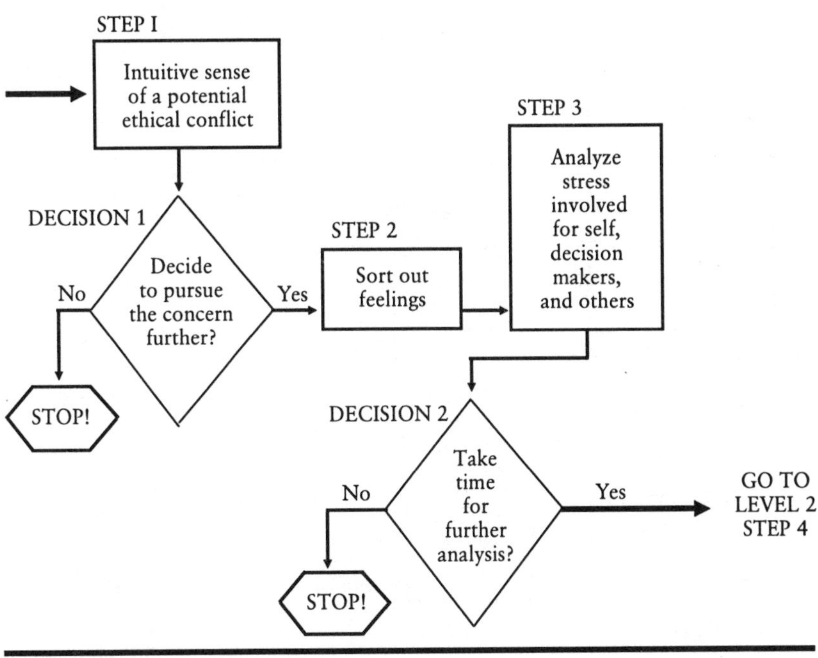

Level 2: Rules

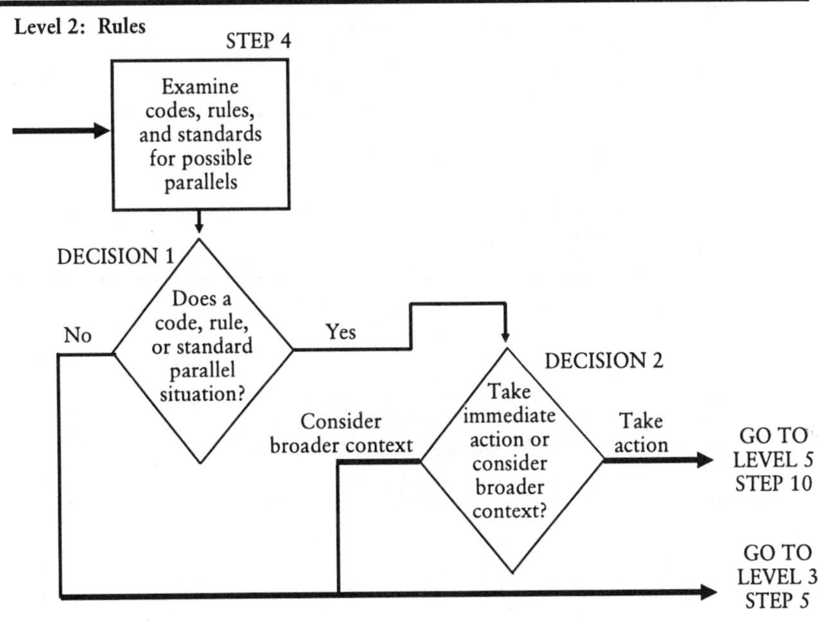

Level 3: Principles and Theory

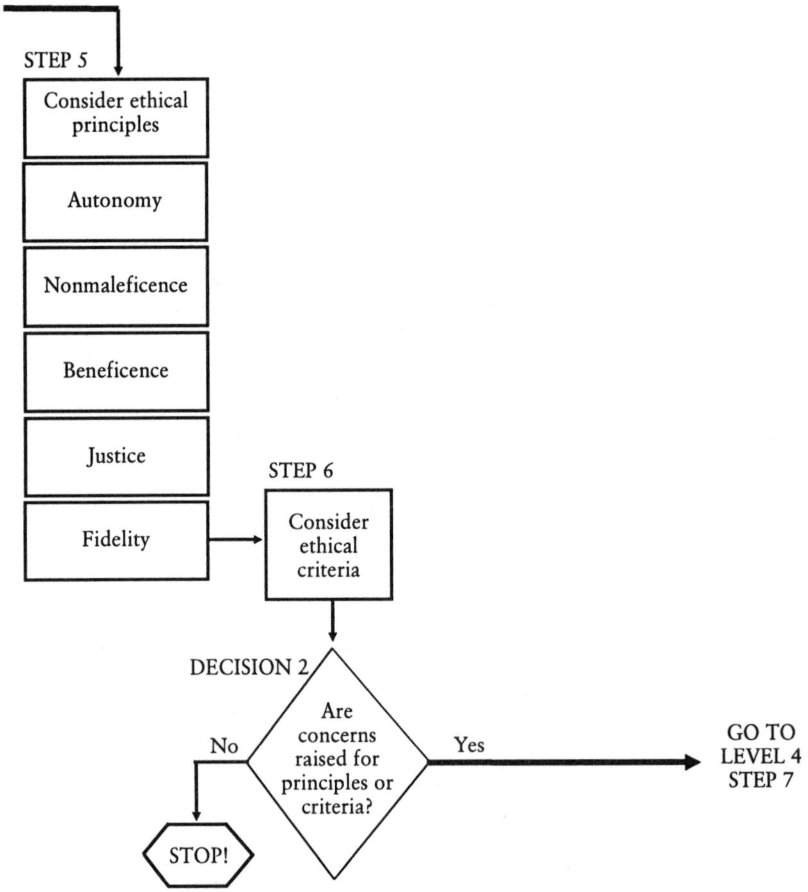

STEP 5
Consider ethical principles
Autonomy
Nonmaleficence
Beneficence
Justice
Fidelity
STEP 6
Consider ethical criteria
DECISION 2
Are concerns raised for principles or criteria?
No
STOP!
Yes
GO TO LEVEL 4 STEP 7

Level 4: Values

STEP 7
Organizational values
STEP 8
Professional values
STEP 9
Personal values
GO TO LEVEL 5 STEP 10

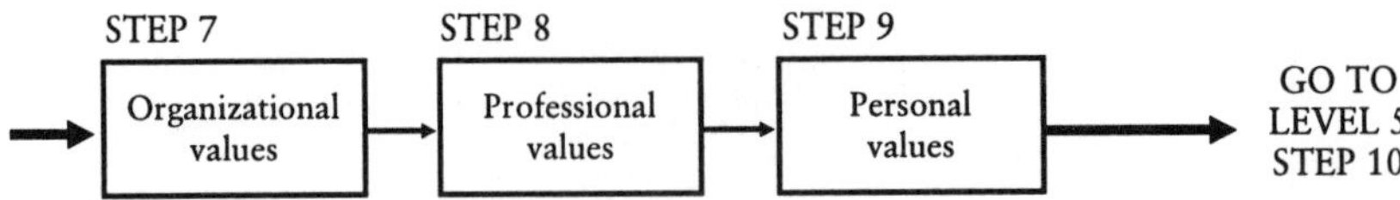

Level 5: Action

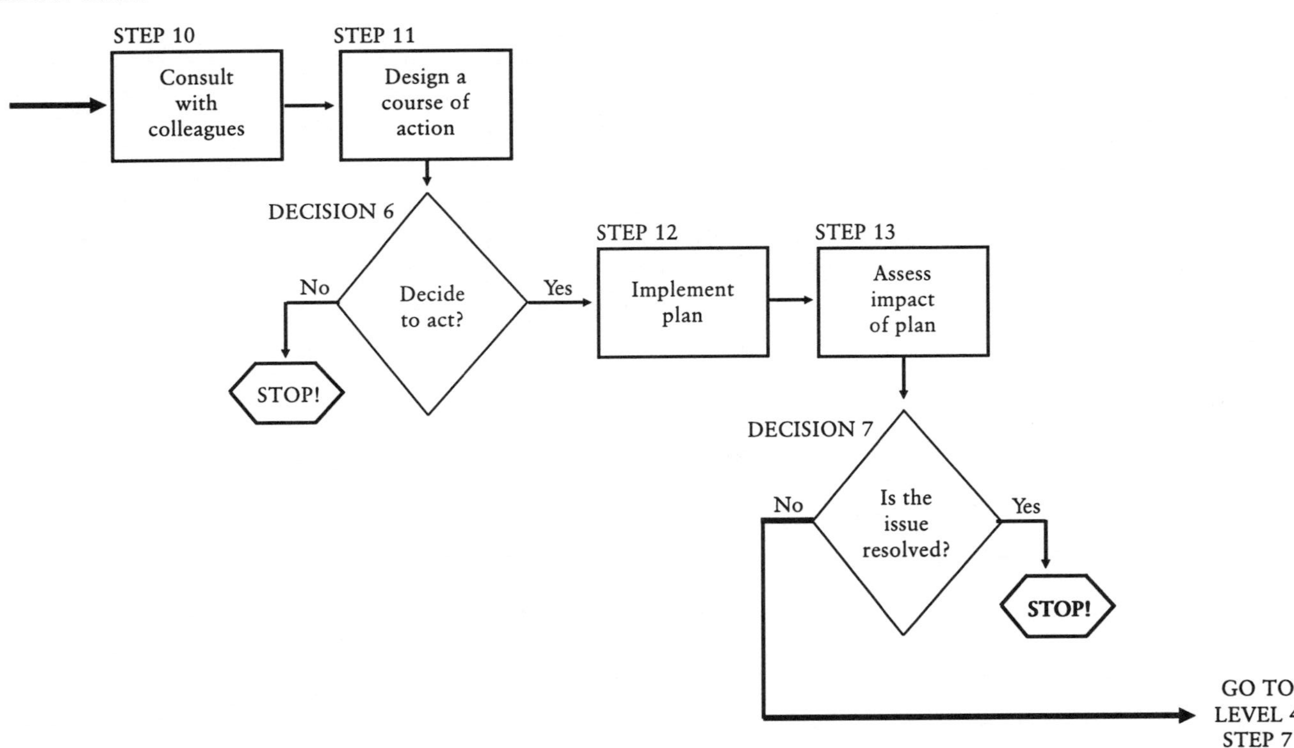

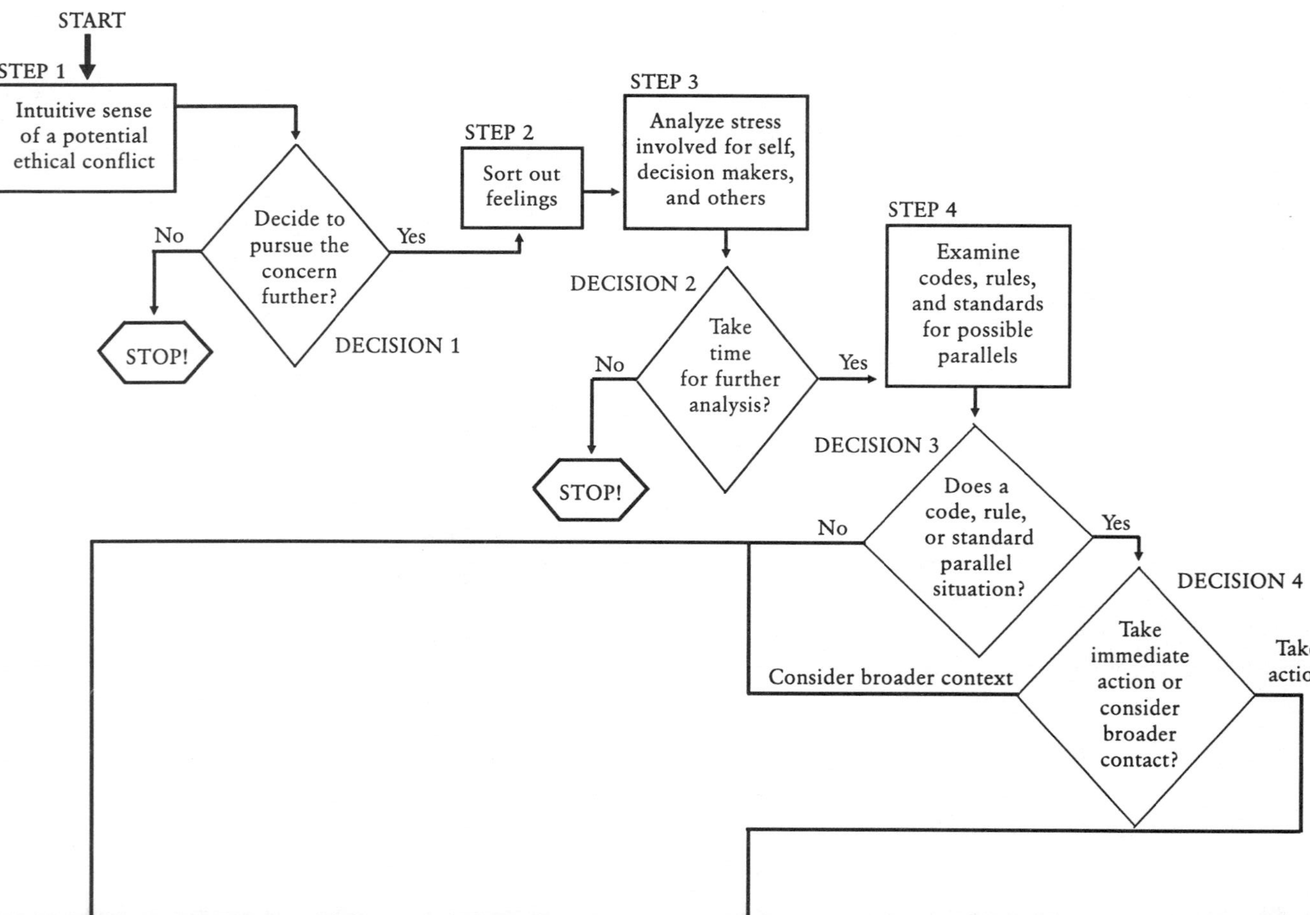
START
STEP 1
Intuitive sense of a potential ethical conflict
Decide to pursue the concern further?
DECISION 1
No
STOP!
Yes
STEP 2
Sort out feelings
STEP 3
Analyze stress involved for self, decision makers, and others
DECISION 2
Take time for further analysis?
No
STOP!
Yes
STEP 4
Examine codes, rules, and standards for possible parallels
DECISION 3
Does a code, rule, or standard parallel situation?
No
Yes
DECISION 4
Take immediate action or consider broader contact?
Consider broader context
Take action

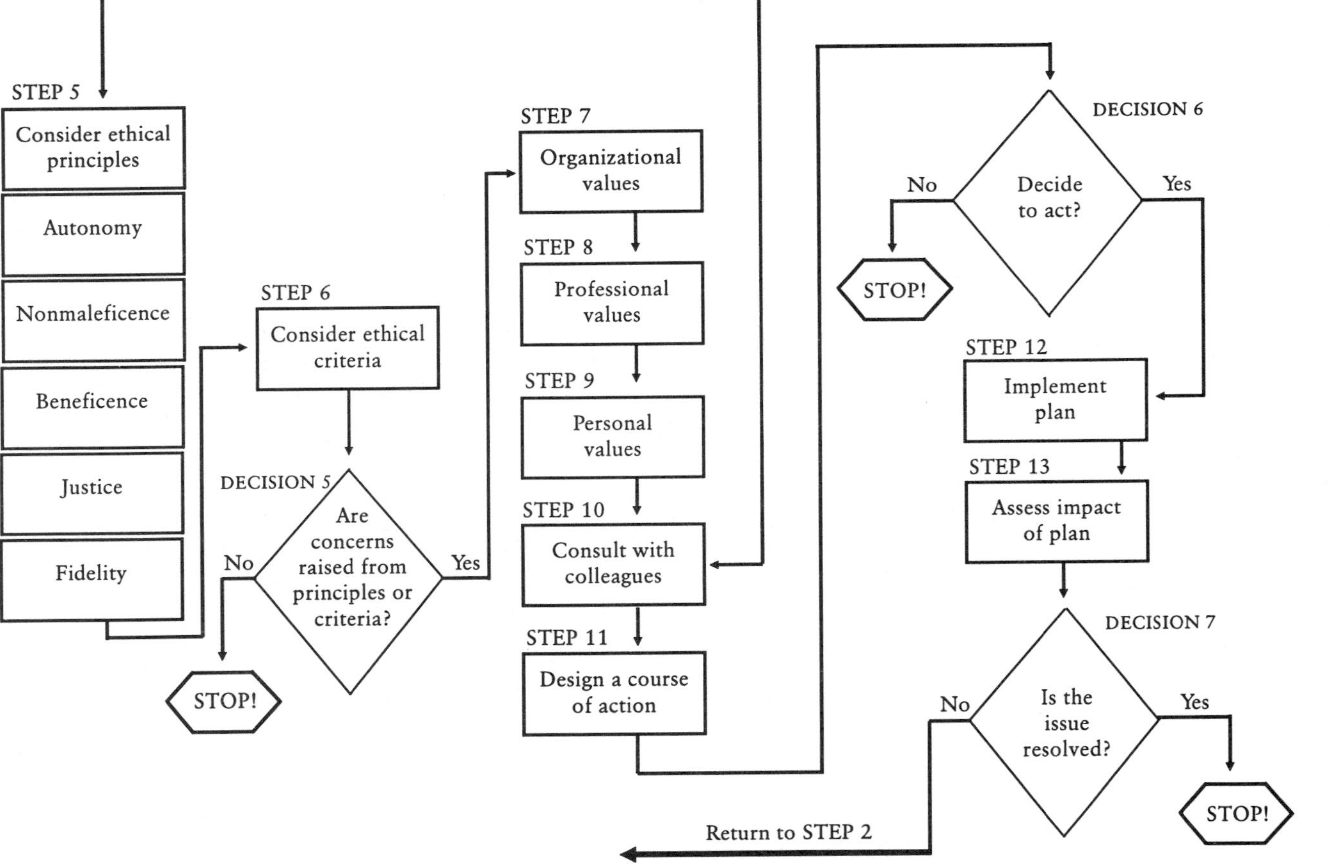
STEP 5
Consider ethical principles
Autonomy
Nonmaleficence
Beneficence
Justice
Fidelity
STEP 6
Consider ethical criteria
DECISION 5
Are concerns raised from principles or criteria?
No
STOP!
Yes
STEP 7
Organizational values
STEP 8
Professional values
STEP 9
Personal values
STEP 10
Consult with colleagues
STEP 11
Design a course of action
DECISION 6
Decide to act?
No
STOP!
Yes
STEP 12
Implement plan
STEP 13
Assess impact of plan
DECISION 7
Is the issue resolved?
No
Return to STEP 2
Yes
STOP!

5

The Effect of Evaluator Role Perceptions on Ethical Decision Making

A Reader's Guide to Chapter 5

This chapter reviews the major roles related to the functions of a program evaluator. Each role is discussed in terms of its expectations, possible ethical dilemmas, and the status of the five principles within that role. Conflicting roles related to the evaluator's status with the project are also discussed. Examples of ethical dilemmas, especially those related to differing role expectations, are provided at the end of the chapter. These may be used to help clarify role definitions and expectations from a practical and realist point of view. Three key points are covered:

- An explanation of roles and how they are acquired
- Five major evaluation roles, their expectations
- Ethical conflicts related to evaluators' status with the program

Vignette 5.1 Pleasing the Client

Sarah Kimball serves as a program planner for a state agency. She has just granted three locally funded service agencies monies to conduct an analysis of their communities' needs using the newly developed community contact questionnaire methodology (CCQM). If CCQM proves to be successful at these three sites, Sarah will have a methodological tool ready to provide to other local agencies, thus saving future evaluation costs and making it easier for her agency to combine site data. To determine if the method is successful, Sarah hires Tom Smith to serve as an external evaluator. Tom's goal is to determine if CCQM is a valid and useful method of conducting needs analyses. Tom spends time examining both the instrument and its implementation at the three sites. He reports back to Sarah that theoretically the instrument is well constructed and should serve as a useful tool; however, his observations indicate that the instrument was modified at all three sites and that none of them adequately followed proper survey methodology. Therefore, Tom recommends that, although the CCQM is an excellent tool, it should not be used. Sarah suggests that he rephrase the recommendation to state that the CCQM works but needs strict implementation. Tom agrees that the CCQM should work, and that if it were properly implemented probably would work. Two weeks later, Tom submits his report with the original recommendation for nonuse. Sarah is upset. She has a methodology that should work but a report that says not to use the method.

- Did Tom meet the client's need? Should he have modified his report?
- Did Tom avoid harm while maintaining his autonomy? Should or could he have provided additional aid to the client?

When evaluators examine a program, they are rarely serving a single interest, a single audience, or a single client. Instead, evaluators find themselves serving as representatives of many interest groups. They are representing the client who commissioned the evaluation, the decision maker who will be using the information, the participants who provide the information, taxpayers who may have funded the program, and consumers who need the program. They also represent the profession of evaluation, the theoretical discipline in which the program is founded, and society at large.

An important question, then, among practicing evaluators, is how to meet the expectations of all these demands and what happens when the expectations are in conflict. A reexamination of the vignettes in Chapter 1 indicates that if the evaluator were to function as a representative of only one group, to serve only one interest, the conflict would be resolved. Most evaluators, however, do not have the luxury of representing only one constituency. Philosophical, theoretical, professional, and personal values pressure the evaluator to represent more than one group; thus, the evaluator is faced with multiple roles, multiple expectations, and conflicting demands that result in ethical dilemmas.

This chapter discusses the ethical issues affecting program evaluators as a result of multiple role expectations. First, we discuss what roles are and how they are acquired, including how this acquisition is viewed by various participants in the evaluation process. Next, ethical conflicts commonly associated with several prominent roles in program evaluation are presented, followed by a brief discussion of conflicting roles related to the evaluator's status with the project.

WHAT ARE ROLES, AND HOW ARE THEY ACQUIRED?

Prior to examining the specific roles, it is important to examine what roles are and how they are acquired. Koor (1982) defines role as "the expectations for how a person should behave or the person's actual behavior while in a particular position" (p. 53). In general, role taking is seen as a communication process typified by a focal person, the one for whom the role is being identified—in this situation, the evaluator—and by role senders, the ones who interact with or have expectations of that person's behavior. In the case of evaluation, there may be one role sender (i.e., the primary evaluation client) or many (i.e., all stakeholders). These role senders develop and attempt to communicate expectations, both prescriptive and proscriptive, that delineate the expected evaluator behavior. As is common in most communication processes, the specifics of the role are affected by all aspects of the communication process, including contextual factors: interpersonal, attributes of the senders and receivers, and organizational. Alkin and Associates' (1985) summary of contextual factors related to evaluation has been expanded by several researchers, including Newman, Brown, and associates.

Role Acquisition

Theoretical attention to the effect of role on professional and personal decision making can be traced to literature in both the social and psychological sciences. Much of this literature is devoted to two specific areas: how a particular role is acquired and how multiple roles interact to create conflicting demands. Thornton and Nardi (1980) identified three methods by which a focal person receives a role. When using the first method, role identification and acquisition are viewed as a one-step process. The role receiver is considered a recipient of expectations from those who are in power, and role acquisition is accomplished when the receiver meets those expectations. Using this perception of role acquisition, an evaluator would identify the appropriate role by meeting with the client, determining expectations for process and product, and fulfilling those expectations. When the client's expectations have been met, the evaluator's role is met. Under this method of role acquisition, the evaluator would adopt the client's ethical standards and would use these standards to settle ethical conflicts. In this setting, the principle of fidelity, especially to the client, would dominate.

The limitation of this type of role acquisition is that it ignores the fact that people rarely conform to expected roles. Most individuals and professionals, including evaluators, are not open to total role definition on the part of another. Most individuals acknowledge that they have some prior conception of what their role should or could be. In fact, a review of current texts used for training evaluators (e.g., Brinkerhoff, Brethower, Hluchyj, & Nowakoski, 1983; Posovac & Carey, 1989; Shadish, Cook, & Leviton, 1991; Worthen & Sanders, 1987) indicates an emphasis on forming conceptions of what evaluation should be. Despite this emphasis when training evaluators, this first mode of role definition and acquisition frequently is found when working with clients. Many clients expect this "blank slate" approach to role definition on the part of the evaluator, especially in organizations where the evaluator is located internally within an extremely hierarchical system or is external to a system that has conducted few evaluations. Vignette 2 in Chapter 1 is an example of this type of client-evaluator interaction. In this setting, the client views the evaluator as a staff member whose primary function is to respond to administrative requests on an as-needed basis. By pulling members off current projects and delaying others' reports without consultation, Joe is perpetuating the administrator's perception that the evaluator can readily adapt to the Bureau Director's individual needs.

The second mode of role acquisition discussed by Thornton and Nardi (1980) reflects a developmental process. In this setting, the person acquiring the role—the evaluator—does not immediately assume all aspects of the expected role; rather, the role is acquired through a series of steps or phases. The emphasis in this method of acquisition is on communication between the role senders and the focal person, culminating in the focal person gradually conforming to the expectations of the senders. Although this model of role acquisition does at least have a temporal dimension and recognizes the need for more communication between the evaluator and client, it still emphasizes client messages that result in the evaluator accepting the role expected by the client. There is an assumption that the evaluator will be willing to comply, over time, to the client's expectations.

This method of acquiring the evaluator role is reflected in much of the literature on ethical problem solving for internal evaluators (e.g., Adams, 1985; Mathison, 1991). In this mode of role acquisition, although internal evaluators initially may not be cognizant of all the values and ethical systems for their sponsoring organization, it is expected that they will gradually conform and become loyal team players. Vignette 5.1 is an example of clients' expectations for this type of role acquisition. Sarah Kimball, the program planner, is willing to discuss the issue of inadequate validity and test development but, in the end, expects the evaluator to conform to her preference for a recommendation.

The third method of role acquisition, proposed and supported by Thornton and Nardi (1980), views role acquisition as a multiway developmental process. It might be better termed role negotiation. Using this procedure, the evaluator and the client interact and communicate, jointly changing and defining their perception of the evaluator's role. This process includes the temporal and developmental aspects of the second method but also implies that both the client and the evaluator will alter their respective expectations of the evaluator's role. Using this process, identification and acquisition of the evaluator role changes from identifying and meeting the clients' needs and performing to their expectations to a more involved process of finding common congruity between multiple needs and expectations. This includes finding congruity between differing ethical systems.

Thornton and Nardi suggest several stages for identification and acquisition that parallel evaluation processes. These include anticipating the need for role definition, formulating one's own (the evaluator's) expectations, learning the client's expectations, reacting to any incongruities between the expectations, and working with the client to reconcile these differences until a common role is defined. This mode of role acquisition is the most beneficial to both evaluator and client, but it is complex and time-consuming. It is this method of role identification and acquisition, however, that results in the multiplicity and variations of role expectations for and among evaluators, including variations in ethical decision making. When this method of role acquisition is used, the evaluator has time to meet with the client and discuss ethical problems, eventually deriving a mutually acceptable solution. The evaluator is neither "doing what the client wants" to keep a job or contract nor being forced to resign from a project. Instead, both the evaluator and the client develop a new sense of ethics related to the project. Using this model, the evaluator and client in Vignette 5.1 would spend more time discussing the pros and cons of test development, possibly come up with an alternate plan of test validation, and then work toward a joint statement on the utility of the instrument.

Role Interactions

Complexity of role definition and acquisition occurs when individuals fulfill multiple roles at the same time. At any given moment, those could include our ascribed roles (e.g., expectations due to our biological or semibiological status, such as age, gender, kinship, and social class) or our achieved roles (e.g., those due to our occupational, political, or avocational needs) (Ostlund, 1973). Research on evaluation use has indicated that ascribed roles affect stakeholders' expectations of evaluators. Braskamp, Brown, and Newman (1978) found variations in expectations by evaluator status, and Newman, Brown, and Littman (1979) and Newman and Bull (1986) found variations in expectations of effectiveness according to evaluator gender and ethnicity.

As the discipline of evaluation has evolved, five achieved roles for evaluators also have evolved. Sieber (1980) summarized four—the evaluator as scientist, administrator, member of society, and individual—and indicated that each of these roles contains inherent ethical systems. The scientist role includes expectations based on appropriate design and methodological issues besides the ability to implement the evaluation design. Administrator expectations include managing the evaluation, being aware of political and feasibility issues, and interacting with program administration. The societal role reflects evaluators' philo-

TABLE 5–1 Role of Evaluators and Ethical Conflicts

Role of Program Evaluator	*Ethical Conflicts*
Objective scientist	
Interpersonal aspects of data collection	Justice and beneficence versus fidelity
Technical aspects of data collection	Autonomy versus fidelity
Analysis of data	Nonmaleficence/beneficence versus escape to autonomy
Interpretation of data	Justice and fidelity (to whom?)
Reporter	Beneficence and justice (to whom?) Evaluator autonomy versus fidelity to client
Administrator/program manager	Autonomy versus fidelity
Member of a profession	Autonomy/fidelity (to which profession?)
Member of society	Beneficence for greater good, justice versus fidelity to profession/client Autonomy of client

sophical perception of the discipline, their view of evaluation's function in serving society, and their perception of evaluation's status as a profession. The individual role includes both ascribed variables and the evaluator's personal philosophy pertaining to self and the larger world. The fifth role, evaluator as reporter, is identified through a series of separate expectations related to the evaluator as information broker, communicator, and change agent (Patton, 1986).

Although it is difficult to determine to what degree each of these roles will be required for a specific project, it is possible to delineate some of the expectations of each role and to discuss where conflicts may arise. The following sections discuss the expectations and conflicts resulting from the five evaluator roles as they relate to ethical decision making. Table 5–1 provides a brief summary of this section. Later in this chapter, we briefly address ethical issues related to conflicts created by evaluators' relationship to the program.

CONFLICTS RELATED TO THE ROLE OF OBJECTIVE SCIENTIST

The most commonly accepted role of the evaluator is that of the objective scientist (Bermant & Warwick, 1978; Goodrich, 1978; Sieber

& Sanders, 1978). Sieber (1980) points out that if an evaluator's work is to be accepted and valued, it is important that it be viewed as objective. There are, however, multiple viewpoints on what constitutes a definition of objective, and these viewpoints frequently conflict. Originally, objective measurement was defined as reliable, accurate, valid, and unbiased assessment. Goodrich (1978), however, redefined the term such that objective evaluation does not entail the exact measurement of a physical, affective, or cognitive characteristic but, instead, determines the truth about the object as experienced by those around it. Guba and Lincoln (1989) broadened the definition of objective to include not only the properties of all those who are affected by the program but all aspects of the program, including social and economic consequences.

There are four major decision areas where the evaluator's role of objective scientist can result in ethical conflicts. These are decisions related to the (a) interpersonal aspects of data collection, (b) technical aspects of data collection, (c) analysis of data, and (d) interpretation of data.

Interpersonal Decisions

Decisions related to the interpersonal aspects of data collection are represented by evaluators' degree of involvement with program staff. It is in this role of data collector/researcher that evaluators have the most direct contact with program staff, participants, consumers, and other stakeholders. Although program staff members are frequently the most knowledgeable about a program's strengths and weaknesses, they are also the most biased for personal and economic reasons. It is possible, at this point of the evaluation, for the staff to "sell" the evaluator on the project based solely on their personality and dedication to the project. Program consumers' perception of the social utility of a program and their ability to convince the evaluator of that utility may also cause conflicts in decision making for evaluators. When involved in these decisions, the evaluator may have to weigh the importance of justice and beneficence with fidelity to the client.

Technical Decisions

Technical decisions made by the evaluator as part of the scientific role also lead to ethical dilemmas. These include decisions related to timeliness and accuracy of data collection, the scope of collected materials, and inclusion of information from all audiences. Although the evaluator in the objective/scientific role may expect random sampling and piloted surveys, or balanced observations preceded by focus groups, the evaluator in the administrator role may be watching the clock and the budget. Also, the client's perception of what is considered technically adequate may vary greatly from the perceptions of the evaluator. This difference in role expectation may force the evaluator to make decisions related to technical issues that satisfy client expectations but not professional evaluator expectations. The principle of autonomy may become important in this instance, and the decisions can become even more difficult if audiences have differing levels of technical sophistication.

Analysis of Data

Once collected, the analysis of data also creates expectations that the evaluator will have to balance when fulfilling the role of objective scientist. These include decisions on what is worth coding, what should be analyzed, and the appropriateness of different types of analyses. For instance, professional evaluators, clients, funding agencies, and program staff may all have different expectations of types of analyses. When studying early childhood programs for the disabled, Lobosco and Newman (1992) found that administrators at the federal and state levels preferred quantitative analyses but that local care providers and parents preferred descriptive data backed by anecdotal information. Again, variations in experience among clients will create conflicting role expectations. Nonmaleficence and beneficence may be key principles at this point as the evaluator tries to avoid overanalyzing information while providing what decision makers want. Some evaluators may use the principle of autonomy to avoid the entire issue.

Interpretation of Results

Interpretation of results is also an area of conflict for the evaluator/scientist when multiple audiences have different needs. Interpretation involves valuing the information and necessitates a comparison against a value standard. At this point, evaluators become acutely aware of the different value systems they are expected to portray and may find themselves having to choose a particular system at the expense of another. Issues pertaining to justice and fidelity may become important. Brinkerhoff et al. (1983) suggest that at this point, the evaluator should examine the different referent points and attempt to explore and present as many viewpoints as possible. This could include looking for confirmation from multiple sources or involving the audience in the interpretation. In the end, however, the evaluator may be forced to select one or two particular points of view at the cost of the others.

CONFLICTS RELATED TO THE ROLE OF REPORTER

The role of information reporter is one of the most hazardous for evaluators. Patton (1986) identified several subroles within this domain: communicator, presenter, discussant, salesperson, and diplomat. According to Worthen and Sanders (1987), this role is the most important of all evaluator roles, yet it receives the least amount of attention in terms of both time and funds. Newman (1988) found that educational administrators and teachers perceived inadequate reporting to be a frequent occurrence in program evaluation.

When examining expectations for the role of reporter, there are multiple areas in which conflict can arise: who should get a report, what content should be included, how the information should be delivered, what responsibility toward use is included in the reporter's role, and what responsibilities pertaining to misuse or abuse of information rest with the reporter.

Professional evaluators' perceptions of the expectations of the role of reporter would appear to differ from those of clients. Most professional evaluators would agree that the purpose of reporting information is to communicate the findings of the evaluation to interested audiences and help them make use of this information (Brinkerhoff et al., 1983; Guba & Lincoln, 1989; Patton, 1986; Worthen & Sanders, 1987). Even within the discipline of evaluation, however, there are variations in expectations related to the role of reporter. Some evaluation approaches view the reporting process as a separate, formalized role involving only the act of communicating specific pieces of information in a specific mode using structured techniques. Accreditation reports, for instance, or statistical summaries of federally funded programs frequently have an accepted method of reporting that has come to be accepted by all participants. In this setting, clients' expectations of evaluator autonomy and fidelity may clash when the evaluator is instructed to be objective and loyal. Other approaches to evaluation, however, do not perceive the role of reporter as a static, one-shot process, nor do they view it as having to be a product (Guba & Lincoln, 1989; Stake, 1978). In these approaches, the third mode of role acquisition is more common, and the evaluator and client will frequently negotiate ethical differences pertaining to the reporting process.

General expectations among most report receivers indicate that reports should be timely, open, frank, and balanced (Cronbach & Associates, 1980; Worthen & Sanders, 1987). Role senders, however, may vary in their definitions of these terms: Administrators may prefer a one-shot report, with decisions of use left to them; program participants may prefer a series of reports where they can be involved in the formulation of use; and program receivers or consumers may prefer a report that provides a rating of services, using self-selected criteria, that will allow them to place a value on services. In the ideal world of evaluation reporting, each of these would be possible; however, most evaluators are faced with both a limited timeline and a limited budget. Hence, the evaluator is caught between the various role expectations of clients, users, and other evaluators and may have to consider the principle of justice when reporting. Using this principle, a possible solution to the multiplicity of expectations is to provide minority viewpoints and to use alternative methods of reporting information that should lead to greater use of the information and better service to all users. If time and budget are a problem, however, Cronbach and Associates (1980) may offer the best alternative: a comprehensive report instead of an exhaustive one. A report may be considered comprehensive when it balances the principles of justice for all stakeholders with nonmaleficence while maintaining evaluator autonomy.

CONFLICTS RELATED TO THE ROLE OF ADMINISTRATOR/MANAGER

Ethical dilemmas related to the role of evaluator as administrator/manager are similar to those found in most management settings. They involve responsibilities related to program management, personnel and staffing issues, fiscal responsibility, and public relations. Evaluators' degree of involvement in administrative functions varies depending on the organizational setting, the project under review, and the evaluators' personal inclinations. An evaluator may be the actual program administrator or the administrator of an evaluation unit, of a single evaluation, or of a small subcomponent of an evaluation for which the evaluator alone constitutes the entire staff. The administrator role of an internal evaluator may go beyond these to also include working as a program staff member, serving as program administrator, and helping the organization use the information. Administrators of internal evaluation units will receive conflicting expectations due to their dual role and will frequently be in conflict over loyalty issues. Administrative role expectations for external evaluators parallel those of the internal evaluators in many ways; however, because the client base is shifting constantly, the external administrators will have additional role expectations related to maintaining their own organization and their own public relations besides those of the client and funding agency. The principles of autonomy and fidelity frequently may be in conflict when evaluators are in an administrative role.

CONFLICTS RELATED TO THE ROLE OF MEMBER OF A PROFESSION

An evaluator's role as a member of a profession reflects our perception of belonging to a peer group involved in a common task. Professional role expectations typically include an interactive relationship with others who have similar training, perform similar tasks, espouse similar vocational goals, and portray a similar philosophy of what our function in society should be. By virtue of our membership in a profession, others expect us (and we expect it of ourselves) to share a common philosophy representing our joint interests and to follow appropriate guidelines regulating or structuring our practice. Membership in a profession is frequently denoted by involvement in an organization whose primary purpose is to support and strengthen the profession. Although not binding, membership in an organization is symbolic of our acceptance of the expectations of the role as defined by the organization. The American Evaluation Association, Division H of the American Educational Research Association, and Division 18 of the American Psychological Association are representative of such organizations. Each promotes the professional status of evaluators through sponsorship of research, training, standards, and discussion of ethical issues. As a consequence, each promotes a set of expectations, including ethical systems, of what it means to be a professional evaluator.

These expectations can be the cause of ethical dilemmas for evaluators for two reasons: First, evaluators are frequently viewed as members of two or more professions, and second, the discipline of evaluation has no clearly defined professional philosophy and frequently promotes multiple, conflicting expectations.

In the early stages of program evaluation's history, practitioners were trained first in a discipline and second in a methodology that only later was termed evaluation. This led to the expectation that the evaluator was first and foremost a member of a contextual discipline. It was expected that primary professional role identification and loyalty would be with the contextual discipline. The ethics of the discipline would guide evaluation practice. For instance, if you were an evaluator in the mental health area, you were first and foremost a mental health professional and second, a methodologist. Consequently, APA guidelines for ethical practice were used by evaluators to monitor their practice.

As evaluation has evolved, however, evaluators have come to be perceived as members of an inquiry-based discipline with one or more supporting areas from the contextual disciplines; that is, one is an evaluator who practices in the mental health area. This shift has led to dual professional role expectations for evaluators. The first role encompasses the expectations of how we practice evaluation, and the second role encompasses the expectations of how we will support the contextual discipline in which we practice evaluation. In discussing roles of evaluators, Mathison (1991) summarizes the conflicts inherent in this dual relationship. She indicates that evaluators are faced with dual professional conflicts related to decisions on which methodologies are appropriate, what association journals and guidelines to use for continuing education, what measures to use for assessment of the quality of our own performance, which group we should disseminate our findings to, and whether or not we should restrict the types of programs we evaluate.

The lack of standardized training and practice within the discipline of evaluation leads to conflicts for members. Because the training of

Vignette 5.2 The Methodology Dilemma: Examples

Mike Stone is Vice President for Personnel Training for a large manufacturing company. He is instituting a new safety training program for the entire staff. He writes a request for proposals that is sent to multiple evaluation contractors. After reviewing the incoming proposals, Stone must choose between two that have almost identical dollar amounts. The proposed evaluation tasks, however, are very different. In the first, the evaluation would be conducted by an in-house evaluation team, trained by the evaluators, that would spend a lot of time on-site, viewing and participating in activities. This plan would include formative information and would be very popular with staff and union representatives. Also, the role of the personnel office would be enhanced among the rank and file. The second evaluation would use an expert review methodology. The evaluation, external in nature, would consist of a team of nationally recognized safety experts visiting the project twice a year for 2 years. This method would give the company some good public relations, make other administrators more open to future training programs, and advance Mike's visibility with upper management. Mike is not sure what to do. Ideally, he would like to hire both evaluators, but he cannot afford two teams. To add to his confusion, he finds out through a third source that the two prospective evaluation contractors know each other and have shared their proposals with each other.

- How should Mike weigh the competing needs of staff and administration?
- How much weight should he put on his own professional needs and/or those of his office?
- Does the fact that the two contractors shared their proposals with each other enter into the decision making? Mike feels that it is "unfair." Is it?

evaluators is lodged primarily within the contextual disciplines, there is frequently disagreement among evaluators over why we do evaluation, what constitutes proper methodology, and how we determine the usefulness of results. Although the discipline of evaluation is slowly developing a broader view of what is acceptable in these domains, the expectations still vary enough to cause both the client and the evaluator difficulties in decision making.

The recent and continued debate over appropriateness of qualitative or quantitative methodologies is an example of how this lack of consensus leads to ethical dilemmas among clients. A subcomponent of Vignette 5.2 is an example of this dilemma. The first evaluator has proposed a methodology that is formative in nature, would be popular with staff members, and would give the evaluator more internal visibility. The second evaluator has proposed a method that is summative, would be popular with administration, and would advance the evaluator's external credentials. Both approaches are acceptable, but the client is left with a dilemma: Which is correct? The evaluators have made no attempt to help the client resolve this issue, and in all probability the client will select the method that "feels the best," discarding the other as incorrect. Both evaluators have retained their autonomy to present what they believe is a correct methodology, but because neither has practiced beneficence (helping the client to grow and expand in knowledge) both may in fact have done harm if the client is left with the impression that one method is "right" and the other "wrong."

Development of standards to guide practice of evaluation and the use of meta-evaluation are two proposed solutions for conflicts created by the variations in professional expectations. Both the ERS and Joint Committee Standards attempt to delineate what constitutes acceptable practice for evaluation. A weakness of both sets of standards, however, is that they are only guidelines, are not always accepted by evaluators and clients, and, indeed, are frequently not known by either group. The use of meta-evaluation as a means of determining quality of evaluation is a growing field and holds promise for the practice of evaluators monitoring evaluators. A weakness of meta-evaluation, however, is knowing what to do with information of misconduct or poor practice if it is found. Vignette 7 in Chapter 1 typifies this situation. In this setting, the meta-evaluator has strong evidence that another evaluator is grossly overcharging a client for services received but does not know what to do with this information. For instance, should the meta-evaluator judge only the quality of the work produced, or should the client be informed of the overbilling? Should the meta-evaluator discuss the issue with the original evaluator and inform other professionals or simply ignore the information?

CONFLICTS RELATED TO THE ROLE OF MEMBER OF SOCIETY

As indicated in Chapter 1, overriding all of the evaluator roles related to functions, professions, and status within organizations is our perception of ourselves as individual members of society and what that may mean in terms of the practice of our vocation. As discussed in Chapter

2, our philosophy toward the world and our place in it provide different perceptions of what constitutes acceptable behavior. D'Onofrio and Ward (1992) suggest that in ethical situations where two or more divergent actions have been deemed acceptable, further debate is "hampered by the participants' ignorance of the fact that they are really disagreeing not only about the rightness of a particular action, but about the grounds on which any determination of rightness or wrongness is to be made" (p. 9).

These different perceptions of ways to determine right and wrong cause conflicts when we evaluate others' programs, others' evaluations, and our own behavior. The dilemmas resulting from these conflicts include placing limitations on our selection and scope of projects; modifying designs to accent our own values, thereby overriding those of the client; presenting self-biased interpretations of information; denying the value of information from alternate views; and literally withholding information because we do not see its value. Because evaluators cannot practice in a value-free mode, they must make every effort to acknowledge their own values and expectations of a program to themselves and to their clients. Vignette 9 in Chapter 1 is an example of this type of dilemma. The evaluator has valued the outcomes of one program over another and is in a position to actually transfer funds to the more preferred project. She does not feel that this would affect her performance on the evaluation of the first project but that it would enhance the effect and improve the standing of the more valued project. Using the principle of beneficence, the evaluator is overlooking her own bias toward the one project. Because she sees this project as more valuable to society at large, she is devaluing the effects of the other project and violating the principles of justice and fidelity.

There also will be times in the course of an evaluation when flagrant violations of legal or accepted social mores come to the attention of the evaluator. These violations will have nothing to do with the goals of the program or the agency but will reflect actions that are considered unacceptable because of our culture's moral code. Our own expectations of our role as a citizen or member of society will be in conflict with our expectations related to objective scientist or unbiased reporter. When evaluators are in this situation, they must make a decision about their responsibility as citizens and members of society. The cause of social justice or beneficence may outweigh fidelity to the client. Vignette 10 in

Chapter 1 is an example of this type of ethical dilemma. The evaluator has received information indicating that individuals are being harmed in a way that is not acceptable to society and so becomes involved in a conflict over the interests of the harmed parties, his interests to his client, and his interests to the larger society.

CONFLICTING ROLES RELATED TO THE EVALUATOR'S STATUS WITH THE PROJECT

As indicated earlier in this chapter, a number of contextual and organizational variables can affect evaluators' ethical decision-making process. Each of these variables will interact with the above role expectations in unique ways. One category of contextual variables—the evaluator's perceived status with the program—can result in several different roles or sets of expectations: internal evaluator, program advocate, whistle-blower, and gatekeeper. Each of these roles is discussed briefly in terms of conflicts created by the organization's expectations of the evaluator and the evaluator's self-perception of that role.

Evaluator as Internal Evaluator

Worthen and Sanders (1987) use the term *internal* to denote evaluations conducted by program employees and the term *external* to indicate those conducted by outsiders. Love (1991) expands the definition of internal evaluation to include an ongoing process with responsibility to management concerns. According to Mathison (1991), one of the difficulties of functioning as an internal evaluator is the multiplicity of role expectations. Not only must internal evaluators meet the dual expectations of membership within both the evaluation and substantive area professions, they must also meet the expectations of membership within the organization where the program is housed.

Adams (1985) identified four major ethical concerns evolving from the conflicting expectations of evaluator role and the organizational role:

- Pressure to play down negative results and emphasize positive results
- Reinforcement for using only nonthreatening activities in the design and conduct of evaluation

- Interest, and sometimes pressure, on the part of administration to make the evaluation unit appear visible without supporting use of the information
- Threat of reducing access to the political power of the organization and subsequent decision making if these expectations are not met

Additional dangers for internal evaluators are serving within an organization for too long a time period, thereby ultimately becoming an extension of program administration (Mathison, 1991), and lack of peer review (Love, 1991).

The differing expectations between the dual professional roles of evaluation specialist and content specialist create additional ethical dilemmas when the evaluator is internal. Not only are evaluators faced with their own expectations and the expectations of the respective disciplines, they are also faced with pressure from the organization to fulfill one or both roles. As discussed in the section pertaining to conflicts related to the role of a professional, all evaluators are confronted with the dilemma of fulfilling the role of both evaluation specialist and content specialist. For the internal evaluator, however, organizational expectations create additional pressure. When serving in an internal capacity, the evaluator is expected to maintain a reputation of being an expert in evaluation as a way of reinforcing autonomy and maintaining credibility. This results in the evaluator attempting to present information pertaining to evaluation methodology and design to other evaluators. As internal members of an organization, however, evaluators experience pressure to use their professional dissemination skills in presenting the information to groups that are more closely connected to the substantive area of the program. Over time, this can result in an evaluator being categorized as a specialist with skills appropriate for only a specific type of program.

Because the organization frequently controls the temporal and financial aspects of dissemination and continuing education, it often becomes difficult for the evaluator to maintain professional contacts with organizations representing the profession of evaluation. Thus, the evaluator gradually becomes loyal to the organization, and its expectations, as a means of financial reality. In other words, because of financial and social pressures, the principle of autonomy is given less weight and the principles of nonmaleficence and fidelity are given more.

An example of this situation is an evaluator employed by a school district who is continuously assigned all projects related to special education. Although the evaluator's task appears to be self-controlled, it can, instead, become controlling: In the eyes of others, the evaluator's area of expertise is limited to only those programs. As a consequence, the evaluator may become dependent on the status of those programs and the personnel involved with them. This may lead to gradual dissociation from other evaluators, a loss of autonomy, and a self-perception that is context dependent.

Evaluator as Program Advocate

Frequently, evaluators, whether external or internal, find themselves in the role of program advocate. Based on the expectations of this role, the evaluator is seen as a proponent of a program, usually because of its social consequences or philosophical underpinning but sometimes because of its financial ramifications. In this setting, the evaluator has moved beyond the expectations ascribed to the roles of objective scientist and balanced reporter to involvement with the political and social context of decision making.

The evaluator's role as program advocate is viewed differently by different role senders. Program developers and program staff frequently perceive this role as the sign of a positive, effective evaluator (fidelity) and are more willing to involve the evaluator in future studies. Program funders, consumers, and other evaluators, however, may perceive this role in a negative manner (lacking autonomy and/or justice), viewing it as harmful to the credibility of the current program, the agency, and the profession. Sieber (1980) states that evaluators are frequently called on by clients to act as program advocates in the data they collect, the interpretation of information, and the reports they write. Examples of advocate behavior are evaluating programs that follow particular philosophies, designing studies that look at only certain types of information, interpreting and valuing information according to only the advocacy viewpoint, and including or excluding information such that the results support the advocate position.

Several authors (e.g., House, 1988; Mathison, 1991) have questioned whether this type of advocacy is really evaluation or the substitution of values. Because not all interest groups are represented, there is no longer credibility and independence of the evaluator's facts; thus any report user may be led to doubt the entire process. Braskamp (1994) differs in his perception of the evaluator as advocate, stating that the role can have positive consequences if the evaluator's stance is honestly disclosed. In these instances, advocacy can imply caring and recognition of context, reinforcing the purpose of evaluation as promoting improvement, not just accountability. Braskamp goes on to indicate that the role of evaluator as program advocate may become more common in situations where participatory or empowerment evaluations are conducted. In these situations, program staff and program users will bring their values and needs with them as they take on the role of evaluator and will expect to view information from this vantage point.

Evaluator as Whistle-Blower

One ethical dilemma that creates great stress for an evaluator can be likened to that of the "whistle-blower" found in many industrial organizations. In this setting, the evaluator is aware of actions or processes that are not ethically acceptable, usually according to society's standards (Simon, 1978). These actions or processes include observations of interpersonal activities, presentation of false information, and misuse of information. The perceived consequences of these actions are harmful either personally, socially, or economically to individuals who either are not aware of the harm or are powerless to prevent it, yet the persons or organization are in a position to reveal and/or cease doing harm. In this setting, the evaluator is faced with the dilemma of revealing the harm or threat of harm while attempting to remain loyal to the evaluation client.

In a situation resulting in limited repercussions, the evaluator may be able to solve the dilemma by making the client aware of the situation and eventually working in cooperation with the client to stop further harm from occurring. At times, however, more serious scenarios will cause increased conflict for the evaluator, especially if the evaluator is aware of individuals or groups who have suffered long-term damage from the action or process. In this situation, the evaluator may have to decide between the responsibilities of privileged information and the public's right to know.

Kimmel (1988) indicates that the evaluator is obliged to report information about potential harm to the appropriate authorities and cites the *Tarasoff* decision as a landmark. In this decision (*Tarasoff v. Regents of the University of California,* 1976), the issue of breaching confidentiality was examined for mental health counselors. The findings resulted in a "duty to warn" decision that indicated that if knowledge of potential harm was known, it must be reported. Kimmel suggests that the conflicting role of the evaluator is even more perilous in that, although evaluators frequently promise confidentiality, the profession has no legal right to ensure confidentiality if it is known that harm is being done. Thus the interpretation of confidential interviews and data sources becomes difficult to maintain in the face of both public and client pressure.

Johnson (1985) suggests that evaluators consider the perceived violation in light of the organizations' goals; if the violation occurs in an area the organization is committed to correcting, then the information should be reported. The weakness of Johnson's approach, however, is that it assumes that evaluators are acquiring the ethical expectations of clients while having none of their own or not valuing any of society's or clients' expectations. In most situations, discovery of the ethical violation is a side effect and may create conflicts between meeting the clients' needs and serving society. The evaluator will be caught between conflicting ethical expectations.

An alternate ethical dilemma that may lead to whistle-blowing occurs when evaluators perceive that information, particularly negative information, is not reaching all audiences. Typically, in this setting, the evaluator has obtained and included information in the report that will be viewed negatively by various audiences. At this time, the evaluator may perceive the client(s) attempting to censor the negative findings or keeping the findings from reaching those audiences who have a "right to know." When this occurs, the evaluator is faced with a conflict between loyalty to client and loyalty to truth. Issues related to ownership of information, right to privileged information, and evaluator/client autonomy may be raised. In the long run, the evaluator may be forced to choose between loyalty to the client, loyalty to society, and loyalty to the objectivity of the profession.

Evaluator as Gatekeeper

A role frequently found in many organizations is that related to the status of gatekeeper. A gatekeeper is a member of a group who filters information and selects what information will be passed on to other members of the group for decision making. Because gatekeepers have access to all information, they are given the power by the group to both forward the information only to those individuals who need it and select how that information will be forwarded (Harrel, 1986). Although this role is inherent in that of the evaluator as reporter, it carries additional expectations when the evaluator is internal to the organization. In the internal setting, it is expected that the evaluator will be loyal to the organization's interest when selecting and channeling the information. This may be counterproductive to the role expectations of the evaluator as unbiased reporter and/or member of society. The evaluator may be faced with the dilemma of knowing that certain aspects of a program are not working but is expected to present that information only to selected members of the group. For internal evaluators, the principle of fidelity may conflict with those of justice and beneficence.

CONCLUSION

The roles of an evaluator are many and varied. The complexity of assuming these multiple roles and meeting their demands frequently creates conflicts for the evaluator that result in ethical dilemmas. A consciousness of these expectations and awareness of where the conflicts occur may help the evaluator in the decision process detailed in Chapter 4. If an evaluator must choose between differing actions, it is beneficial to know why the conflict arose and to explore the expectations behind the conflicts. Although it is not possible for an evaluator to maintain a role-free evaluation, it is possible to know the expectations that will be sent by the different stakeholders. Through knowing, understanding, and valuing these expectations, evaluators will be better able to establish their own roles. This chapter concludes with additional examples of role-related ethical dilemmas that can be used to further the discussion of ethical practice as it is affected by multiple expectations.

Vignette 5.3 Conflicting Roles

As part of an evaluation of an on-campus media project, the evaluator and her staff visit Professor Jones's classroom. In an attempt to be unobtrusive, they arrive 10 minutes before class and take seats in the back of the room. Throughout the next 10 minutes, the classroom quickly fills up, leaving only three vacant chairs. At 9:05, five students walk into the room. Three scramble for the vacant chairs; the other two sit on the floor by the door.

- Were the evaluators justified in taking up classroom space in order to remain unobtrusive?
- If moving would disrupt the classroom and the teacher, creating a less valid observation, should the evaluators remain in the chairs?
- Is there a better solution to the problem? How does the role of data collector interfere with the roles of evaluator administrator and member of society in this setting? How could—or should—the evaluator report this dilemma?

Janice Dorian is evaluating a new state-funded program for preschool disabled children. According to grant guidelines, she is to evaluate achievement of program goals related to improved motor coordination and speech ability. Although it is not part of the required observation, Janice visits the new and traditional sites several times, observing the children and talking to parents and staff members. She notes that children enrolled in the new program have better socialization skills and less emotional problems when handling new situations. Parents and staff at the new site say they have noticed the same things. As part of the required evaluation, she conducts standardized tests and compares the new program results with a control group consisting of children who did not get the new services. Analysis of the standardized comparison data indicates no change in students' speech or motor coordination skills. Janice is not sure what to do. She believes that the program is helping the students, but she is not sure how. She has no reliability or validity for her own observations, and there is no parent information from the traditional school. Also, the program developer based the "claim to fame" of the program on the fact that it would change two areas that did not change but is already promoting it as such.

- What roles conflict in this setting?
- How does Janice balance her own observations with those of the program developer?
- Would her role expectations vary if Janice were an internal evaluator? What if her observations showed negative changes instead of positive ones?

Jack is the local director of an intra-agency group that conducts evaluations for other sections of the agency. In September, he is contacted by Tom with a request for an evaluation of a federally funded project. An agreement is reached regarding scope of evaluation, date of delivery, dollar amount, and methods of transferring funds. Jack has his group commence the evaluation. In January, Jack receives a phone call from the budget office indicating that, although an account has been set up, no funds for the evaluation have yet been received. Jack calls Tom and indicates that the budget office needs the funds. Tom assures Jack that the matter has been taken care of by his office. The evaluation continues. In March, the budget office calls again. Jack calls Tom; Tom sends Jack a copy of a letter, dated February, requesting transfer of funds. Jack assumes that the budget office is behind on paperwork and continues the evaluation. In April, with the data collected and a draft report written, Jack gets another phone call from the budget office. The budget office has no paperwork requesting transfer of funds and will no longer provide funds to complete the project. Jack calls Tom and says there will be no report unless the money is transferred immediately. Tom replies that after all this badgering there will be no money transferred until he gets the final report. The next day Jack is called into the agency director's office and asked why he is obstructing agency progress.

- What evaluator roles are in conflict in this setting? How do the client's and the agency head's expectations match with Jack's?
- What could Jack have done differently at the beginning of the project? At the middle? What should he do now?
- How will Jack stop his negative experience as evaluator/administrator from affecting or biasing his role of evaluator/reporter?

An evaluation agency simultaneously bids on several large projects from different funders. Each is national or international in nature and will be very visible projects. The bids all refer to the use of Dr. I. M. Wellknown as the full-time project director if the bid is accepted. Much to the agency head's surprise and joy, they are offered three contracts. Dr. Wellknown informs the agency that she is happy to take on any one of the projects, but she obviously cannot direct all three. For both status and credibility purposes, the funding agencies all want Dr. Wellknown as director. In order to not lose the contracts, the agency offers Dr. Wellknown reduced time on all three or offers to pay her to allow her name to be nominally associated with two while working 90% on the project of her choice.

- What should Dr. Wellknown do?
- How will her role change within the three projects? Will her role expectations conflict with those of the evaluation agencies? The funding agency?

Alternate scenarios:

- Would the situation change if the three projects were not high-visibility tasks?
- Would the situation change if Dr. Wellknown were instead Dr. Notknown?
- What would you do if you were the reviewer for multiple agencies and you saw Dr. Wellknown's name on project bids 2 months later?

6

Context, Methodology, and Ethics

A Reader's Guide to Chapter 6

Evaluators use a rich variety of methods derived from educational and psychological research, political science, anthropology, ethnography, and sociology, to name only a few, and they employ them in equally diverse geographical, service, and cultural settings. Do the different methods and contexts have implications for the ethical issues confronting evaluators? What special concerns should evaluators have, depending on the methods they use and the settings in which they are conducting an evaluation? This chapter examines unique ethical concerns within two contextual settings:

- Multicultural and international settings
- Corporate settings

It also discusses ethical issues related to two methodological approaches:

- Evaluations that use qualitative methods
- Evaluations that have research purposes and require examination by institutional review boards

CONTEXTS AND ETHICAL ISSUES

Multicultural and International Evaluation Settings

Vignette 6.1 No One Wants to Comment

An evaluator of a school project in an Asian country uses a methodology requiring a control group and an experimental group and in so doing tries to get both groups to be competitive with each other. The evaluator also interviews students and tries to get them to disclose what is not going well for them in the project. After the first two interviews, other students refuse to be interviewed. The evaluator cannot understand what is happening.

- Under what false assumptions is the evaluator operating?
- What are possible reasons for the students' noncooperation?

In this global society, evaluators often conduct program evaluations in different countries with highly divergent cultures and values or are involved with programs in the United States that are designed for participants with different cultural heritages. Indeed, even with the omnipresence of television fostering increased homogeneity in this country, significantly profound regional differences in attitudes and expectations exist among U.S. citizens. Racial, ethnic, and social class differences within American cities of any size are so profound that evaluators can easily find themselves in a multicultural setting within one school district, one political district, and even crossing from one section of town to another. Of course, evaluators who are used to working in an educational setting will find different values and perspectives operating when they undertake an evaluation in a medical or business setting. Evaluators find themselves in different cultural environments, even within what, on the surface, appears to be the mundane environment of public policy, where conflicts between the interests of basic researchers, the corporate world, and the public regulators can be a shock to those evaluators who are politically naive (Archer, Pettigrew, & Aronson, 1992). So, whether they are conducting evaluations in an exotic foreign country or across the street in a different neighborhood, they will likely be involved in multicultural activities.

Corey, Corey, and Callahan (1988) suggest that cultural diversity reflects differences in the characteristics of institutions, language, values, religious ideals, and patterns of social relationships. These facets of a culture are influenced by ethnicity, gender, age, socioeconomic status, and lifestyle. After examining existing ethical codes pertinent to therapists, Corey et al. concluded that the codes were insensitive to other cultures, that multiplicity had been neglected, and that, generally, the codes could be considered "culturally encapsulated." We doubt if even the recent revisions of APA and AERA ethical codes and the new AEA code would rate a much better judgment.

We, the authors, are white, middle-class U.S. citizens. Although we have a rich experiential background in evaluation activities, the bulk of our experience has been in settings dominated by the current majority culture in this country. Even though our own heritage and experiences limit our perspective, we do recognize the need to try to understand others' perspectives and so think it essential to illustrate those differences and how they might affect an evaluator's behavior.

Demographers have projected that in the not-too-distant future, the current majority will be in the minority. Thus, it is essential that evaluators attend to cultural differences. From the perspective of social justice, such attention is imperative. We believe that the same questions and principles are applicable to any setting in which the evaluator's background and experience are different from that of the evaluation context. Although many of our examples reflect extreme cultural differences represented by international work, the same issues apply when we are evaluating programs within our own city, county, state, or nation that serve persons of different cultural, ethnic, racial, gender, or religious backgrounds. Merryfield (1985) has noted three specific issues—informed consent, privacy, and deception—that need special attention when conducting an evaluation in a different cultural setting. Each of these issues is discussed in turn.

Informed Consent

Even in an evaluation or research project with no international and multicultural dimensions, researchers and evaluators in the United States are seldom as forthright about obtaining informed consent as they might be. Too often, the emphasis is on obtaining consent, and how "informed" the participant is may be questionable. You may have experienced reading consent forms for participation in medical studies that were so jargon-filled you could not understand them or were so explicit in their warnings (e.g., "Flu shots can result in serious complications [vomiting, high fever, heavy cough] for some patients") that you really questioned your decision to participate (we have)—but you went ahead anyway because you trust people wearing a white lab coat (we did). Making sure that consent is truly informed and that information about possible effects is candid and clear is critical for evaluations conducted in international and multicultural settings. Other cultures may not be as accustomed to surveys, interviews, observations, or even the concept of evaluation as we in the United States are. This novelty effect may lead to resistance to participate, or it may stimulate the naive but curious to participate.

Autonomy, one of the five ethical principles discussed in Chapters 2 and 4, may not be either as highly valued or as readily attainable in another culture as it is in ours. In a cultural setting where loyalty to the group receives primary consideration in contrast to the concerns of the individual, informants may be confused about what their appropriate, and safe, response should be to a process asking them to make critical and candid comments about employers or an organization. U.S. participants are familiar with surveys and filling out evaluation forms after a workshop, conference, or instructional session that ask for their feedback, criticisms, and suggestions. This may not be true for program participants from different cultures where it is customary to be more subtle and where helping the program designers and administrators save face is more important and more typical than confronting program planners with criticisms. Difficulties occur when the evaluator is viewed as a foreigner (Seefeldt, 1985), such as the evaluator in Vignette 6.1 who mistakenly assumed that competition would be accepted naturally by the participants and they would welcome the opportunity to offer constructive critiques.

Evaluators cannot assume automatically that their techniques and tools will transfer directly to another culture. Cultures vary in the importance they give to independence, competition, conflict, democracy, individuality, maturity, and other variables that have an impact on not only the effectiveness of the evaluator in a different country but also the ethical implications of the evaluator's actions. An evaluator should not assume that the concept of formal evaluation itself can be transported to another culture without special efforts to avoid misunderstanding.

Evaluators working in a different country or in a different cultural setting will find that their first important task is to learn about the culture and its implications for the program evaluation. Their second important task is to inform participants about their (evaluators') beliefs about evaluation, its purpose, the evaluator's role, and the participant's role before planning the evaluation even begins.

Participants in more authoritarian cultures may be accustomed to acquiescing to requests for information coming from supposed official representatives. They may fear recriminations if they do not participate. This may be the case particularly when representatives other than the evaluator provide instructions to participants and when someone else oversees the data-collection process. As an evaluator, you might be pleased initially when you receive a 100% return rate on your evaluation survey but be dismayed when you discover that participation was almost forced, thus causing the results to have questionable validity.

Informed consent implies more than simply obtaining a signature at the bottom of a form. It means ensuring that participants fully understand what is involved and ensuring that there is no coercion, subtle or otherwise. It means that the focus has to be on truly informing the participants rather than on obtaining the largest participation rate possible.

Privacy

What is viewed as private differs among cultures. In some cultures, the woman's face must not be viewed in public. A study of our U.S. history of clothing fashion reminds us that not too long ago, exposure of a woman's ankle was considered risqué. To cite another example, in some cultures it is acceptable to note prominent persons' sexual liaisons but not their incomes. Cultural *faux pas* lie in wait like mines in a warring nation's sea harbor for the naive evaluator working in another country. The resulting explosions could be equally disastrous.

Privacy is particularly important when writing reports and identifying individuals or groups in the report. Evaluators and researchers have been reasonably successful in masking individuals' identity in reports by using fictitious names. Where there is the slightest possibility, however, that the report could be controversial in a public setting, evaluators must exercise extreme caution. If you reflect on prominent, headline-making trial cases in which reporters were successful in finding out which juror voted which way, and as a result sometimes significantly embarrassing those jurors, you will recognize the need to be protective of your sources.

Privacy in a multicultural context has relevance beyond the individual; it can also pertain to one's race or ethnicity or even to the neighborhood group. Naming a group, when discussing criminal or immoral behavior, can reinforce negative stereotypes when cultural identification is irrelevant to the evaluation question. Evaluation reports that contain negative information about a particular neighborhood or cultural group hold the potential for harm that the evaluator must weigh against other possible benefits.

Uses of Reports

Can evaluators write their reports and then wash their hands of the uses made of the report? This is a question faced by all evaluators, but it has special implications for evaluators conducting multicultural studies that may have political ramifications. Even the most highly positive report may indirectly provide information for policymakers and administrators that could be used to manipulate those in the culture being studied. If evaluators know at the outset that the information collected will be used for such purposes, they should make contractual arrangements to avoid this possible outcome. Keeping the information secret or limiting its dissemination is a last resort but sometimes necessary.

We are continually being told that "information is power," and it is important that evaluators recognize the potential implications of this truism. Will the evaluation information significantly strengthen the power of some individuals or groups within or outside the evaluation context? Changes in power may not dramatically affect the participants, but such changes will not go unnoticed by the participants, who will, as a result, shy away from future evaluations because of this experience. How much caution and concern should this cause evaluators? Having good intentions about involving participants early and distributing the information power base more broadly helps, but actualizing these can be difficult. Coimbra (1986) describes the difficulties encountered when conducting implementation-oriented evaluations in Brazil, where no prior tradition existed for having evaluations be both impartial and implementation oriented. As a result, it was extremely difficult to convince participants that the evaluation could provide information that would directly benefit them.

An overriding guiding principle for all evaluations might be, as we noted in Chapter 2, what benefit does the evaluation have for the participants in the program being evaluated as well as for society at large? This principle is particularly applicable for evaluations conducted in cultures that are less economically developed and perhaps less educationally advanced than the evaluators' culture. Montejo, Modol, and Ramirez (1986), describing the methods used in an evaluation of social programs in Costa Rica, note the importance of understanding the "social realities" of the evaluation context. They strongly recommend avoiding implementation of the same evaluation design in two different communities, even within the same country. Evaluators must consider the living standards, resources available, and public opinion within each community when they plan evaluations. Evaluators who use only their own scale of values are likely to produce an evaluation that is shallow, simplistic, and generally useless. To avoid this, Montejo et al. suggest obtaining community involvement early in the planning stages.

The evaluator must be responsive to the needs of the cultural community being evaluated. These needs can be met in several ways. Writing an evaluation report and anticipating how the report will be used is not being sufficiently responsive. The evaluator might have faith that the agency or organization for whom the evaluation is being conducted will be responsive to the needs of the cultural community, but we know that "having faith" is not sufficient even within settings where evaluation is a commonplace activity. If appropriate within evaluators' perception of their role, evaluators need to consider an advocacy role and make a special effort to see that the community's needs are being noted by others in positions of power who might be more responsive (House, 1993). Finally, evaluators themselves may be able to provide direct technical assistance to the community—for example, assisting in interpretation of data, providing consultation about change strategies within the community, or sharing knowledge about similar programs and processes in other settings.

Ideally, the evaluator does not wait until the evaluation is completed and a report made to consider how to be responsive to the community's needs. These questions should be considered in the earliest stages possible when planning the evaluation. The evaluator can improve the chances of the evaluation having a positive impact on the community by involving community members early in the evaluation process. What information could be collected that would help them understand themselves? What information would they like to know? How best might the collected evaluation information be communicated, and to whom? These questions can be answered by involving the community in project planning and planning the evaluation. Marino (1980), for example, notes that persons planning rural development projects in different countries must be aware that these projects will not succeed unless there is community involvement. He suggests that the same holds true for evaluation.

Including community members in the planning and execution of an evaluation is also important for evaluations involving diverse cultural groups in the United States. Madison (1992) describes how cultural bias can misinform social theory and how terms such as *hardcore unemployable*, *economically disadvantaged*, *at-risk population*, and *culturally deprived* are negative social descriptors that carry with them prejudices when they are used as concepts to plan and evaluate social programs. She, like House (1990, 1993) and others, questions whether or not evaluation can be cultural-free. Cultural factors can influence data collection methods and data verification strategies. Inclusion of program participants in the evaluation process can serve two purposes: provide credibility to the evaluation findings and provide an opportunity to note whether or not moral questions relating to social justice have been addressed (Madison, 1992).

Inclusion of stakeholders in planning and conducting an evaluation and attending to cultural expectations in different countries, however, requires more than good intentions. Thompson (1989) notes, for example, that in the Maghreb region of North Africa, the evaluator can best function as a power broker who mediates and sometimes takes blame for things unsaid by those in the culture who prefer not to ask or answer direct questions, but this requires extensive experience. Being successful in the power broker role means more than bringing stakeholders together for a meeting; this may result in only superficial collaboration. Thompson finds the power broker role most similar to the Fourth Generation evaluation method used by Guba and Lincoln (1989). The evaluator must attempt to gather together the views of all stakeholders and be particularly attentive to the voices of the most disenfranchised. Indeed, Guba and Lincoln see this as a moral imperative. This is not easy for the novice evaluator, and, as Mason (1989) comments, a proactive evaluator may be seen as an interloper and even, in some instances, as a subversive.

In one way or another, all of the ethical principles discussed in Chapters 2 and 4 have relevance for conducting international and multicultural evaluations. The autonomy of the participants must be considered along with how they view autonomy and authority. The evaluator must avoid doing harm. The evaluator must keep promises, some of which implicitly go beyond the timeline of the evaluation itself. Of particular importance, from our perspective, are the principles of beneficence and justice. What good can the evaluator do that is not patronizing and that does not jeopardize the culture? What is fair, and what is responsive to the needs of the culture? Diener and Crandall (1978) note that too often anthropological studies of other cultures have been premised on what they call "academic colonialism," an assumption that we know what is best. Instead, they suggest, we gain far more through respect and reciprocity. The traditions of another culture exist for a reason, and it is quite possible that we can learn as much, if not more, from the people in the other culture as they can learn from us. We believe that this holds true for evaluation studies, and the obligation to be fair and to do good weigh particularly for the evaluator conducting international and multicultural evaluations.

Kirkhart (1995) describes three threats to the validity of evaluations in multicultural settings: time, culturally unsophisticated evaluators, and arrogant complacency. In Chapter 4, we illustrated how time affects stress, which in turn affects decision making in evaluation situations, no matter the context. We hope that our discussion in this chapter demonstrates that we share Kirkhart's concerns about the impact of unsophisticated and arrogant evaluators not only for the threats they represent to validity but also for the barriers they represent to conducting an ethical evaluation.

Patton (1985), who has participated in numerous evaluations in different cultural settings, asserts what he calls the one "nongeneralization" about cross-cultural evaluations: namely, that one should not generalize about the specific interactions of culture and evaluation but always be attentive and be able to respond to the specific situation. Thus, "nongeneralization" might well be appropriate for all evaluations in whatever setting.

Corporate or Organizational Responsibility

Vignette 6.2 Good Intentions but Negative Results

Jane works with an evaluation team within a large, nonprofit organization. The team conducts internal and external evaluations. At a staff meeting, one of the team members suggests watering down the negative findings for a federally funded project because it is doing good work but in the competitive world of grants, any negative comments might place continued funding at risk. None of the other five team members speak up, so Jane remains quiet, although the decision does bother her.

- How often have you said or heard the same thing about reporting negative findings or writing negative references?
- What principles are being violated?
- What would you suggest Jane do?

So far, much of our discussion has focused on ethical decision making by individual evaluators. In our discussion in Chapter 4 of the need to consider the organizational context when making decisions, we focused on the individual evaluator within the organization or larger system but did not discuss organizational ethics or organizational responsibility. We will do so here.

There are three important questions to be considered when examining organizational ethics:

- Is there a corporate or organizational ethical climate? That is, can we say that an agency or organization is ethical or unethical, or must we not personify the organization and only talk about individuals within the corporation being ethical?
- Do organizations have ethical responsibilities? Again, not the individuals within the organization but the organization as a whole.
- What can an organization do to improve its ethical climate?

We examine these questions briefly as they relate to program evaluation.

Existence of an Ethical Climate in Organizations

Organizations and companies have reputations. These reputations include attributes like being dependable, standing by their products, and being responsive to consumers. On the negative side, others have reputations for overcharging or not providing good service. If most of us examine closely the reasons why we buy the cars we do, wear the clothes we do, and use certain brand-name products, we probably won't have to scratch our heads too much to discover that among the reasons are these: "Everyone in my family bought Buicks because of their road dependability and their reputation for quality service," "My sisters and I always wear clothes from Land's End because they are known for their long wear life," and "Don't buy one of that company's appliances because the motors always break down." These statements involve products, but they reflect on the services and, ultimately, the reputation of the organizations that designed and manufactured them.

Multiple programs of research offer support for the concept of there being an organizational climate and that these climates can be differentiated as to the degree to which they can be considered ethical (Brown, 1985a; Moos, 1979; Stern, 1970).

One example of differentiation is provided by Victor and Cullen (1988), who speculated about the components of organizational ethics and postulated what different types of ethical climates might be like. They hypothesized nine ethical climates derived from cross-tabulation of two dimensions:

- The ethical criteria used for organizational decision making. Were decisions based on what was good for the organization itself (self-interest), what was good for the clients/customers (benevolence), or what was consistent with general moral principles (principles)?
- The locus of the referent. Was the focus on the concerns of the individual employees, the local firm (employer and employees), or those employed in the same industry across the country?

Results of their research indicated that it was possible to categorize organizations by the first dimension, ethical criteria used for decision making. Organizations could be classified as being primarily focused on self-interest, doing good, or moral principles as the criteria for making ethical decisions. Only at the moral principle level did Victor and Cullen find differences based on the second dimension, that is, the individual, local, or industrywide referents. It is interesting to note that they found no differences in employee satisfaction levels related to the ethical criteria. They surmised that if there were bad fits, then employees either left or were indifferent to these concerns.

What are the implications of organizational ethics for the program evaluator? Acknowledgment of the presence of organizational ethical climates should suggest that the evaluator get a feel for this climate as early as possible in the process of negotiating the evaluation contract. We noted in Chapter 4 the value of assessing the stress levels of those involved in the program being evaluated because they will affect how they process and use information. Find out who and what is at risk. The same is true for the ethical climate. What is the perceived mission of the organization? Who is it serving? How does it resolve issues? What are the criteria for its decision making? Does this ethical climate match that of the evaluator? Are they compatible? We don't pretend that this is an easy process, especially in the limited time usually available to establish and agree on a contract. We do believe, however, that the ethical climate of the organization is something to which the evaluator needs to be alert throughout the evaluation process.

Ethical Responsibility of Organizations

If organizations have an ethical climate, a follow-up question that should be addressed is "Should (or can) organizations be ethically responsible?" There is not agreement on the answer to this question (Carr, 1989; McCoy, 1989; Mirvis & Seashore, 1982). Goodpaster (1989) and Goodpaster and Matthews (1989) outline the pros and cons enumerated by the business community in its response to this question. Critics of the view that organizations have moral responsibility question the validity of this position, sometimes view this stance as "subversive," and question the ability to blend social responsibility with economic decision making. According to this view, the powers of the marketplace provide enough incentive eventually to purify self-interest.

Goodpaster and Matthews (1989) believe that corporations can have a conscience and so can be held morally responsible. They recognize the complexities of today's bureaucracies, but in response to nine possible objections to the concept of a moral organization, they state the following:

- We think of organizations as having goals and strategies, so why can't we think of them as having a collective conscience as well?
- Moral responsibility does not need to be a replacement for economic self-interest but, rather, is viewed as a containment.

- The political process remains the primary mechanism for protecting public interest, but there is no reason why this role cannot also be assumed by private organizations.
- The charge of shareholders is not for organizations to use any means possible to obtain a profit.
- Even neutral stances by organizations represent a moral stand, so therefore the question is not whether corporations exert moral force but, rather, how critically they should choose to do so.
- Although we have not reached a moral consensus on many issues in this country, we do share some common values, and an organization can reflect these.
- Ultimate responsibility rests with individuals within an organization, but an organization is more than the sum of its parts; it represents a cooperative system aiming at cooperative purposes.
- In today's world, the large, modern corporation must be recognized as a significant moral force, although not a substitute for other forces, such as the individual and the state.
- Strict self-interest in the real world is not always congruent with the common good.

Goodpaster and Matthews (1989) conclude that organizations must show respect for persons as ends and not as means to organizational purposes. In our view, they present strong arguments for asserting that organizations do have ethical responsibilities.

Improving an Organization's Ethical Climate

There are parallels between why an organization should strive to be ethical and why an individual person should be ethical. In both cases, a primary motivator is to promote self-interest and achieve success. Although individuals and organizations may define them differently, both have goals of success and have self-interests to address. Maintaining an ethical approach should be part of the goal for each. However, several complexities make it more problematical for an organization. The layers of responsibility limit communication and make it possible for individuals within the organization to use these layers as an excuse for not taking ethical action. Because of varying loyalties within an organization and often because of the sheer numbers of people involved, it is difficult to arrive at a clear consensus of what needs to be done.

Fear of being ostracized or worse, such as being viewed as the "whistle blower" discussed in Chapter 5, can be a major inhibitor to candor and an open dialogue. As noted by Honea (1991), evaluators who were members of a team believed being part of a team would be sufficient to make them more ethical, but in reality being a team member only served as another reason for not discussing ethics. Like Jane in Vignette 6.2, evaluators can be influenced by the silence of others.

Andrews (1989) suggests that, although it is difficult, it is possible to overcome these obstacles and have an organization that is ethical. Of primary importance is the personal deportment of the head of the organization. The actions of the chief executive officer speak louder than existing written policies. When the CEO admits a mistake, orders that a poor product be recalled or repaired, or asks questions about the ethical appropriateness of an action, these behaviors proliferate through the organization. Casual judgments, informal jokes, and even silences can speak loudly and forcefully to others in the organization. If members of the organization are to believe the sincerity of their leadership's pledge to be truly ethical, leaders must model appropriate behavior, and the ethical intentions of an organization need to be discussed, managed, and monitored at the highest levels of the organization rather than left untended. Staff development training programs need to foster clear understanding of policies and discussions through case presentations or discussions of simulated ethical dilemmas. Finally, swift action must be taken when an ethical violation occurs. Ethical principles, such as fidelity and justice, can be tempered with compassion for the individuals involved in violations, but the organization must demonstrate its commitment by not tolerating unethical actions.

Indeed, for some, these suggestions are more than just possible actions for administrators within an organization, they are moral mandates. Drucker (1992) says that the purpose of an organization is to enable common people to do uncommon things. This is a high ideal that goes beyond the principle of nonmaleficence (doing no harm) and clearly approaches beneficence (doing good).

Evaluators have at least two organizations whose motives and policies affect their activities and that, in turn, they have a responsibility to influence: the organization they represent and the organization they are evaluating. Besides attending to their own individual ethical behavior, if Drucker's mandate is accepted, evaluators must attend to ethical responsibilities of the organizations with which they are involved as employees or as evaluators. This is a heavy responsibility.

METHODOLOGY AND ETHICAL ISSUES

Evaluations Using Qualitative Methods

Vignette 6.3 Guess Who Said That?

John conducts an intensive evaluation of a whole language program in elementary schools in a district. The evaluation involves interviews with teachers and parents. He does a superb job of establishing rapport with the teachers, who discuss with him other concerns about their school. He reports all this directly to the superintendent, including information that makes it readily possible for the superintendent to identify the particular schools involved.

- What do you think about John's report?
- What should John do differently?

The ethical issues and dilemmas discussed thus far apply, for the most part, to evaluations employing either quantitative or qualitative methodologies or both. Because much of the initial heritage of evaluation and the training of many evaluators has resided in quantitative methods, the literature on ethical concerns and related codes (American Educational Research Association, 1992; American Psychological Association, 1992) focuses extensively on ethical concerns that arise in evaluations using traditional (quantitative) methods. Except to look at these concerns from the perspective of Kitchener's (1984) ethical principles and our suggested criteria, we do not feel the need to replicate here a discussion of the typical issues involving quantitative methodology. Other resources are available (e.g., Lobosco & Newman, 1992; Ryan, 1995). However, we do feel the need to ask if there are ethical issues unique to evaluations using qualitative methods as compared to those using quantitative methods. Are there unique ethical issues when an evaluator interviews staff members, observes program participants involved in the program, or becomes a participant observer? There are differing perspectives on whether or not the ethical issues for evaluators using qualitative methods are unique or simply highlighted more (Lincoln, 1991; Soltis, 1990a, 1990b). We believe that at least certain ethical issues are more prominent, if not unique, when using qualitative methods, and these issues merit attention by evaluators using such methods.

What are the ethical issues to which you need to pay particular attention when you use qualitative methods? Few standards or ethical codes address this specific issue. The Guiding Principle for Evaluators encompasses both qualitative and quantitative methodologies in all statements. Association standards do likewise. The Joint Committee Standards (1994) has distinct sections in their Accuracy Standards devoted to the analysis of qualitative information and the analysis of quantitative information. Because analysis procedures for qualitative information cannot always be specified ahead of time and because of the nature of the data, the standards call for a different process of verification. The aim of the analysis standard, however, for both qualitative and quantitative information is to avoid inaccurate conclusions. In essence, the Standards suggest that you pay particular attention to confirmability of your data and conclusions.

Evaluators and researchers who frequently use qualitative methods suggest that there are ethical concerns that should be considered (e.g., Deyhle, Hess, & LeCompte, 1992; Eisner, 1986; Eisner & Peshkin, 1990). These concerns center around the relationship between the evaluator and the informants, deception, reciprocity, obtrusiveness, and reporting.

Relationships With Informants

Many relationship issues are attributable to the qualitative evaluator's attempts to get inside the program for a fuller understanding of the program and, indeed, an attempt to get inside the informants' heads. This is in contrast to the evaluator who uses exclusively quantitative methods and who tries to remain outside the program and the participant in an attempt to maintain objectivity. Trying to get inside the program and inside the informants' heads means establishing closer ties to the program and the individual stakeholders—ties that can result in close friendships between the evaluator and the informants.

You might wonder why anyone would want to be a close friend of an evaluator, but even prisoners develop close relationships with polite guards, and interrogators take advantage of this phenomenon to gain the trust of criminals to help them obtain more information. So perhaps we should not be surprised when friendships form between evaluators and their informants. During interviews when the evaluator appears concerned and interested, informants may become particularly vulnerable and reveal more than they might under different circumstances. When the evaluator assumes a fake persona as a participant observer, friendships can develop without other participants being aware of the evaluator's dual role. As discussed in Chapter 5, these roles may lead to divergent expectations—for example, informants' expectations of the evaluator may not match those of the evaluator.

Deception

Evaluators who serve as participant observers in the guise of fake personae and do not inform other participants of this dual role are in essence living a lie. It is not unusual to read a newspaper account by a journalist who assumed the role of a homeless person, a hospital patient, or a college student in a residence hall so as to write a portrayal of what life is like on the streets, in a hospital, or in a college residence hall. The goal of this data collection strategy besides obtaining "inside" information is to provide the reader with a vicarious experience of what it is like to be a true participant in the program. Using the actual voices of the participants, such as Susko (1992) does in letting the homeless and psychiatric hospital survivors speak for themselves, is powerful, but when participant observers put their own feelings into print, the validity of these perceptions is questionable because the authors are not homeless, or ill, or facing a final exam. How can they truly understand and portray the plight of these individuals?

Other questions arise for evaluators: Is it ethical to assume a participant observer role without informing others? What information about the study should be given to the informants? What information from the study can be passed on to others? In the case of participant observation, informants have not been provided with the informed consent option prior to the study and so might divulge information they would not have if they knew a study was being conducted. What is the implicit social contract between the participant observer and the informants and others being observed? Wouldn't two friends in these situations expect mutual confidentiality? What happens if, in the course of your study, you observe illegal behavior or believe that someone is being harmed?

The opportunities to lie when conducting evaluations are extensive. Bok (1978, 1982) writes eloquently about lying both by professionals and by many of us in everyday life. She stresses the need to be public about what we do and say. For her, an empathic understanding is necessary—to have a sense of what reasonable persons would see as deception and to discern what is and is not intrusive. In much the same vein, Lincoln (1991) argues that deception is basically derived from a positivist perspective; from a constructivist perspective, deception is "inimical to the research effort" (p. 280). In her mind, having a perspective of searching for the one truth is much more likely to lead to support for deception than is a naturalistic, constructivist perspective that is more likely to value relationships.

Reciprocity

In a qualitative study in which you conduct intensive interviews, what does the informant expect from you as an evaluator and what obligations do you have to the informant? It is not easy to study unique populations without the presence of mutual promises and expectations. Will you be expected to become an advocate for the particular informant group? Does this potentially compromise your candidness or honesty in your report? In many interview situations, it is not unusual for evaluators to justify their presence and questions by prefacing their remarks with statements such as "The information I collect will be used to help improve the lives of others in situations like yours." Is this a deceptive ploy designed solely to gain the informant's trust, or is it truly a contract made with the informant that the evaluator intends to follow?

Deyhle et al. (1992) suggest that some investigators see a covenantal ethics as an attractive way to look on their roles (May, 1980). The covenantal ethical role emphasizes the gratitude, fidelity, and care that typifies relationships between intimate friends. This role warrants consideration and is consistent with our discussion of beneficence and social justice throughout this book; however, as Deyhle et al. (1992) note, a researcher or evaluator has potentially multiple covenantal relationships (e.g., with the client, with other stakeholders), and so sorting out these roles is not always straightforward. To whom the evaluator owes justice, fidelity, and beneficence is a difficult question to answer.

Obtrusiveness

Issues related to obtrusiveness are not exclusive to using qualitative methods, but they may be more apparent than when using quantitative methods. Both the outside observer in the back of the classroom and the surveyor passing out a questionnaire in the hallway are obtrusive, but most would agree that the observer from the outside is more obtrusive. We are concerned here with the issue of intrusion having a detrimental effect on the participants rather than methodological questions regarding the validity of the data obtained.

We have all seen televised coverage of news reporters pestering victims of tragedies with inane but intrusive questions such as "How does it feel to have survived this great catastrophe?" or "How does it feel to lose your loved ones?" We doubt that evaluators are customarily this intrusive, but nevertheless, cautions are warranted. Has our presence as evaluators in a hospital setting affected the patients' dignity or the quality of services they receive? Have our interviews with school students prompted them to question the mutual trust they have among themselves? In some contexts, such as prisons, maintaining confidentiality and obtaining accurate information are constantly in a state of tension, if not contradictory to each other (Klein, 1981). These are questions that evaluators must confront when peaking through the keyhole of life trying to record their perception of reality.

Reporting

Two issues warrant attention regarding reporting: confidentiality and who should receive reports. Special efforts must be employed to protect confidentiality and anonymity when reporting qualitative data obtained through interviews and observations. In contrast to quantitative data, which when reported in summation form is difficult or impossible to match with a particular individual, qualitative reports of interviews and observations may inadvertently reveal the identity of the individuals involved. When describing the clothes a person is wearing or the way an office is furnished or when quoting an informant, you may provide clear clues regarding the person's identity. Providing fictitious names is not a sufficient safeguard. In Vignette 6.3, the evaluator paid more attention to gaining interview rapport than to protecting confidentiality.

Serious consideration should be given to sharing quoted information with persons quoted and obtaining their permission to print the specific quote prior to any release of a report. In fact, it is a helpful policy to promise this procedure and protection when collecting information. Anthropologists, ethnographers, and sociologists have in recent years examined the risks associated with quotations and attempts to portray the lives and capture the meaning of other persons (Sankar, 1991; Schepter-Hughes, 1982; Stacey, 1990). Extreme measures need to be taken to mask the identity of individuals and individual evaluation entities (e.g., schools, classrooms, agencies) when making evaluation information public. After reviewing these issues, Colombo and Merithew (1992) decided to give teachers in their evaluation study four choices regarding quotations:

- Refuse to permit the quotation to be used
- Permit the quotation to be used but change the wording
- Offer a substitute
- Permit the quotation to be used as is

Like many ethical concerns, major problems can be averted by discussing these issues ahead of time with clients and significant others. Delineating who the different audiences are for the report may be necessary as some identifiers may be appropriate for certain audiences but not for others. Perhaps the nursing director might be appropriately informed of what is going on in a specific ward of the hospital, but it is not necessary for the hospital administrator to know the specific ward. Perhaps the department chair should know the name of a particular faculty member who has concerns, but the college dean does not need the name. These distinctions would have to be clearly understood by the informants. It is not sufficient to expect individual informants or agencies to look out for their own best interests when revealing information, it is up to the evaluator to see to it that informants are at least aware of the risks they are taking.

Another issue relating to reporting is, How much information should be given back to the informants? Responses to this question range from providing different reports to different audiences to providing one report to all audiences. We discussed some of these issues in Chapter 5. In our view, the best stance to take in most situations is to provide informants full access to the entire report. "Full access" in our usage does not mean providing a naive layperson with a highly technical report. It means providing a report whose potential implications for decisions that could affect an informant's life are clearly understandable to that informant. This is appropriate in all evaluations but is particularly so when the voices of the informants, through quotes, form a major portion of the report. Audiences should be permitted to form their own interpretations from the voices of the participants, but there is always the risk that the evaluator is knowingly or inadvertently expressing a subjective interpretation through selected presentation of the participants' voices.

Not surprising, there is not 100% agreement among those who comment on ethical issues related to qualitative methods in regard to specific issues nor in regard to general principles. Smith (1991) describes six ethical principles for qualitative researchers:

- Professional and personal positions ought to be congruent.
- The principle of informed consent needs to be extended to a principle of "dialogue" so that there is a mutual shaping of the research results.
- The inquiry itself must be worth doing.
- Each decision and act must be considered from an ethical perspective.
- Moral positions should be consistent across public roles (social and political) as well as professional and personal roles.
- Principles may not be absolute, but an individual needs to make a commitment to some principles.

In her discussion of these principles, Lincoln (1991) added two of her own based on Kant's categorical imperatives: "Act in such a way that you would not be distressed to discover that the principle undergirding your own action were now a law that could be enacted by others upon you" (p. 291) and treat all persons as ends in themselves and never solely as means.

Williams (1986) compared the Joint Committee Standards (1981) with a synthesis of standards for naturalistic inquiry. His standards for naturalistic inquiry included making sure results were credible, applicable, and ethical. His standards for ethical results included providing for ethical treatment of participants (e.g., confidentiality respected), being as unintrusive as possible, and making a clear contribution to knowledge and/or to solving problems. When comparing the two sets of standards on 510 possible intersections (30 evaluation standards and 17 naturalistic criteria), he found 43% of the comparisons complementary, 54% neither complementary nor conflictual, and only 3% potentially conflictual. The potential conflicts centered on report dissemination, report timeliness, and practical procedures. Only two standards related to ethics conflicted. The formal obligation propriety standard for evaluations conflicted with the inductive emergent issues criteria for naturalistic inquiry. The evaluator using naturalistic inquiry would have difficulty specifying ahead of time all evaluation activities in a formal contract. The criteria of unintrusiveness and unobtrusiveness for the naturalistic inquirer and the evaluation standard for reliable measurement were seen to conflict, owing to the fact that the naturalistic inquirer prefers to observe phenomena as they occur and so is not able to enter into the evaluation with already devised, highly reliable measures. These conflicts, for the most part, are due to the openness of the naturalistic inquiry method and the difficulty in specifying ahead of time the parameters, instruments, and possible outcomes. Williams (1986) believes, and we agree, that these potential conflicts can be avoided by open discussions and negotiations between the evaluator and the evaluand, or contractor, early in the process.

Despite the similarities between the ethical issues of importance for evaluators conducting quantitative or qualitative studies, it would be an oversimplification to say they are not different. That would be like telling a child who has experienced eating an apple but never a watermelon that both have seeds, so they warrant no different concerns when eating them. What isn't explained are the differing location and quantity of the seeds in the apple and the watermelon. Although the potential ethical issues arising in a quantitative or qualitative evaluation do not differ substantively, they differ sufficiently in their emphasis to warrant special attention.

Institutional Review Boards

Vignette 6.4 Is a Signed Consent Form Enough?

Peter is helping a research hospital evaluate its intake procedures. In the process, he notices that few, if any, patients read the permission forms giving the hospital approval to conduct certain experiments. The patients seem nervous at the time and anxious to move on. Peter believes that all the experiments are for the good of society and so does not raise this as an issue of concern.

- Have you experienced similar feelings when asked to complete consent forms?
- What are the trade-offs of making sure participants fully understand the consent form process?

Institutional/internal review boards (IRBs) or human subjects committees were mandated in 1974 by the National Research Act (Public Law 93-348). Each university or other organization that conducts medical or behavioral research involving human subjects and receives federal funding must have a committee whose role it is to review all proposals for human research before the research is conducted (Sieber, 1992). The major concerns of IRBs are the following:

- Obtaining voluntary informed consent and providing debriefing of research participants
- Protecting the privacy of research participants
- Ensuring confidentiality
- Taking special care when using deception in research
- Assessing the relative risks and benefits derivable from the research

Sieber (1992) provides a detailed discussion of these concerns in her guide for students and IRBs, and Kimmel (1988) also discusses many of the same issues. Rather than reiterate principles and ideas that have been discussed elsewhere in detail, we focus briefly on illustrative issues that pertain particularly to evaluators. Readers are advised to become familiar with works such as those by Kimmel (1988) and Sieber (1992) and the policies and procedures within their own institution or organization.

Two sets of questions must be addressed: Do IRB requirements apply to program evaluators? What provisions need to concern program evaluators the most? Regarding the first question, we have no direct empirical data, but informal observations and anecdotal information paint at least a clouded picture. Most researchers in academic settings are aware that they are required to obtain approval from an IRB before engaging in research using human subjects. Our experience, however, tells us that too many students and faculty members either profess unawareness of this requirement or have no strong interest in complying with the requirement. Often, they do not see their surveys, interviews, or whatever as "that kind of research," which apparently they envision primarily as experimental manipulation or deception with human subjects.

This is particularly true among persons conducting program evaluations. Review boards generally exempt projects that require participants (e.g., students in an educational setting or patients in a hospital setting) to do no more than they would under a normal evaluation process, particularly if these requirements do not call for collection of sensitive information and do not put participants at risk for physical or psychological harm. Say, for example, an educational curriculum is being evaluated. If the students are not required to take different tests nor the staff required to fill out different forms than they would if the curriculum was not being evaluated, the effort is usually considered exempt from the review board's full scrutiny. Supposedly "minor" variations from these expectations for participants and staff, particularly in school settings, are sometimes ignored, so evaluators assume they are exempt in all their activities. This assumption, we believe, is not due to intentional flaunting of rule expectations but, rather, is due to ignorance, poor modeling by other researchers and evaluators, and insensitivity to ethical issues. If our perception of the frequency of this blasé attitude is inaccurate, we stand corrected, but at this point we remain deeply concerned.

Although the Joint Committee on Standards (1994) does not discuss institutional/internal review boards or human subjects committees directly, its Propriety Standard P3 (Rights of Human Subjects) is quite explicit about what is expected. The guidelines within this standard emphasize the need to obtain permission of parents or guardians when testing children, the requirement to obtain permission to access records, guaranteeing confidentiality, if not anonymity, and ensuring that volunteer participants can withdraw at any time without penalty. These concerns are almost identical to the expectations that an IRB would have, although the IRB regulations are clearer in noting that these stipulations must be spelled out before the research begins (the Joint Committee Standards also suggest that the evaluator examine ethical and legal principles prior to initiating the evaluation) and that, of course, an external body (the IRB) must review the study proposal prior to the study's start date. Our interpretation of this Joint Committee standard and the subsequent guidelines is that evaluators are strongly advised to follow the guidelines outlined by the IRBs.

If no IRB exists, we recommend that evaluators clear their proposed studies through any available formal process. If a school, hospital, or other agency does not have a formal review board and review process established, the evaluator should encourage the institution or agency to establish one, and the evaluator's project should be reviewed before the evaluation begins.

What are examples of IRB concerns that might have particular relevance for program evaluators? In our view, IRB concerns that apply to program evaluations are not necessarily different in substance from those that apply to research, but a few examples illustrate how they differ at least in emphasis. One major IRB guideline is obtaining voluntary consent of the participants, which also includes the understanding that participants can withdraw at any time without prejudice. The spirit of this guideline may be difficult to fulfill in some program evaluations, particularly for program staff members. Evaluations may be mandated from above; thus everyone is expected to "cooperate" with the evaluators by answering questions, filling out surveys, or being available for observation. A roll call might not be taken, but participation may be subtly forced on staff members. Not "cooperating" by refusing to answer some questions, for example, could be viewed negatively by program administrators. Extra steps may have to be taken by program administrators and the evaluators to ensure that participation is truly voluntary and there are no repercussions for not participating or withdrawing.

Privacy and confidentiality concerns can be particularly troublesome for evaluators who have informed staff they are "evaluating the program and not the personnel" and discover several staff to be incompetent or not fulfilling their job responsibilities. This was the illustration we discussed in Chapter 4. In this instance, the evaluator has made a promise to the staff member and owes fidelity to the staff member to keep that promise. At the same time, from a duty perspective, the evaluator also has loyalty to the client whose program's success may be jeopardized by the staff member's poor performance. Situations like this can never be completely avoided, but many problems can be avoided if expectations are clearly spelled out ahead of time. Staff members or program participants should not be told **carte blanche** that nothing they personally say or do in the presence of the evaluator will ever be made public unless that is absolutely true. If there are provisos related to illegal behavior, negligence, or incompetence, then these should be made known to the staff members or participants when their consent for participation is being obtained.

In research protocols that outline the potential risks and benefits of the proposed research, the focus is primarily on the potential direct impact on the research participants. IRB members must consider questions such as these: What is the potential harm to a participant who was deceived in a research project or who was placed in a placebo group rather than the treatment group through random assignment? What are the potential negative side effects of a particular treatment? These risks are weighed against the potential benefits to both individual participants and society. Sieber (1992) notes that this is a difficult task: It is not easy to assess all the potential risks, some of which may be completely unanticipated. Perhaps this is why the focus is more on the known risks to known individuals—the research participants.

Research results, even those conducted in laboratory situations, can have policy implications that affect many lives. This is particularly true for evaluation efforts conducted within the public domain for highly visible programs. The evaluator needs to be sensitive to possible misinterpretations and overgeneralizations that policymakers and the public are prone to make. Data obtained for one purpose can be misused to characterize an institution, a community, or a subpopulation within the community. Negative stereotypes can be strengthened through oversimplification of interpretations. Data related to substance abuse (Piazza & Yeager, 1990) or child abuse or sexually transmitted disease may be subject to subpoena (Harding, Gray, & Neal, 1993; Melton & Gray, 1988), and evaluators must be attentive to these possibilities when collecting data or guaranteeing confidentiality. Researchers who are engaged in laboratory work and communicate with each other primarily in jargon-filled research journals may be excused for their naiveté or forgiven if they believe they are in pursuit of truth without accompanying political implications. Evaluators, however, cannot afford to be that naive and therefore must be alert and sensitive to how their findings and conclusions will be used.

Much of the discussion in the psychological research literature on issues related to voluntary consent, deception, and confidentiality focus on the tension between the validity of scientific research and the rights of the participants (Blanck, Bellack, Rosnow, Rotheram-Borus, & Schooler, 1992; Grisso et al., 1991; Pope & Vetter, 1992; Sieber & Sorenson, 1992). We fear that the collective impact of these articles and others could leave the reader with the perception that IRB rules are perhaps a necessary nuisance, standing in the way of progress (see Peter in Vignette 6.4). This conclusion would not be surprising to us, but it would be unfortunate. At a minimum, it runs the risk of placing the value of scientific progress on an equal plane with individual rights. At its worst, it runs the risk of putting researcher/evaluators on a pedestal—above everyone else as they seek the truth—and perhaps less than subtly gives the impression that science and truth are above individual rights. These choices must be examined carefully using the ethical principles and criteria suggested in Chapters 2 and 4.

CONCLUSION

It is clear to us that if an evaluator is to be ethical in practice, simply having an awareness of ethical rules, codes, principles, and theory is insufficient. An ethical evaluator must constantly be alert to how the evaluation context affects the perceptions and behaviors of participants and other stakeholders in the evaluation. Does their culture affect their expectations and behaviors? How will they perceive the program and the evaluation differently from the evaluator? An ethical evaluator must also be conversant with how the methodology used affects relationships between the evaluator and the participants being interviewed, surveyed, or observed and, in turn, their expectations. Different methodologies warrant a double check regarding what is ethically appropriate behavior for the evaluator. The ethical principles and criteria presented in Chapters 2 and 4 can help the evaluator sort out what is appropriate and make decisions regarding what action to take.

7

Improving the Ethical Practice of Evaluation

A WORKING AGENDA FOR THE PROFESSION

A Reader's Guide to Chapter 7

To encourage a continuing dialogue, which is one of the primary purposes of this book, we suggest an agenda of action items appropriate for the following:

- Professional associations
- Graduate programs and instructors of evaluation courses
- Directors of evaluation agencies and evaluation units within organizational settings
- Researchers on ethical practice
- Evaluation clients and stakeholders

We also include a section on myths about ethics and evaluation that we believe are prevalent in practice. We propose these items as a working agenda and, in placing the agenda before you, we ask:

- What would you like to add to the agenda?
- How might agenda items that interrelate be clustered together for efficient discussion and action?
- How would you prioritize the items on the agenda?

Implicit, if not explicit, in the agenda items are our biases and perspectives that come from our own training, experience, readings, and values. Occasionally, we may appear prescriptive. We take that risk because we believe deeply that evaluators hold the potential to have an impact on many lives, so it is incumbent on them to ensure that many voices are heard and consensus reached. Also, someone must start the process by stepping forward and saying "This is what I think." The following chapter presents our current thinking.

Improving the ethical practice of evaluation is a major challenge facing those involved in the next stage of evaluation's evolution as a profession. Efforts focused on improvement of ethical practice need to receive equal prominence with those concerned with role definitions and technical advances in measurement. Considerable discussion in the past quarter-century has centered on what role evaluators can and should serve and what assessment criteria and tools are appropriate (McLaughlin & Phillips, 1991). Development of evaluation standards (Rossi, 1982; Stufflebeam, 1991) and the tentative establishment of evaluation principles represent a significant step forward in providing evaluators with guidelines for being ethical in their practice. For further progress to occur, concerted efforts need to be taken by all the significant stakeholders who have an investment in evaluation as an ethical endeavor. Some stakeholders have more responsibility and power than others, but all must be involved.

PROFESSIONAL ASSOCIATIONS

The field of evaluation has shown clear signs of reaching adulthood and the maturity and stability associated with this stage of professional development. The American Evaluation Association (AEA) has existed for more than 10 years, the result of the merger of the Evaluation Research Society and the Evaluation Network. Publications devoted to evaluation issues (e.g., the journals *Evaluation Research, Educational Evaluation and Policy Analysis, Evaluation and Program Planning, Evaluation Practice,* and *Evaluation Review*) are recognized outlets for discussion of evaluation issues. Retrospectives are in vogue (McLaughlin & Phillips, 1991), and anthologies of evaluation literature are available. The topic of professional ethics is becoming a common theme addressed throughout all these developments. The question that now should be addressed is, Where does the profession need to go now?

The AEA has recently adopted a broad set of ethical principles that can serve as general guidelines for determining ethical practice, and the Joint Committee Standards provide excellent guidelines for evaluators in education. As these documents are disseminated more widely and employed, the field of evaluation will reach new levels of maturity. However, we believe that special attention needs to be given to standards and ethical issues by professional associations, particularly the AEA. The principles discussed in this book represent one formulation that may be helpful; other formulations might also be appropriate.

A profession and an association involved actively in the making of value judgments needs to be straightforward about reaching a consensus and stating its own values. An entire conference devoted to ethical issues is an appropriate step. It is also worthwhile to have a theme track at each annual meeting that focuses on one or more ethical issues, ranging from conflict of interest to reporting.

Journals should consider periodically devoting special issues to ethics, such as the special issue of *Evaluation and Program Planning,* edited by Nick Smith (1985) and containing thought-provoking articles by Adams (1985), Bank (1985), Bunda (1985), Hendricks (1985), and Kirkhart

(1985). *Evaluation Practice* could have a special section, perhaps using a "Dear Abby" format, in each issue devoted to ethical questions and issues. Instructional units, similar to those appearing in *Educational Measurement: Issues and Practice,* could be developed concerning ethics and standards and published in *Evaluation Practice.*

We believe that the AEA needs to begin work on adopting its own ethical code or set of ethical standards based on its guiding principles. This code in essence might be a full embracement of the Joint Committee Standards, extension of the Standards to all disciplines, or development of a separate set. Examples need to represent settings broader than educational ones and encompass all aspects of evaluation, not just program evaluation. Currently, the dichotomy between the two Joint Committee Standards (Program Evaluation and Personnel Evaluation) gives many practitioners a false impression of separateness even as the profession is beginning to recognize similarities (Stufflebeam, 1991). Most professional associations of which we are aware have their own ethical code. The American Nurses Association has its own code of ethics; it does not say that because nurses are in the health profession they should simply use the broader code of the American Medical Association. There is value in going through the process of establishing codes, even though at times it may appear we are reinventing the wheel. However, wheels come in different sizes and weights. Professional codes are one of the primary sources of information that professionals have regarding professional ethics (Gibson & Pope, 1993).

The existence of principles and codes is a starting place, but, we believe, eventually certification and an enforcement process are necessary. These are difficult issues, but they can be approached in stages. The first stage would ensure that every AEA member has a copy of the principles and code. The next stage might have members sign a statement saying that they have read the code and plan to abide by it. A detailed casebook might be published by the association. If a certification or licensing process ever becomes a reality, certification of knowledge regarding ethical issues should be a part of the process. Ultimately, an enforcement process is needed, which would necessitate the existence of an active ethics committee. Independent of serving a watchdog function, this committee could prove useful by providing an avenue for dialogue, developing educational programs, and providing counsel to individual members. The American Psychological Association annually prints the names of expelled or suspended members. Although it will be some time before the profession of evaluation reaches this level of ethical development, the AEA must continue its discussion on ethical practice. However, it will have to find its own process.

We do not pretend that these steps will ensure universal ethical behavior in evaluation any more than they do in medicine or psychotherapy, but the process would help sensitize evaluators and perhaps our clientele to these issues. Continuing the dialogue will provide a powerful message to those within and outside the profession.

GRADUATE PROGRAMS AND TEACHING ETHICAL PRACTICE

Despite the proliferation of new ethics courses in professional training programs for students preparing for careers in law, medicine, business, psychology, and other fields, an underlying cynicism remains as to whether or not it is possible to teach ethics. A historical perspective on the relative effectiveness or ineffectiveness of the family, the church, and the school in fostering moral behavior makes pessimism understandable. These institutions might have been influential in the past, but their influence in today's society is debatable. Higher education in this century has avoided ethical issues, for the most part, leaving them to the philosophers. Many philosophers, in turn, have said there is no such thing as "applied ethics"; only theoretical discussions are appropriate. Finally, skeptics question how a democratic, multiethnic, and pluralistic society can ever hope to arrive at a consensus about what behavior is ethical. Because course offerings in ethics for professionals in many fields have increased in the past decade, it is time for evaluation training programs to expand their offerings.

Training programs for evaluators need to supplement their focus on evaluation technology and the politics of being an evaluation consultant with equally lively discussions of what the role of the evaluator is in helping society define and pursue the common good (e.g., What is the role of the evaluator in actively promoting social justice?). Discussions in publications by Schwandt (1992), Sirotnik (1990), and House (1993), among others, on social justice issues and evaluation should have a significant place in courses and seminars. House (1993) believes that trying to balance all stakeholder interests and criteria in an evaluation and determining how far to carry the efficiency criterion remain two of the most difficult tasks confronting evaluators. Evaluators must be full participants in this dialogue and not passive observers. What better place to start the dialogue than in training programs?

If instructors are to be successful in fostering ethical development in training programs, they must have a minimal understanding of developmental levels and how developmental change can be fostered. Brown (1985b) proposed a developmental model for supervising evaluation practicum students derived from the work by Loganbill, Hardy, and Delworth (1982), and Brown and Dinnel (1992) explored further the applicability of this model for supervising evaluation practicum students.

The model comprises three developmental levels: naiveté and rigidity, disequilibrium, and assimilation and integration. One of its eight developmental tasks is development of ethical competence. In the initial stage (naiveté and rigidity), the student is aware of ethical guidelines and standards but tries to apply them rigidly to all situations. In Stage 2 (disequilibrium), the student is confronted with an ethical dilemma not easily resolved through direct application of an ethical rule and so becomes confused and perhaps disheartened. Finally, in Stage 3 (assimilation and integration), the student recognizes that flexibility is necessary in the application of rules and so begins to search for broader ethical principles. This model is comparable to those proposed specifically for looking at moral and ethical development within developmental psychology that also provide helpful concepts regarding student development and instructional strategies applicable to instructors of evaluation seminars and supervisors of field experiences who wish to increase their students' level of ethical awareness and sensitivity.

The implications of a developmental perspective for teaching ethics in evaluation focus on the process of how a person moves through these levels. Three characteristics of this process are particularly relevant for teaching ethics:

- The levels or positions can be viewed as stages of development through which a person moves sequentially without skipping any stage.
- Change occurs through the appropriate balance between being challenged and being supported.
- The challenge must be one stage or step beyond the person's current position.

The sequential stage concept has implications for curriculum development. Undergraduate and beginning graduate students looking at ethical issues in evaluation would likely make judgments reflective of the naive and rigid stage. At this level, right behavior is viewed as that which shows deference to authority, rules, or tradition and emphasizes not "doing wrong." When an evaluator decides not to fudge data because "evaluators are always objective" or insists on a written summary when interim verbal reports would better serve the client's needs, the evaluator is at the naive and rigid stage. For these practitioners, there is a right and a wrong way to do evaluation, and they must meet those requirements. Advanced graduate students would more likely be at the postconventional and principled levels. At these levels, the student or practitioner is confronted with ethical dilemmas and realizes that there is no easy solution to the conflict. Evaluators at Stage 2 (disequilibrium) may become confused and disheartened and will need the assistance of instructors or peers in discussing and working through the issues. The flowchart in Chapter 4 might prove very helpful in this setting. With the assistance of others, the student can work through the confusion and conflict and see possible solutions. In Stage 3 (assimilation and integration), the student or practitioner will have a more developed set of experiences and a broader set of ethical practice to use in resolving ethical conflicts. The difficulties will still be there, but the evaluator will have integrated a pattern of ethical thinking into his or her decision making and use it to determine a course of action.

Students progress through these stages as they confront challenges in their courses and practicum experiences, are encouraged to reflect, and receive supportive mentoring. The challenges to students' thinking must be at the appropriate developmental level. If the challenge is more than one stage higher, the person might be challenged too much and so will make little or no progress and might even regress. If the challenge is at the appropriate level but there is no support, the same outcome may occur. A physical analogy makes this process concrete. A person who wishes to gain strength through weight training must practice lifting weights that present a challenge. Too light a weight (low or no challenge) will not result in gains; too heavy a weight (too high a challenge) will result in failure and perhaps sore or injured muscles (regression). The optimum weight, usually slightly heavier than comfortable, presents a reasonable challenge and leads to the most growth.

The research literature on teaching ethics in different professional fields is still emerging. Instructors of evaluation courses who examine this literature within the developmental framework described earlier here should be able to integrate discussions about ethical issues in evaluation into their curricula and courses in a way that facilitates ethical development.

DIRECTORS OF AGENCIES AND EVALUATION UNITS

In Chapters 4 and 5, we noted that evaluation takes place within a system that is often a highly organized agency or unit. The evaluator may be a part of the organization being evaluated or an agent of another organization involved in conducting the evaluation. Much of the ethical climate is established by the actions of the organization's leadership. This leadership can take several forms. For one, each organization, no matter its size, should adopt and establish its own set of ethical principles and its own code. This applies to the evaluator's own institution or organizational unit and the institution or unit being evaluated.

The starting place for the evaluator's own agency or organization would be to read existing codes, such as the AEA's *Guiding Principles for Evaluators,* the Joint Committee Standards, the American Educational Research Association statement, those of the American Psychological Association, and others. Evaluators should ask their organization if it endorses and/or adopts one or more of these codes as its guidelines for practice. This should be an educational process, involving discussion groups, focus groups, panels, and case illustrations. Even if the organization adopts in full an already-published set of guidelines or a professional code, this process provides the vehicle for provocative questions and permits determination of what additions or exceptions must be made to fit the uniqueness of the organization. By devoting time to these efforts, the organization is providing behavioral testimony to the importance it places on ethical practice.

It may seem presumptuous of the evaluator to require that each organization being evaluated have its own ethical standards, and we would not make it an absolute prerequisite to conducting an evaluation. Nevertheless, it is quite appropriate for the evaluator to inquire if a set of standards exists for purposes of ensuring that the evaluator does not violate organizational policies because it provides a fuller understanding of the organization being evaluated. If no guidelines are available, the evaluator might look to the discipline in which the organization is established. Is it health related? Are there guidelines from another professional organization that might have guided the training and thinking of the client?

An ongoing program of ethical education also needs to be an integral part of staff development programs. As Honea (1991) noted, very little discussion about ethical concerns seems to take place among evaluators. Providing a formal but relaxed forum, including discussions of real or simulated case studies, gives staff members permission to seek confirmation of their own thinking or be challenged in a safe environment.

RESEARCHERS OF ETHICAL PRACTICE

Three topics warrant attention for researchers concerned about ethical practice:

- Descriptive studies of current viewpoints on ethical issues in practice and what occurs in practice
- Studies of how practitioners go about making ethical decisions—what are their thinking processes?
- Assessment of the worth and effectiveness of different strategies for training evaluators about ethical practice

Most of the literature on ethical practice in all professions consists of thought pieces and anecdotal portrayals. These pieces are needed to stimulate our thinking about the issues. Some research studies that examine current practice and thinking about ethical issues by practitioners are listed in the "For Further Reading" section of the references provided near the end of the book. We are not strong believers in having researchers conduct massive surveys regarding ethical practice, but our current knowledge base is some distance from that threshold. The work of Newman and Brown (1992) and Morris and Cohn (1993) represents a beginning. Examples from other professions are studies by psychologists (Pope, Tabachnick, & Keith-Spiegel, 1987; Pope & Vetter, 1992) and counselors (Gibson & Pope, 1993). Until we reach that threshold, it is important that researchers continue to get a sense of what is happening among evaluation practitioners. What are the major ethical dilemmas? Do the dilemmas differ dramatically from content area to content area? What are the differences between novice and experienced evaluators? How do the issues differ for those in public or private employment? Descriptive information can be used as baseline data and provide helpful cues about needed future directions.

Researchers need not wait until more descriptive data are available, however, to begin studying the thinking processes involved when evaluators make ethical decisions. Tentative exploratory studies can be conducted. Can one of the moral development theories provide a useful framework for examining how evaluators go about making ethical decisions? At what stage of moral development are different types of evaluators? Is their level of thinking about their evaluation practice different from their developmental level in making other ethical judgments? What are significant correlates of their developmental level? Are educational background, field setting, and evaluation philosophy related to their moral development level and other facets of their ethical reasoning?

Research is also needed on the ethical principles and criteria described in Chapter 2 and the decision-making process described in Chapter 4. Descriptive research could examine what principles evaluators use to make their decisions and also could examine the interaction between developmental levels of the decision maker and the relative importance of different principles and criteria. How frequently do ethical issues related to autonomy and beneficence occur in practice? How much weight do evaluators give to different principles when the principles conflict? What consequences weigh most heavily in their thinking: those to the client or those to program participants? What do they see as the duties and obligations of the evaluator? What rights do they see clients and stakeholders having?

Finally, we need research on numerous questions regarding educational and intervention programs for evaluators and for clients and stakeholders. How can we best sensitize evaluators to ethical issues? How can we heighten their awareness of what constitutes ethical issues? How can we help them understand that many rather than few of the professional decisions they make have potential ethical implications? In turn, how can we help clients and stakeholders to become aware of their ethical rights? These questions are not unique to the evaluation profession. Doctors, psychotherapists, and other professionals have asked similar questions for decades, some with limited success but also perhaps until recently a limited commitment. The focus of these studies should be on protecting the public and on providing the best evaluation service to the public for their benefit.

Whether the educational strategy is used in undergraduate or graduate classes in evaluation or for potential evaluation consumers or professionals, or whether it takes place in staff development workshops for current professionals in a variety of fields, we need more information about what ethical training practices work, when, by whom, and for whom? How can we best assess developmental levels? What represents appropriate challenges to help move people to higher developmental levels? How effective are case studies?

This research agenda is only illustrative, yet it is a massive undertaking. It is enough to keep many researchers busy for some time.

CLIENTS AND STAKEHOLDERS

What can clients and other stakeholders do to improve the ethical practice of program evaluation? In many ways, clients and stakeholders are potentially all-powerful, but in some ways, they border on being powerless. Not many are likely to read this book, they are probably unfamiliar with published standards or ethical codes, and they have little recourse or few outlets for complaints about ethical behavior unless they perceive the evaluator's behavior as illegal, in violation of an ethical code related to the evaluator's professional identity in another field, or in violation of a contractual agreement. Yet clients have control of the purse strings, and it is interesting to note that when evaluators are asked to describe ethical dilemmas they confront (e.g., Brown & Newman, 1986a, 1986b; Morris & Cohn, 1993), they are likely to describe the behavior or perceived unethical behavior of clients rather than the behavior of fellow evaluators.

Asking clients and stakeholders to educate themselves about ethics and standards in evaluation may be like asking heart patients to know the ethical code and behavioral expectations for heart surgeons or for bank depositors to know the code of ethics for bankers and accountants. It is possible that having this knowledge will enable them to ask appropriate questions and might help, in turn, to monitor and improve ethical medical and financial practices, but it is a lot to expect, and it cannot be placed cavalierly on the shoulders of clients. Doing so provides too much autonomy without ensuring appropriate competency.

Clients who are patients in a medical setting or who are participants in a program evaluation, however, are not completely at the mercy of the physician or the evaluator. This is especially true if something goes wrong. Liability insurance rates for medical malpractice are testimony to this source of power that the medical patient has, but no one-to-one counterpart exists in the evaluation field. Evaluation clients and stakeholders probably have less experience working with an evaluator than they do with a physician, and although they control the fee structure and the power of rehiring the evaluator for future contracts, they still can be highly dependent on the expertise of the evaluator and hence vulnerable.

We believe that the initiative and a major share of the responsibility for increasing clients' and stakeholders' knowledge and awareness of, and sensitivity to, ethical issues in evaluation rests with the evaluator. Responsive approaches to evaluation (Worthen & Sanders, 1987) and other approaches that propose considerable involvement of clients and stakeholders in designing and conducting evaluations (e.g., *Fourth Generation Evaluation* by Guba & Lincoln, 1989) provide opportunities for evaluators to engage in activities designed to educate stakeholders regarding their rights and expectations during an evaluation. Indeed, one of the purposes of the *Fourth Generation* approach is to empower the clients and stakeholders through increasing their understanding of the evaluation process and sorting through the issues involved within the specific context of their program and their evaluation.

Schapiro and Blackwell (1987) describe a partnership approach to evaluation that involves clients playing an active role in almost every evaluation activity but data analysis. Through several experiences, Schapiro and Blackwell note that the power relationships change dramatically. Clients assumed more responsibility for matters ranging from research design to choice of statistical procedures. The evaluator had to learn to accept criticisms of instruments and procedures and had to assume an educator or mentor role more deliberately and intently.

As undergraduate and graduate textbooks and courses in management and administration expand their discussions of program evaluation issues and approaches, we should expect more informed evaluation clients and stakeholders. Textbook learning is insufficient, however, unless it is matched with changes in practice. Therefore, evaluation practitioners must forsake the mantle of all-knowing expert and put on the cloak of the educator, clarifier, and facilitator.

MYTHS ABOUT ETHICS AND EVALUATION PRACTITIONERS

House (1993) proposed a set of ethical fallacies that represented frequent ethical mistakes in evaluation. These included *clientism* (doing whatever the client wants), *managerialism* (seeing program managers as the sole beneficiary), *methodologism* (believing that adherence to good methods is synonymous with being ethical), *relativism* (accepting everyone's opinion equally), and *pluralism/elitism* (giving a priority voice to the more powerful). These fall short of exhausting the list of significant mistaken notions about ethics. In this final section, we present 10 myths about ethics that we believe have relevance for program evaluators and must be kept in mind as each of us struggles to be ethical practitioners. These myths were originally developed by Harry Canon (Canon & Brown, 1985) and are applicable to all professionals. We have taken those most pertinent to evaluators, added a few, and provided examples of how they apply to evaluators.

1. **Personal ethical perfection (or near perfection) is prerequisite to any serious ethical inquiry.** Everyone falls short of being the ethical ideal. Among the ethicists we have cited, it is difficult to identify ethical truths that are considered absolute and universal. This is particularly true for a professional activity like evaluation in which value judgments are an inherent part of the professional activity. Fallibility is more the norm than perfection—at least in our own practices—and trying to do the least harm we can is a sufficient motivator for our inquiries, and in the process, we are challenged to do good as well as avoid harm.

2. **Ethics are just value judgments, and one person's values are as good as another's.** This can be a persuasive myth, especially in an era when we are trying to be attentive to so many voices in our pluralistic society. It is a statement typical of Perry's (1970) multiplistic developmental position. We suspect that no reasonable person among us would place the

value judgments of Adolf Hitler on a par with those of Martin Luther King. We are comfortable asserting that some values are better than others and that we must continue to seek for the consensus that recognizes those values. Taylor (1992) suggests that an authentic ethical belief system is not one in which each of us believes whatever we *feel* like without a rational process involved. An authentic ethical belief system is one that we have carefully thought about and one about which we are genuinely persuaded. It is a belief system that may have originated from intuitive feelings but has gone through a cognitive process, through examination of principles, and through dialogue. Even though this belief system is not absolute, it is the highest level of ethical development to which we can aspire.

3. **The answers to ethical dilemmas lie in our professional ethical codes.** Throughout this book, we have indicated that codes and standards are helpful but will not answer every dilemma we face. Looking at broader ethical principles and theories can help us work through these dilemmas.

4. **Dealing with ethical violations is the job of ethics committees.** Earlier, we proposed that the American Evaluation Association needs an ethics committee to help evaluators with ethical dilemmas and to consider sanctions as a means of enforcement, but we do not believe that a committee can or should deal with every ethical violation. Each evaluation practitioner has to be involved, and this means being willing to contact the violators or bringing questionable behavior to the attention of the potential offender. Canon (Canon & Brown, 1985) suggests that we ask ourselves which we would rather have happen to us: Have a colleague confront us about our questionable behavior, or have the first contact being a call or letter from our professional ethics committee? The personal contact provides us the opportunity to offer an explanation, gives us a chance to change our behavior, and prevents the situation from escalating.

5. **People are either ethical, or they are not. It is as simple as that.** This myth fails to recognize that even the best among us can be blind at times and make decisions that are self-serving. Being empathic and being a

logical thinker are important attributes of an ethical person. These are skills that can be developed and refined.

6. **Ethical discussions are necessary only to deal with major scandals.** Professional evaluators make ethical choices in almost every professional action they take. Deciding which evaluation project to take on, what instruments to use, and what kind of reports to write all have potential ethical implications. Ethics is not something for a special occasion; it is a part of daily practice (Wilensky, 1964).

7. **Evaluation practice affects programs, not people.** We have to admit that for a long time we told evaluation clients "We are here to evaluate your program, not you." As we matured professionally, we realized that separation of program from personnel evaluation is extremely difficult, if not impossible, in the eyes of those whose program is being evaluated. Our example in Chapter 4 dealt with a dilemma resulting from this perspective, and in that discussion we examined several of the ethical implications and principles involved. It is interesting to note that the separate standards for evaluating personnel use the same organizational format as those for program evaluation, although in a different order (Joint Committee on Standards, 1988, 1994). As we noted earlier in this chapter, the profession of evaluation would benefit from a discussion of whether or not these two sets of standards should be merged.

8. **I just don't have time to be reflective about ethical matters.** It is true that it is difficult to ask ourselves basic ethical questions each time we conduct an evaluation. We adopt shortcuts based on experience or expediency. These shortcuts can take any number of forms. One shortcut may be looking out for the best interest of the client, who is usually the program funder or program manager. Another shortcut may mean placing emphasis on outcomes or products using standardized indicators (e.g., in an educational setting, emphasizing results of standardized tests; in the health area, using length of stay as the primary indicator of success). In other contexts, a shortcut may involve calculating dollar costs and dollar benefits as the basis for a decision. One frequent shortcut is to respond to the squeaky wheel: If a stakeholder complains, then we respond; otherwise, we ignore that stakeholder group.

Shortcuts like these and others are not necessarily inappropriate; they can be efficient ways to save time and energy. They become integrated with our style or approach to evaluation; they become second nature. They do not remove us, however, from being responsible for our actions. We cannot be reflective about every moment of every evaluation, but we have a professional obligation to pause periodically and examine the shortcuts, to question the assumptions we make, and to think about the consequences of our actions. Are the interests of certain stakeholders continually ignored, or do our shortcuts fail to consider the broader range of possible good that could result? Periodic self-examination through case conferences and discussions with colleagues may in the long run save us time and avoid future complex and controversial dilemmas.

9. Being ethical is all very fine, but one also has to be practical. Numerous philosophers have examined this same question, and many state their answers in a form suggesting hedonism or egoism as the ultimate root motivational source, regardless of protestations of altruism to the contrary. According to these thinkers, ultimately our rationale for being ethical has our self-interest as its base, even if this self-interest is no more than that we feel good about ourselves. A few authors suggest that being ethical pays off in power and monetary rewards. Kenneth Blanchard (1982), author of *The One Minute Manager,* teamed with Norman Vincent Peale (1952), author of *The Power of Positive Thinking,* to write *The Power of Ethical Management* (Blanchard & Peale, 1988). In a book filled with aphorisms such as "Nice guys may appear to finish last but usually they're running in a different race" and "Managing only for profit is like playing tennis with your eye on the scoreboard and not on the ball," they point out that poor ethical practices lead to an unhappy staff, which in turn leads to disgruntled customers and thus eventually to reduced production, sales, and profits. Though seemingly oversimplified, the book makes useful points about the need to take a long view and the need to take time to be reflective.

We agree that having integrity through being ethical can have professional and even material benefits in the long run for evaluators. Integrity is a prime attribute for successful evaluators; it is an important dimension of credibility, and it in turn relates to the acceptance and usefulness of the evaluator's efforts. So a good case can be made that being ethical is good for business. But we would be remiss if we did not acknowledge that this may not always be the case, especially in the short run, which may be the only run we have. Self-esteem, or self-respect, comes closer to being the ultimate reason for being ethical. As Drane (1982) noted, the ultimate reason for ethical practice is what we value and who we want to be, which are determined by our philosophical and religious values.

10. If people would just follow the ethical codes of their professions, life would be a lot less complicated. We are not so sure. We have repeatedly stated our belief that ethical codes are insufficient to answer all of our ethical dilemmas. In fact, the more immediate and specific the dilemma becomes to us, the more difficult applying a code becomes. Emotions and stress enter in. No one likes to be thought of as being unethical, and so defensiveness becomes a part of our response pattern. In many instances, adhering to the codes alone represents a minimal effort to be ethical.

Being ethical is not simple, and it doesn't make life easier—it makes it complicated. Being ethical is not a state or condition that someone is in; rather, it is a process or a journey. It requires constant effort, continuing exploration and questioning, and ongoing self-confrontation—all with little or no hope of ever arriving at our destination: a completely ethical person.

CONCLUSION

In this chapter, and throughout the book, we have suggested an agenda for everyone who has anything to do with evaluation—whether as a practitioner, an instructor, a consumer, a student, a leader in professional associations, or some combination of these. We have no doubt left out some possible agenda items, and undoubtedly, as practice and needs change, new items must be added or others given higher priority. For now, we hope that all persons involved in evaluations will make their own list and do what they can to keep the dialogue moving.

Epilogue

As we noted in the preface, the intent of this book was threefold: to sensitize evaluators and, we hope, potential clients and stakeholders to ethical issues in program evaluation; to provide a set of principles that can serve as foundational guidelines for making ethical decisions; and to suggest a process that can be used to think about ethics and make ethical decisions about evaluation practice. In the process, we have taken five important stances.

First, we assert that ethical choices are part of the everyday world of the program evaluator; they are not isolated events occurring only during troubled confrontations with a client or stakeholder. From the moment the evaluator begins the consultation process to the time when the evaluator is responding to the last reaction to the evaluation report, ethical choices are being made every day in matters small and large.

Second, we believe that standards and ethical codes are useful but will always be insufficient guidelines in themselves for ethical practice. Evaluators need to make decisions based on principles and using criteria that clearly describe their value positions regarding their professional relationships and obligations. These principles are broader than specific rules, and they provide helpful, although not absolute, guidance when rules conflict and when specific contextual situations demand unique responses.

Third, we believe that making ethical choices is a cognitive process—even as it involves our personal values—that can be enhanced through thinking, reading, discussion, and practice.

Fourth, we believe that being ethical demands more than being like a goaltender in hockey or soccer who fends off attacks when threatened. It is insufficient to work solely to avoid ethical dilemmas; the principle of beneficence, the philosophy of social justice, and the ethics of care perspective suggest the need to step forward and actively promote effective evaluations and, indeed, effective programs aided by good evaluations.

Fifth, we must strive to reduce our collective phobia to confront value issues and to do so in a way that does not substitute an ethical prescription or imperialism but rather evolves into what Gilligan (1982) and Noddings (1984) call the ethics of care.

In summary, we believe that being ethical is more than making good ethical choices regarding isolated incidents or situations. Being an ethical evaluator is a professional way of life and, ultimately, a personal way of life. Like any way of life, it does not remove conflict and stress, and it does not provide a rule book answer to all dilemmas. Rather, being ethical represents the perspective we take on the tasks we face, the process we use to confront issues, and the guides we use to make decisions. Being ethical also takes something we probably have not addressed enough in this book, and that is courage. That courage, on occasion, demands resistance; on other occasions it demands persistence; and on other occasions it may even demand assertiveness. While fostering courage, however, we have to avoid being self-righteous. Courage must be coupled with the humble acceptance that we will not always make the best decision or the best choice, but we will keep trying, and we trust our colleagues and clients will help us by providing constructive criticisms.

Finally, we have a request to make of the readers and users of this work. It is our hope that the book will serve as a stimulus to ethical thinking in practice and to additional research on ethics in program evaluation. As we indicated in Chapter 1, the model we have presented is under development. We would appreciate receiving examples of your use of the model when working through ethical dilemmas along with feedback on the utility of the principles and the model in practice. We also encourage other researchers on evaluation ethics to use the principles and model as part of your own research agenda and request that you let us know how you find the model to function. As the field of evaluation grows, so too does the need for ethical practice and the determination of what constitutes ethical practice. We must all join in this endeavor.

APPENDIX A

Joint Committee on Standards
Program Evaluation Standards

Utility

The utility standards are intended to ensure that an evaluation will serve the information needs of intended users.

U1 **Stakeholder Identification** Persons involved in or affected by the evaluation should be identified so that their needs can be addressed.

U2 **Evaluator Credibility** The persons conducting the evaluation should be both trustworthy and competent to perform the evaluation so that the evaluation findings achieve maximum credibility and acceptance.

U3 **Information Scope and Selection** Information collected should be broadly selected to address pertinent questions about the program and be responsive to the needs and interests of clients and other specified stakeholders.

U4 **Values Identification** The perspectives, procedures, and rationale used to interpret the findings should be carefully described so that the bases for value judgments are clear.

U5 **Report Clarity** Evaluation reports should clearly describe the program being evaluated, including its context, and the purposes, procedures, and findings of the evaluation so that essential information is provided and easily understood.

U6 **Report Timeliness and Dissemination** Significant interim findings and evaluation reports should be disseminated to intended users so that they can be used in a timely fashion.

U7 **Evaluation Impact** Evaluations should be planned, conducted, and reported in ways that encourage follow-through by stakeholders so that the likelihood that the evaluation will be used is increased.

Feasibility

The feasibility standards are intended to ensure that an evaluation will be realistic, prudent, diplomatic, and frugal.

F1 **Practical Procedures** The evaluation procedures should be practical to keep disruption to a minimum while needed information is obtained.

F2 **Political Viability** The evaluation should be planned and conducted with anticipation of the different positions of various interest groups so that their cooperation may be obtained and so that possible attempts by any of these groups to curtail evaluation operations or to bias or misapply the results can be averted or counteracted.

F3 **Cost-Effectiveness** The evaluation should be efficient and produce information of sufficient value so that the resources expended can be justified.

Propriety

The propriety standards are intended to ensure that an evaluation will be conducted legally, ethically, and with due regard for the welfare of those involved in the evaluation, as well as those affected by its results.

P1 **Service Orientation** Evaluations should be designed to assist organizations to address and effectively serve the needs of the full range of targeted participants.

P2 **Formal Agreements** Obligations of the formal parties to an evaluation (what is to be done, how, by whom, when) should be agreed to in writing so that these parties are obligated to adhere to all conditions of the agreement or formally to renegotiate it.

P3 **Rights of Human Subjects** Evaluations should be designed and conducted to respect and protect the rights and welfare of human subjects.

P4 **Human Interactions** Evaluators should respect human dignity and worth in their interactions with other persons associated with an evaluation so that participants are not threatened or harmed.

P5 **Complete and Fair Assessment** The evaluation should be complete and fair in its examination and recording of strengths and weaknesses of the program being evaluated so that strengths can be built upon and problem areas addressed.

P6 **Disclosure of Findings** The formal parties to an evaluation should ensure that the full set of evaluation findings along with pertinent limitations are made accessible to the persons affected by the evaluation and any others with expressed legal rights to receive the results.

P7 **Conflict of Interest** Conflict of interest should be dealt with openly and honestly, so that it does not compromise the evaluation processes and results.

P8 **Fiscal Responsibility** The evaluator's allocation and expenditure of resources should reflect sound accountability procedures and otherwise be prudent and ethically responsible so that expenditures are accounted for and appropriate.

Accuracy

The accuracy standards are intended to ensure that an evaluation will reveal and convey technically adequate information about the features that determine worth of merit of the program being evaluated.

A1 **Program Documentation** The program being evaluated should be described and documented clearly and accurately so that the program is clearly identified.

A2 **Context Analysis** The context in which the program exists should be examined in enough detail so that its likely influences on the program can be identified.

A3 **Described Purposes and Procedures** The purposes and procedures of the evaluation should be monitored and described in enough detail so that they can be identified and assessed.

A4 **Defensible Information Sources** The sources of information used in a program evaluation should be described in enough detail so that the adequacy of the information can be assessed.

A5 **Valid Information** The information-gathering procedures should be chosen or developed and then implemented so that they will ensure that the interpretation arrived at is valid for the intended use.

A6 **Reliable Information** The information-gathering procedures should be chosen or developed and then implemented so that they will ensure that the information obtained is sufficiently reliable for the intended use.

A7 **Systematic Information** The information collected, processed, and reported in an evaluation should be systematically reviewed, and any errors found should be corrected.

A8 **Analysis of Quantitative Information** Quantitative information in an evaluation should be appropriately and systematically analyzed so that evaluation questions are effectively answered.

A9 **Analysis of Qualitative Information** Qualitative information in an evaluation should be appropriately and systematically analyzed so that evaluation questions are effectively answered.

A10 **Justified Conclusions** The conclusions reached in an evaluation should be explicitly justified so that stakeholders can assess them.

A11 **Impartial Reporting** Reporting procedures should guard against distortion caused by personal feelings and biases of any party to the evaluation so that evaluation reports fairly reflect the evaluation findings.

A12 **Meta-evaluation** The evaluation itself should be formatively and summatively evaluated against these and other pertinent standards so that its conduct is appropriately guided and, on completion, stakeholders can closely examine its strengths and weaknesses.

SOURCE: Joint Committee on Standards. (1994). *Program evaluation standards* (2nd ed.).

APPENDIX B

Evaluation Research Society Standards for Program Evaluation

Formulation and Negotiation

1. The purpose and characteristics of the program or activity to be addressed in the evaluation should be specified as precisely as possible.

2. The clients, decision makers, and potential users of the evaluation results should be identified and their information needs and expectations made clear. Where appropriate, evaluators should also help identify areas of public interest in the program.

3. The type of evaluation that is most appropriate should be identified and its objective made clear; the range of activities to be undertaken should be specified.

4. An estimate of the cost of the proposed evaluation and, where appropriate, of alternatives should be provided; this estimate should be prudent, ethically responsible, and based on sound accounting principles.

5. Agreement should be reached at the outset that the evaluation is likely to produce information of sufficient value, applicability, and potential use to justify its cost.

6. The feasibility of undertaking the evaluation should be estimated either informally or through formal evaluability assessment.

7. Restrictions, if any, on access to the data and results from an evaluation should be clearly established and agreed to between the evaluator and the client at the outset.

8. Potential conflicts of interest should be identified, and steps should be taken to avoid compromising the evaluation processes and results.

9. Respect for and protection of the rights and welfare of all parties to the evaluation should be a central consideration in the negotiation process.
10. Accountability for the technical and financial management of the evaluation once it is undertaken should be clearly defined.
11. All agreements reached in the negotiation phase should be specified in writing, including schedule, obligations, and involvements of all parties to the evaluation, and policies and procedures on access to the data. When plans or conditions change, these, too, should be specified.
12. Evaluators should not accept obligations that exceed their professional qualifications or the resources available to them.

Structure and Designs

13. For all types of evaluation, a clear approach or design should be specified and justified as appropriate to the types of conclusions and inferences to be drawn.
14. For impact studies, the central evaluation design problem of estimating the effects of nontreatment and the choice of a particular method for accomplishing this should be fully described and justified.
15. If sampling is to be used, the details of the sampling methodology (choice of unit, method of selection, time frame, and so forth) should be described and justified, based on explicit analysis of the requirements of the evaluation, including generalization.
16. The measurement methods and instruments should be specified and described, and their reliability and validity should be estimated for the population or phenomena to be measured.
17. Justification should be provided that appropriate procedures and instruments have been specified.
18. The necessary cooperation of program staff, affected institutions, and members of the community, as well as those directly involved in the evaluation, should be planned and assurances of cooperation obtained.

Data Collection and Preparation

19. A data collection preparation plan should be developed in advance of data collection.

20. Provision should be made for the detection, reconciliation, and documentation of departures from the original design.

21. Evaluation staff should be selected, trained, and supervised to ensure competence, consistency, impartiality, and ethical practice.

22. All data collection activities should be conducted so that the rights, welfare, dignity, and worth of individuals are respected and protected.

23. The estimated validity and reliability of data collection instruments and procedures should be verified under the prevailing circumstances of their use.

24. Analysis of the sources of error should be undertaken, and adequate provisions for quality assurance and control should be established.

25. The data collection and preparation procedures should provide safeguards so that the findings and reports are not distorted by any biases of data collectors.

26. Data collection activities should be conducted with minimum disruption to the program under study and with minimum imposition on the organizations or persons from whom data are gathered.

27. Procedures that may entail adverse effects or risks should be subjected to independent review and then used only with informed consent of the parties affected.

28. Data should be handled and stored so that release to unauthorized persons is prevented and access to individually identifying data is limited to those with a need to know.

29. Documentation should be maintained of the source, method of collection, circumstances of collection, and processes of preparation for each item of data.

30. Appropriate safeguards should be employed to ensure against irrecoverable loss of data through catastrophic events.

Data Analysis and Interpretation

31. The analytic procedures should be matched to the purposes of the evaluation, the design, and the data collection.

32. All analytic procedures, along with their underlying assumptions and limitations, should be described explicitly, and the reasons for choosing the procedures should be clearly explained.

33. Analytic procedures should be appropriate to the properties of the measures used and to the quality and quantity of the data.

34. The units of analysis should be appropriate to the way the data were collected and the types of conclusions to be drawn.

35. Justification should be provided that the appropriate analytic procedures have been applied.

36. Documentation should be adequate to make the analysis replicable.

37. When quantitative comparisons are made, indications should be provided of both statistical and practical significance.

38. Cause-and-effect interpretations should be bolstered not only by reference to the design but also by recognition and elimination of plausible rival explanations.

39. Findings should be reported in a manner that distinguishes among objective findings, opinions, judgments, and speculation.

Communication and Disclosure

40. Findings should be presented clearly, completely, and fairly.

41. Findings should be organized and stated in language understandable by decision makers and other audiences, and any recommendation should be clearly related to the findings.

42. Findings and recommendations should be presented in a framework that indicates their relative importance.

43. Assumptions should be explicitly acknowledged.

44. Limitations caused by constraints on time, resources, data availability, and so forth should be stated.

45. A complete description of how findings were derived should be accessible.

46. Persons, groups, and organizations who have contributed to the evaluation should receive feedback appropriate to their needs.

47. Disclosure should follow the legal and proprietary understandings agreed upon in advance, with the evaluator serving as a proponent for the fullest, most open disclosure appropriate.

48. Officials authorized to release the evaluation data should be specified.

49. The finished database and associated documentation should be organized in a manner consistent with the accessibility policies and procedures.

Use of Results

50. Evaluation results should be made available to appropriate users before relevant decisions must be made.

51. Evaluators should try to anticipate and prevent misinterpretations and misuses of evaluative information.

52. The evaluator should bring to the attention of decision makers and other relevant audiences suspected side effects—positive and negative —of the evaluation process.

53. Evaluators should distinguish clearly between the findings of the evaluation and any policy recommendations based on them.

54. In making recommendations about corrective courses of action, evaluators should carefully consider and indicate what is known about the probable effectiveness and costs of the recommended courses of action.

55. Evaluators should maintain a clear distinction between their role as an evaluator and any advocacy role they choose to adopt.

SOURCE: ERS Standards Committee, "Evaluation Research Society Standards for Program Evaluation" (pp. 12-15) in P. H. Rossi (Ed.), *Standards for evaluation practice* (New Directions for Program Evaluation No. 15), 1982, San Francisco: Jossey-Bass.

APPENDIX C

American Evaluation Association Guiding Principles for Evaluators

Systematic Inquiry

Evaluators conduct systematic, data-based inquiries about whatever is being evaluated.

1. Evaluators should adhere to the highest appropriate technical standards in conducting their work, whether that work is quantitative or qualitative in nature, so as to increase the accuracy and credibility of the evaluative information they produce.

2. Evaluators should explore with the client the shortcomings and strengths both of the various evaluation questions it might be productive to ask and the various approaches that might be used for answering those questions.

3. When presenting their work, evaluators should communicate their methods and approaches accurately and in sufficient detail to allow others to understand, interpret, and critique their work. They should make clear the limitations of an evaluation and its results. Evaluators should discuss in a contextually appropriate way those values, assumptions, theories, methods, results, and analyses that *significantly* affect the interpretation of the evaluative findings. These statements apply to all aspects of the evaluation—from its initial conceptualization to the eventual use of findings.

Competence

Evaluators provide competent performance to stakeholders.

1. Evaluators should possess (or, here and elsewhere as appropriate, ensure that the evaluation team possesses) the education, abilities, skills, and experience appropriate to undertake the tasks proposed in the evaluation.

2. Evaluators should practice within the limits of their professional training and competence and should decline to conduct evaluations that fall substantially outside those limits. When declining the commission or request is not feasible or appropriate, evaluators should make clear any significant limitations on the evaluation that might result. Evaluators should make every effort to gain the competence directly or through the assistance of others who possess the required expertise.

3. Evaluators should continually seek to maintain and improve their competencies in order to provide the highest level of performance in their evaluations. This continuing professional development might include formal coursework and workshops, self-study, evaluation of one's own practice, and working with other evaluators to learn from their skills and expertise.

Integrity/Honesty

Evaluators ensure the honesty and integrity of the entire evaluation process.

1. Evaluators should negotiate honestly with clients and relevant stakeholders concerning the costs, tasks to be undertaken, limitations of methodology, scope of results likely to be obtained, and uses of data resulting from a specific evaluation. It is primarily the evaluator's responsibility to initiate discussion and clarification of these matters, not the client's.

2. Evaluators should record all changes made in the originally negotiated project plans and the reasons why the changes were made. If those changes would significantly affect the scope and likely results of the evaluation, the evaluator should inform the client and other important stakeholders in a timely fashion (barring good reason to the contrary before proceeding with further work) of the changes and their likely impact.

3. Evaluators should seek to determine, and where appropriate be explicit about, their own, their clients', and other stakeholders' interests concerning the conduct and outcomes of an evaluation (including financial, political, and career interests).

4. Evaluators should disclose any roles or relationships they have concerning whatever is being evaluated that might pose a significant conflict of interest with their role as an evaluator. Any such conflict should be mentioned in reports of the evaluation results.

5. Evaluators should not misrepresent their procedures, data, or findings. Within reasonable limits, they should attempt to prevent or correct any substantial misuses of their work by others.

6. If evaluators determine that certain procedures or activities seem likely to produce misleading evaluative information or conclusions, they have the responsibility to communicate their concerns, and the reasons for them, to the client (the one who funds or requests the evaluation). If discussions with the client do not resolve these concerns, so that a misleading evaluation is then implemented, the evaluator may legitimately decline to conduct the evaluation if that is feasible and appropriate. If not, the evaluator should consult colleagues or relevant stakeholders about other proper ways to proceed (options might include, but are not limited to, discussions at a higher level, a dissenting cover letter or appendix, or refusal to sign the final document).

7. Barring compelling reason to the contrary, evaluators should disclose all sources of financial support for an evaluation and the source of the request for the evaluation.

Respect for People

Evaluators respect the security, dignity, and self-worth of the respondents, program participants, clients, and other stakeholders with whom they interact.

1. Where applicable, evaluators must abide by current professional ethics and standards regarding risks, harms, and burdens that might be engendered to those participating in the evaluation; regarding informed consent for participation in the evaluation; and regarding informing participants about the scope and limits of confidentiality. Examples of such standards include federal regulations about protection of human subjects and the ethical principles of such associations as the American Anthropological Association, the American

Educational Research Association, or the American Psychological Association. Although this principle is not intended to extend the applicability of such ethics and standards beyond their current scope, evaluators should abide by them where it is feasible and desirable to do so.

2. Because justified negative or critical conclusions from an evaluation must be explicitly stated, evaluations sometimes produce results that harm client or stakeholder interests. Under this circumstance, evaluators should seek to maximize the benefits and reduce any unnecessary harms that might occur, provided this will not compromise the integrity of the evaluation findings. Evaluators should carefully judge when the benefits from doing the evaluation or in performing certain evaluation procedures should be foregone because of the risks or harms. Where possible, these issues should be anticipated during the negotiation of the evaluation.

3. Knowing that evaluations often will negatively affect the interests of some stakeholders, evaluators should conduct the evaluation and communicate its results in a way that clearly respects the stakeholders' dignity and self-worth.

4. Where feasible, evaluators should attempt to foster the social equity of the evaluation so that those who give to the evaluation can receive some benefits in return. For example, evaluators should seek to ensure that those who bear the burdens of contributing data and incurring any risks are doing so willingly and that they have full knowledge of and maximum feasible opportunity to obtain any benefits that may be produced from the evaluation. When it would not endanger the integrity of the evaluation, respondents or program participants should be informed if and how they can receive services to which they are otherwise entitled without participating in the evaluation.

5. Evaluators have the responsibility to identify and respect differences among participants, such as differences in their culture, religion, gender, disability, age, sexual orientation, and ethnicity, and to be mindful of potential implications of these differences when planning, conducting, analyzing, and reporting their evaluations.

Responsibilities for General and Public Welfare

Evaluators articulate and take into account the diversity of interests and values that may be related to the general and public welfare.

1. When planning and reporting evaluations, evaluators should consider including important perspectives and interests of the full range of stakeholders in the object being evaluated. Evaluators should carefully consider the justification when omitting important value perspectives or the views of important groups.

2. Evaluators should consider not only the immediate operations and outcomes of whatever is being evaluated but also the broad assumptions, implications, and potential side effects of it.

3. Freedom of information is essential in a democracy. Hence, barring compelling reason to the contrary, evaluators should allow all relevant stakeholders to have access to evaluative information and should actively disseminate that information to stakeholders if resources allow. If different evaluation results are communicated in forms that are tailored to the interests of different stakeholders, those communications should ensure that each stakeholder group is aware of the existence of the other communications. Communications that are tailored to a given stakeholder should always include all important results that may bear on interests of that stakeholder. In all cases, evaluators should strive to present results as clearly and simply as accuracy allows so that clients and other stakeholders can easily understand the evaluation process and results.

4. Evaluators should maintain a balance between client needs and other needs. Evaluators necessarily have a special relationship with the client who funds or requests the evaluation. By virtue of that relationship, evaluators must strive to meet legitimate client needs whenever it is feasible and appropriate to do so. However, that relationship can also place evaluators in difficult dilemmas when client interests conflict with other interests or when client interests conflict with the obligation of evaluators for systematic inquiry, competence, integrity, and respect for people. In these cases, evaluators should explicitly identify and discuss the conflicts with the client

and relevant stakeholders, resolve them when possible, determine whether continued work on the evaluation is advisable if the conflict cannot be resolved, and make clear any significant limitations on the evaluation that might result if the conflict is not resolved.

5. Evaluators have obligations that encompass the public interest and good. These obligations are especially important when evaluators are supported by publicly generated funds, but clear threats to the public good should never be ignored in any evaluation. Because the public interest and good are rarely the same as the interests of any particular group (including those of the client or funding agency), evaluators will usually have to go beyond an analysis of particular stakeholder interests when considering the welfare of society as a whole.

References

Adams, K. A. (1985). Gamesmanship for internal evaluators: Knowing when to "hold 'em" and when to "fold 'em." *Evaluation and Program Planning, 8,* 53-57.

Alkin, M. C., & Associates. (1985). *A guide for evaluation decision makers.* Beverly Hills, CA: Sage.

Amen, C. (1990). Use of the Joint Committee Standards: Benefits gained and lessons learned. *Evaluation Practice, 11*(1), 33-39.

American Educational Research Association. (1992). Ethical standards of the American Educational Research Association. *Educational Researcher, 21*(7), 23-26.

American Evaluation Association. (1995). *Guiding principles for evaluators.* Greensboro, NC: Author.

American Psychological Association. (1992). Ethical principles of psychologists and code of conduct. *American Psychologist, 47,* 1597-1611.

Andrews, K. R. (1989). *Ethics in practice: Managing the moral corporation.* Boston: Harvard Business School Press.

Archer, D., Pettigrew, T. F., & Aronson, E. (1992). Making research apply: High stakes public policy in a regulatory environment. *American Psychologist, 47*(1), 1233-1236.

Bank, A. (1985). Private thought and public actions: A commentary on articles dealing with ethical issues in evaluation. *Evaluation and Program Planning, 8,* 67-72.

Barnhart, C. L. (Ed.). (1966). *The American college dictionary.* New York: Random House.

Baumgarten, E. (1982). Ethics in academic professions: A Socratic view. *Journal of Higher Education, 53,* 282-295.

Beauchamp, T. L., & Bowie, N. E. (Eds.). (1979). *Ethical theory and business.* Englewood Cliffs, NJ: Prentice Hall.

Beauchamp, T. L., & Childress, J. F. (1983). *Principles of biomedical ethics* (2nd ed.). Oxford, England: Oxford University Press.

Bentham, J. (1970). *An introduction to the principles of morals and legislation* (J. M. Burns & H. L. A. Hart, Eds.). London: Athlone. (Original work published 1789)

Bermant, G., & Warwick, D. P. (1978). The ethics of social intervention: Power, freedom, and accountability. In G. Bermant, H. Kelman, & D. P. Warwick (Eds.), *The ethics of social intervention.* New York: John Wiley.

Blanchard, K. (1982). *The one minute manager.* New York: William Morrow.

Blanchard, K., & Peale, N. (1988). *The power of ethical management.* New York: William Morrow.

Blanck, P. D., Bellack, A. S., Rosnow, R. L., Rotheram-Borus, M. J., & Schooler, N. R. (1992). Scientific rewards and conflicts of ethical choices in human subjects research. *American Psychologist, 47*(7), 959-965.

Bok, S. (1978). *Lying: Moral choice in public and private life.* New York: Random House.

Bok, S. (1982). *Secrets: On the ethics of concealment and revelation.* New York: Pantheon.

Brandt, R. B. (1959). *Ethical theory: The problems of normative and critical ethics.* Englewood Cliffs, NJ: Prentice Hall.

Braskamp, L. A. (1994, September). *The role of the advocate.* A panel presentation at the College of Education's 75th Anniversary Symposium. University of Illinois-Urbana.

Braskamp, L. A., Brown, R. D., & Newman, D. L. (1978). The credibility of a local education program evaluation report: Author source and client audience characteristics. *American Educational Research Journal, 15*(3), 441-450.

Braybrooke, D. (1972). The firm but untidy correlativity of rights and obligations. *Canadian Journal of Philosophy, 1,* 351-363.

Brinkerhoff, R. O., Brethower, D. M., Hluchyj, T., & Nowakoski, J. R. (1983). *Program evaluation: A practitioner's guide for trainers and educators.* Boston: Kluwer-Nijoff.

Brown, R. D. (1985a). Creating an ethical community. In H. J. Canon & R. D. Brown (Eds.), *Applied ethics in student services: New directions for student services* (pp. 67-79). San Francisco: Jossey-Bass.

Brown, R. D. (1985b). Supervising evaluation practicum and intern students: A developmental model. *Educational Evaluation and Policy Analysis, 2,* 161-167.

Brown, R. D., & Dinnel, D. (1992). Exploratory studies of the usefulness of a developmental approach for supervising evaluation students. *Evaluation Review, 17*(1), 23-29.

Brown, R. D., & Krager, L. (1985). Ethical issues in graduate education: Faculty and student responsibilities. *Journal of Higher Education, 56*(4), 403-418.

Brown, R. D., Newman, D. L., & Rivers, L. S. (1984). A decision making context model for enhancing evaluation utilization. *Educational Evaluation and Policy Analysis, 6*(4), 393-400.

Brown, R. D., & Newman, D. L. (1986a, March). *Evaluator principles and evaluator behavior: What evaluators do and what clients think.* Paper presented at the annual meeting of the American Educational Research Association, San Francisco.

Brown, R. D., & Newman, D. L. (1986b, November). *Ethical principles: A comparison of the standards and frequency of violations.* Paper presented at the annual meeting of the American Evaluation Association, Kansas City, MO.

Brown, R. D., & Prentice, D. G. (1987). Assessing decision-making risk and information needs in evaluation. *Evaluation Review, 11*(3), 371-381.

Bunda, M. A. (1985). Alternative systems of ethics and their application to education and evaluation. *Evaluation and Program Planning, 8,* 25-36.

Bunda, M. A., & Halderson, C. (1985, October). *Client information requirements vs. program information needs: Applying ERS standards to programs for the gifted.* Paper presented at the annual meeting of the Evaluation Network, Toronto, Ontario.

Canon, H. J., & Brown, R. D. (1985). *Applied ethics for student services* (New Directions in Student Services, No. 30). San Francisco: Jossey-Bass.

Carpinello, S. E. (1989). *The effect of power, consequences, and the experience on nurse decision makers utilization of evaluation information: A dissertation.* Albany: State University of New York Press.

Carr, A. Z. (1989). Is business bluffing ethical? In K. R. Andrews (Ed.), *Ethics in practice: Managing the moral corporation* (pp. 99-108). Boston: Harvard Business School Press.

Cavanaugh, G. F., Moberg, D. J., & Velasquez, M. (1981). The ethics of organizational politics. *Academy of Management Review, 6*(3), 363-374.

Chalk, R., Frankel, M., & Chafer, S. (1980). *AAAS Professional Ethics Project: Professional ethics activities in the scientific and engineering societies.* Washington, DC: American Association for the Advancement of Science.

Coimbra, M. (1986). Methods and techniques used to evaluate social action programmes and projects in Brazil. In E. Solomon (Ed.), *Evaluation in Latin America and the Caribbean: Selected experiences* (pp. 123-146). Paris: UNESCO.

Collopy, B. (1988). Autonomy in long term care: Some crucial distinctions. *The Gerontologist, 28,* 10-17.

Colombo, M., & Merithew, M. (1992, November). *Searching for procedures to guide the use of direct quotations in evaluation reports.* Paper presented at the annual meeting of the American Evaluation Association, Seattle.

Cook, T. D., & Shadish, W. R., Jr. (1986). Program evaluation: The worldly science. *Annual Review of Psychology, 37,* 210.

Corey, G., Corey, M. S., & Callahan, P. (1988). *Issues and ethics in the helping professions* (3rd ed.). Pacific Grove, CA: Brooks/Cole.

Cronbach, L. J., & Associates. (1980). *Toward reform of program evaluation.* San Francisco: Jossey-Bass.

Deyhle, D. L., Hess, G. A., Jr., & LeCompte, M. D. (1992). Approaching ethical issues. In M. D. LeCompte, W. L. Millroy, & J. Preissle (Eds.), *The handbook of qualitative research in education* (pp. 597-641). San Francisco: Jossey-Bass.

Diener, E., & Crandall, R. (1978). *Ethics in social and behavioral research.* Chicago: University of Chicago Press.

D'Onofrio, A., & Ward, D. (1992, November). *A close philosophical consideration of ethical decisions in quantitative and qualitative research.* Paper presented at the annual conference of the American Evaluation Association, Seattle.

Drane, J. F. (1982). Ethics and psychotherapy: A philosophical perspective. In M. Rosenbaum (Ed.), *Ethics and values in psychotherapy* (pp. 15-50). New York: Free Press.

Drucker, P. F. (1992). *Managing for the future: The 1990s and beyond.* New York: Dutton.

Eisner, E. W. (1986, March). *Ethical tensions in qualitative research.* Paper presented at the annual meeting of the American Educational Research Association, San Francisco.

Eisner, E. W., & Peshkin, A. (Eds.). (1990). *Qualitative inquiry in education: The continuing debate.* New York: Teachers College Press.

Ericson, D. P. (1990). Social justice, evaluation, and the educational system. In K. A. Sirotnik (Ed.), *Evaluation and social justice: Issues in public education* (pp. 5-22). San Francisco: Jossey-Bass.

Farley, J., & Mertens, D. M. (1993, November). *Feminist perspectives in evaluation methodology.* Paper presented at the annual meeting of the American Evaluation Association, Dallas.

Feinberg, J. (1973). *Social philosophy.* Englewood Cliffs, NJ: Prentice Hall.

Feinberg, J. (1984). *Harm to others.* New York: Oxford University Press.

Gibson, W. T., & Pope, K. S. (1993). The ethics of counseling: A national survey of certified counselors. *Journal of Counseling and Development, 71*(3), 330-336.

Gilligan, C. (1982). *In a different voice.* Cambridge, MA: Harvard University Press.

Goodpaster, K. E. (1989). Ethical imperative and corporate leadership. In K. R. Andrews (Ed.), *Ethics in practice: Managing the moral corporation* (pp. 212-228). Boston: Harvard Business School Press.

Goodpaster, K. E., & Matthews, J. B., Jr. (1989). Can a corporation have a conscience? In K. R. Andrews (Ed.), *Ethics in practice: Managing the moral corporation* (pp. 155-166). Boston: Harvard Business School Press.

Goodrich, T. J. (1978). Strategies for dealing with the issue of subjectivity in evaluation. *Evaluation Quarterly, 2,* 631-645.

Grisso, R., Baldwin, E., Blanck, P. D., Rotheram-Borus, M. J., Schooler, N., & Thompson, R. (1991). Stands in research: APA's mechanism for monitoring the challenges. *American Psychologist, 46*(6), 758-766.

Guba, E., & Lincoln, Y. (1989). *Fourth generation evaluation.* Newbury Park, CA: Sage.

Haddad, A. M., & Kapp, M. B. (1991). *Ethical and legal issues in home health care.* Norwalk, CT: Appleton & Lange.

Harding, A. K., Gray, L. A., & Neal, M. (1993). Confidentiality limits with clients who have HIV: A review of ethical and legal guidelines and professional policies. *Journal of Counseling and Development, 71*(3), 290-296.

Hare, R. (1981). The philosophical basis of psychiatric ethics. In S. Bloch & P. Chodoff (Eds.), *Psychiatric ethics* (2nd ed., pp. 33-46). Oxford: Oxford University Press.

Harrel, G. D. (1986). *Consumer behavior.* San Diego: Harcourt Brace Jovanovich.

Hendricks, M. (1985). Should evaluators judge whether services are appropriate? *Evaluation and Program Planning, 8,* 37-44.

Honea, G. (1990, November). *Ethical dilemmas in evaluation: Interviews of evaluators.* Paper presented at the annual meeting of the American Evaluation Association, Washington, DC.

Honea, G. (1991, November). *Evaluation, policy and ethics: Mixing oil and water?* Paper presented at the annual meeting of the American Evaluation Association, Chicago.

House, E. (1976). Justice in evaluation. In G. V Glass (Ed.), *Evaluation studies review annual* (Vol. 1, pp. 75-79). Beverly Hills, CA: Sage.

House, E. (1980). *Evaluating with validity.* Beverly Hills, CA: Sage.

House, E. (1988). *Jesse Jackson and the politics of charisma: The rise and fall of the PUSH/Excel program.* Boulder, CO: Westview.

House, E. (1990). Methodology and justice. In K. Sirotnik (Ed.), *Social justice: Issues in public education* (New Directions for Program Evaluation No. 45). San Francisco: Jossey-Bass.

House, E. (1991). Evaluation and social justice: Where are we? In M. W. McLaughlin & D. C. Philips (Eds.), *Evaluation and education: At quarter century* (19th Yearbook of the National Society for the Study of Evaluation, pp. 233-247). Chicago: University of Chicago Press.

House, E. R. (1993). *Professional evaluation: Social impact and political consequences.* Newbury Park, CA: Sage.

Hume, D. (1983). *Enquiry concerning the principles of morals* (J. B. Schneewind, Ed.). Indianapolis, IN: Hackett. (Original work published 1751)

Janis, I. L., & Mann, L. (1977). *Decision making: A psychological analysis of conflict, choice, and commitment.* New York: Free Press.

Jatulis, L. L., & Newman, D. L. (1991). The role of contextual variables in evaluation decision making: Perceptions of potential loss, time, and self-efficacy on nurse managers' need for information. *Evaluation Review, 15*(3), 364-377.

Johnson, P. L. (1985). Ethical dilemmas in evaluating programs with family and related clients. *Evaluation and Program Planning, 8,* 45-51.

Joint Committee on Standards. (1981). *Standards for evaluations of educational programs, projects, and materials.* New York: McGraw-Hill.

Joint Committee on Standards. (1988). *The personnel standards: How to assess systems for evaluating educators.* Newbury Park, CA: Sage.

Joint Committee on Standards. (1994). *Program evaluation standards* (2nd ed.). Thousand Oaks, CA: Sage.

Kant, I. (1956). *Critique of practical reason* (L. W. Beck, Trans.). New York: Liberal Arts Press. (Original work published 1788)

Kimmel, A. J. (1988). *Ethics and values in applied social research* (Applied Social Research Methods Series, Vol. 12). Newbury Park, CA: Sage.

Kirkhart, K. E. (1985). Analyzing mental health evaluations: Moral and ethical dimensions. *Evaluation and Program Planning, 8,* 13-23.

Kirkhart, K. E. (1995). Seeking multicultural validity: A postcard from the road. *Evaluation Practice, 16*(1), 1-12.

Kitchener, K. S. (1984). Intuition, critical evaluation and ethical principles: The foundation for ethical decisions in counseling psychology. *The Counseling Psychologist, 12*(3), 43-56.

Kitchener, K. S. (1985). Ethical principles and ethical decisions in student affairs. In H. J. Canon & R. D. Brown (Eds.), *Applied ethics in student affairs* (New Directions for Student Services No. 30, pp. 17-30). San Francisco: Jossey-Bass.

Klaidman, S., & Beauchamp, T. L. (1986). *The virtuous journalist.* New York: Oxford University Press.

Klein, M. W. (1981). On frustration tolerance and self-flagellation: The decision to evaluate. In W. S. Davidson II, J. R. Koch, R. G. Lewis, & M. D. Wresinski (Eds.), *Evaluation strategies in criminal justice* (pp. 249-261). New York: Pergamon.

Koor, W. S. (1982). How evaluators can deal with role conflict. *Evaluation and Program Planning, 5,* 53-58.

Kozol, J. (1991). *Savage inequalities: Children in America's schools.* New York: Crown.

Krager, L. A. (1985). A new model for defining ethical behavior. In H. J. Canon & R. D. Brown (Eds.), *Applied ethics in student services* (New Directions for Student Services No. 30, pp. 31-48). San Francisco: Jossey-Bass.

Krager, L. A., & Brown, R. D. (1991). Decision making strategies by student affairs administrators: What factors make a difference. *National Student Personnel Administrators Journal, 29*(2), 121-130.

Kytle, J., & Millman, E. J. (1986). Confession of two applied researchers in search of principles. *Evaluation and Program Planning, 9,* 167-177.

Lincoln, Y. S. (1985). The ERS standards for program evaluation: Guidance for a fledgling profession. *Evaluation and Program Planning, 8,* 251-253.

Lincoln, Y. S. (1991). Toward a categorical imperative for qualitative research. In E. W. Eisner & A. Peshkin (Eds.), *Qualitative inquiry in education: The continuing debate* (pp. 277-295). New York: Teachers College Press.

Lincoln, Y. S., & Guba, E. G. (1989). Ethics: The failure of positivist science. *Review of Higher Education, 12*(3), 221-240.

Lobosco, A. F., & Newman, D. L. (1992). Stakeholder information needs: Implications for evaluator practice and policy development in early childhood special education. *Evaluation Review, 16*(5), 443-463.

Loganbill, C., Hardy, E., & Delworth, W. (1982). Supervision: A conceptual model. *The Counseling Psychologist, 10*(1), 3-42.

Love, A. J. (1991). *Internal evaluation: Building organizations from within* (Applied Social Research Methods Series, Vol. 24). Newbury Park, CA: Sage.

Madison, A. (1992). Primary inclusion of culturally diverse minority program participants in the evaluation process. In A. Madison (Ed.), *Minority issues in program evaluation* (New Directions for Program Evaluation No. 53, pp. 35-43). San Francisco: Jossey-Bass.

Marino, A. L. (1980). Evaluation of a rural development project in Colombia. In E. S. Solomon (Ed.), *Evaluating social action projects* (pp. 51-99). Paris: UNESCO.

Mason, J. P. (1989). Commentary: Issues in the Maghreb. In R. E. Conner & M. Hendricks (Eds.), *International innovations in evaluation methodology* (New Directions for Program Evaluation No. 42, pp. 49-50). San Francisco: Jossey-Bass.

Mathison, S. (1991). Role conflicts for internal evaluators. *Evaluation and Program Planning, 14,* 173-179.

May, W. F. (1980). Doing ethics: The bearing of ethical theories on fieldwork. *Social Problems, 27*(3), 358-370.

McCoy, B. H. (1989). The parable of the Sadhu. In K. R. Andrews (Ed.), *Ethics in practice: Managing the moral corporation* (pp. 201-207). Boston: Harvard Business School Press.

McKillip, J., & Garberg, R. (1986). Demands of the Joint Committee's standards for educational evaluation. *Evaluation and Program Planning, 9,* 325-333.

McLaughlin, M. W., & Phillips, D. C. (Eds.). (1991). *Evaluation and education: At a quarter century.* Chicago: University of Chicago Press.

Melton, G. B., & Gray, J. W. (1988). Ethical dilemmas in AIDS research. *American Psychologist, 43*(1), 60-64.

Merriam Webster's ninth new collegiate dictionary. (1988). Springfield, MA: Merriam Webster, Inc.

Merryfield, M. (1985). The challenge of cross-cultural evaluation: Some views from the field. In M. Q. Patton (Ed.), *Culture and evaluation* (New Directions for Program Evaluation No. 25, pp. 3-18). San Francisco: Jossey-Bass.

Mertens, D. M. (1994, November). *Implications for evaluation practice from a multicultural, feminist perspective on ethics.* Paper presented at the annual meeting of the American Evaluation Association, Boston.

Mill, J. S. (1962). *Utilitarianism: On liberty* (M. Warnock, Ed.). Cleveland, OH: World. (Original work published 1863)

Miller, B. (1981). Autonomy and the refusal of lifesaving treatment. *Hastings Center Report, 11*(4), 22-28.

Mirvis, P. H., & Seashore, S. E. (1982). Creating ethical relationships in organizational research. In J. E. Sieber (Ed.), *The ethics of social research: Surveys and experiments* (pp. 68-84). New York: Springer-Verlag.

Montejo, A., Modol, M., & Ramirez, G. (1986). Analysis of the evaluation methods used in social action projects in Central America. In E. Solomon (Ed.), *Evaluation in Latin America and the Caribbean: Selected experiences* (pp. 75-122). Paris: UNESCO.

Moos, R. H. (1979). *Evaluating educational environments.* San Francisco: Jossey-Bass.

Morris, M., & Cohn, R. (1993). Program evaluators and ethical challenges: A national survey. *Evaluation Review, 17,* 621-642.

Neilsen, W. A. (Ed.). (1936). *Webster's new international dictionary of English language* (Unabridged 2nd ed.). Springfield, MA: G. C. Merriam.

Newman, D. L. (1988, April). *Teachers' willingness to participate in evaluation: The effect of past participation and perceptions of usefulness.* Paper presented at the annual meeting of the American Educational Research Association, New Orleans.

Newman, D. L., & Brown, R. D. (1992). Violations of ethical standards: Frequency and seriousness of occurrence. *Evaluation Review, 16*(3), 219-234.

Newman, D. L., Brown, R. D., & Littman, M. I. (1979). Evaluator, report, and audience characteristics which influence the impact of evaluation reports: Does who says what to whom make a difference? *CEDR Quarterly, 12*(2), 14-18.

Newman, D. L., Brown, R. D., & Rivers, L. S. (1987). Factors influencing the decision-making process: An examination of the effect of contextual variables. *Studies in Educational Evaluation, 13,* 199-209.

Newman, D. L., Brown, R. D., Rivers, L. S., & Glock, R. F. (1983). School boards' and administrators' use of evaluation information: Influencing factors. *Evaluation Review, 7,* 110-125.

Newman, D. L., & Bull, K. S. (1986, August). *The effects of evaluator gender and ethnicity on educational evaluation.* Paper presented at the annual meeting of the American Psychological Association, Washington, DC.

Noddings, N. (1984). *Caring: A feminine approach to ethics and moral education.* Berkeley: University of California Press.

O'Neill, P., & Hern, R. (1991). A systems approach to ethical problems. *Ethics & Behavior, 1*(2), 129-143.

Ostlund, L. E. (1973). Role theory and group dynamics. In S. Ward & T. S. Robertson (Eds.), *Consumer behavior: Theoretical sources* (pp. 230-275). Englewood Cliffs, NJ: Prentice Hall.

Patton, M. Q. (Ed.). (1985). *Culture and evaluation* (New Directions for Program Evaluation No. 25). San Francisco: Jossey-Bass.

Patton, M. Q. (1986). *Utilization-focused evaluation* (2nd ed.). Beverly Hills, CA: Sage.

Peale, N. V. (1952). *The power of positive thinking.* Englewood Cliffs, NJ: Prentice Hall.

Perloff, R., & Perloff, E. (1980). Ethics in practice. In R. Perloff & E. Perloff (Eds.), *Values, ethics, and standards in evaluation* (New Directions for Program Evaluation No. 7, pp. 77-83). San Francisco: Jossey-Bass.

Perry, W. G. (1970). *Forms of intellectual and ethical development in the college years.* New York: Holt, Rinehart & Winston.

Pflum, G., & Brown, R. D. (1984). The effects of conflict, quality, and time on small group information use and behavior in evaluative decision making situations. *Evaluation and Program Planning, 7,* 35-43.

Piazza, N. J., & Yeager, R. D. (1990). Federal confidentiality regulations for substance abuse treatment facilities: A case in applied ethics. *Journal of Mental Health Counseling, 12*(2), 120-128.

Pope, K. S., Tabachnick, B. G., & Keith-Speigel, P. (1987). Ethics of practice: The beliefs and behaviors of psychologists as therapists. *American Psychologist, 42*(6), 993-1006.

Pope, K. S., & Vetter, V. A. (1992). Ethical dilemmas encountered by members of the American Psychological Association: A national survey. *American Psychologist, 47*(3), 397-411.

Posovac, E. J., & Carey, R. (1989). *Program evaluation: Methods and case studies* (3rd ed.). Englewood Cliffs, NJ: Prentice Hall.

Powell, C. J. (1984). Ethical principles and issues of competence in counseling adolescents. *The Counseling Psychologist, 12*(3), 57-73.

Rawls, J. (1971). *A theory of justice.* Cambridge, MA: Belknap Press of Harvard University Press.

Ross, W. D. (1930). *The right and the good.* New York: Oxford University Press.

Rossi, P. H. (Ed.). (1982). *Standards for evaluation practice* (New Directions for Program Evaluation No. 15). San Francisco: Jossey-Bass.

Ryan, K. E. (1994, November). *Using feminist strategies for addressing issues of social justice: Do they help?* Paper presented at the annual meeting of the American Evaluation Association, Boston.

Ryan, K. E. (1995). *Values and privilege: Ethical considerations in quantitative research.* Paper presented at the annual meeting of the American Educational Research Association, San Francisco.

Ryan, K. E., & Ory, J. C. (1993, November). *Evaluation ethics: Contributions from feminine moral thinking.* Paper presented at the annual meeting of the American Evaluation Association, Dallas.

Sankar, A. (1991). *Dying at home: A family guide for caregiving.* Baltimore, MD: Johns Hopkins University Press.

Schapiro, J. A., & Blackwell, D. L. (1987). Large-scale evaluation on a limited budget: The partnership experience. In J. Nowakowski (Ed.), *The client perspective on evaluation* (New Directions for Program Evaluation No. 36, pp. 53-62). San Francisco: Jossey-Bass.

Schepter-Hughes, N. (1982). *Saints, scholars, and schizophrenics: Mental illness in rural Ireland.* Berkeley: University of California Press.

Schwandt, T. A. (1989, November). Recapturing moral discourse in evaluation. *Educational Researcher,* pp. 11-16, 35.

Schwandt, T. A. (1992). Better living through evaluation: Images of progress shaping evaluation practice. *Evaluation Practice, 13*(2), 135-144.

Scriven, M. (1972). Pros and cons of goal-free evaluation. *Evaluation Comment, 3*(4), 1-4.

Seefeldt, F. M. (1985). Cultural considerations for evaluation consulting in the Egyptian context. In M. Q. Patton (Ed.), *Culture and evaluation* (New Directions in Program Evaluation No. 25, pp. 69-78). San Francisco: Jossey-Bass.

Shadish, W. R., Jr., Cook, T. D., & Leviton, L. C. (1991). *Foundations of program evaluation: Theories of practice.* Newbury Park, CA: Sage.

Sheinfeld, S., & Lord, G. L. (1981). The ethics of evaluation researchers: An exploration of value choices. *Evaluation Review, 5*(3), 377-391.

Sieber, J. E. (1980). Being ethical? Professional and personal decisions in program evaluation. In R. Perloff & E. Perloff (Eds.), *Values, ethics and standards in evaluation* (New Directions for Program Evaluation No. 7, pp. 51-61). San Francisco: Jossey-Bass.

Sieber, J. E. (1992). *Planning ethically responsible research: A guide for students and internal review boards* (Applied Social Research Methods Series, Vol. 31). Newbury Park, CA: Sage.

Sieber, J. E., & Sanders, N. (1978). Ethical problems in program evaluation: Roles, not models. *Evaluation and Program Planning, 1,* 117-120.

Sieber, J. E., & Sorenson, J. L. (1992). Ethical issues in community-based research and intervention. In J. Edwards, R. D. Tindale, L. Heath, & E. J. Posavac (Eds.), *Social psychological applications to social issues: Vol. 2. Methodological issues in applied social psychology* (pp. 110-137). New York: Plenum.

Simon, G. C. (1978). The psychologist as whistle blower: A case study. *Professional Psychology, 9,* 322-340.

Singer, P. (1993). *Practical ethics* (2nd ed.). Cambridge, England: Cambridge University Press.

Sirotnik, K. A. (Ed.). (1990). *Evaluation and social justice: Issues in public education* (New Directions for Program Evaluation No. 45). San Francisco: Jossey-Bass.

Smith, L. M. (1991). Ethics in qualitative field research: An individual perspective. In E. W. Eisner & A. Peshkin (Eds.), *Qualitative inquiry in education: The continuing debate* (pp. 258-276). New York: Teachers College Press.

Smith, N. L. (1985). Some characteristics of moral problems in evaluation practice. *Evaluation and Program Planning, 8,* 5-11.

Snow, D. L., & Gersick, K. E. (1986). Ethics and professional issues in mental health consultation. In F. V. Manino, E. J. Trickett, M. F. Shore, M. G. Kidder, & F. G. Levin (Eds.), *Handbook of mental health consultation* (pp. 393-431). Rockville, MD: National Institute of Mental Health.

Soltis, J. D. (1990a). The ethics of qualitative research. In E. W. Eisner & A. Peshkin (Eds.), *Qualitative inquiry in education: The continuing debate* (pp. 247-257). New York: Teachers College Press.

Soltis, J. D. (1990b). Response to the commentary by Lincoln. In E. W. Eisner & A. Peshkin (Eds.), *Qualitative inquiry in education: The continuing debate* (pp. 302-308). New York: Teachers College Press.

Stacey, J. (1990). *Brave new families.* New York: Basic Books.

Stake, R. E. (1978, February). The case study method in social inquiry. *Educational Researcher,* pp. 5-8.

Stein, J., & Su, P. Y. (Eds.). (1978). *The Random House dictionary.* New York: Ballantine.

Stern, G. G. (1970). *People in context.* New York: John Wiley.

Stockdill, S. H. (1987). Evaluation standards: A study of their appropriateness in business and education. *Dissertation Abstracts International, 47*(8), 2967A.

Stufflebeam, D. L. (1991). Professional standards and ethics for evaluators. In M. W. McLaughlin & D. C. Phillips (Eds.), *Evaluation and education: At quarter century* (19th Yearbook of the National Society for the Study of Education, pp. 249-282). Chicago: University of Chicago Press.

Susko, M. A. (Ed.). (1992). *Cry of the invisible: Writings from the homeless and survivors of psychiatric hospitals.* New York: Conservatory Press.

Tarasoff v. Regents of the University of California, *California Reporter,* 131, 14 (1976).

Taylor, C. (1992). *The ethics of authenticity.* Cambridge, MA: Harvard University Press.

Thompson, R. J. (1989). Evaluator as power broker: Issues in the Maghreb. In R. E. Conner & M. Hendricks (Eds.), *International innovation in evaluation methodology* (New Directions for Program Evaluation No. 42, pp. 39-47). San Francisco: Jossey-Bass.

Thornton, R., & Nardi, P. M. (1980). The dynamics of role acquisition. *American Journal of Sociology, 80*(4), 870-878.

Toms, K. T. (1993). *A Canadian-American cross national study of the personal and professional ethical structure of evaluators.* Unpublished doctoral dissertation, State University of New York at Albany.

Upcraft, M. L., & Poole, T. G. (1991). Ethical issues and administration politics. In P. L. Moore (Ed.), *Managing the political dimension of student affairs* (New Directions for Student Services No. 55, pp. 75-92). San Francisco: Jossey-Bass.

Van Hoose, W. H., & Kottler, J. A. (1977). *Ethical and legal issues in counseling and psychotherapy.* San Francisco, CA: Jossey-Bass.

Victor, B., & Cullen, J. (1988). The organizational bases of ethical climate. *Administrative Science Quarterly, 33*(1), 101-126.

Wilensky, H. L. (1964). The professionalization of everyone? *American Journal of Sociology, 70,* 137-158.

Williams, D. D. (1986). Naturalistic evaluation: Potential conflict between evaluation standards and criteria for conducting naturalistic inquiry. *Educational Evaluation and Policy Analysis, 8*(1), 87-99.

Winston, R. B., Jr., & McCaffrey, S. S. (1983). Ethical practices in student affairs administration. In T. K. Miller, R. B. Winston, Jr., & W. R. Mendenhall (Eds.), *Administrative leadership in student affairs: Actualizing student development in higher education* (pp. 167-191). Muncie, IN: Accelerated Development.

Worthen, B. R., & Sanders, J. R. (1987). *Educational evaluation: Alternative approaches and practical guidelines.* New York: Longman.

For Further Reading

Brown, R. D., & Newman, D. L. (1983, April). *A decision making context model for enhancing evaluation utilization.* Paper presented at the annual meeting of the American Educational Research Association, Montreal.

Brown, R. D., & Newman, D. L. (1985, October). *Ethical principles and evaluator roles.* Paper presented at a joint meeting of the Evaluation Network and Evaluation Research Society, Toronto.

Brown, R. D., & Newman, D. L. (1987, April). *Developmental task assessment scale for research and evaluation students.* Paper presented at the annual meeting of the American Educational Research Association, Washington, DC.

Brown, R. D., & Newman, D. L. (1988, April). *Developmental research task assessment scale: Independence of the domains and validity.* Paper presented at the annual meeting of the American Educational Research Association, New Orleans.

Brown, R. D., & Newman, D. L. (1992a, November). *A model for ethical decision making for evaluators.* Paper presented at the annual meeting of the American Evaluation Association, Seattle.

Brown, R., D., & Newman, D. L. (1992b). Ethical principles and evaluation standards: Do they match? *Evaluation Review, 16*(6), 650-663.

Brown, R. D., Newman, D. L., & Rivers, L. S. (1981, October). *A model for utilizing decision theory in evaluation.* Paper presented at the annual meeting of the Evaluation Network, Austin, TX.

Brown, R. D., Newman, D. L., & Rivers, L. S. (1985). An exploratory study of contextual factors as influences on school board evaluation information needs for decision making. *Educational Evaluation and Policy Analysis,* 7(4), 437-445.

Newman, D. L. (1986). *Evaluation standards: Are they related to ethical principles and evaluator roles?* Paper presented at the annual meeting of the Canadian Evaluation Society, Banff, Alberta.

Newman, D. L. (1988, October). *Decision making and interpersonal influence theory: A framework for research on utilization.* Paper presented at the annual meeting of the American Evaluation Association, San Francisco.

Newman, D. L. (1989, March). *Administrators' willingness to participate in evaluation: Effect of past participation.* Paper presented at the annual meeting of the American Educational Research Association, San Francisco.

Newman, D. L., Bauer, S. M., Toms, K. T., & Rinne, C. (1990, November). *Does it help or hurt? What teachers think about program evaluation.* Paper presented at the annual meeting of the American Evaluation Association, Washington, DC.

Newman, D. L., & Brown, R. D. (1987a, April). *Violations of ethical standards: Do they occur and are they serious?* Paper presented at the annual meeting of the American Educational Research Association, Washington, DC.

Newman, D. L., & Brown, R. D. (1987b, October). *Ethical reasoning and the standard for evaluation: Do the guidelines represent ethical principles?* Paper presented at the annual meeting of the American Evaluation Association, Boston.

Newman, D. L., & Brown, R. D. (1993, April). *Ethics in program evaluation: Transferring the theoretical to practice.* Paper presented at the annual meeting of the American Educational Research Association, Atlanta.

Newman, D. L., Jatulis, L., & Carpinello, S. E. (1990). What is evaluation? Nurse decision makers' perceptions of program evaluation. *Journal of NYSNA, 21*(3), 10-14.

Ziobrowski, E. M. (1992). *Teacher perceptions of opportunities and willingness to be involved in program evaluation decision making.* Unpublished doctoral dissertation, State University of New York at Albany.

Ziobrowski, E. M., & Newman, D. L. (1992, November). *Opportunities for participation in program evaluation: The role of shared decision making.* Paper presented at the annual meeting of the American Evaluation Association, Seattle.

Ziobrowski, E. M., & Newman, D. L. (1993, April). *Teacher perceptions of program evaluation: Opportunities for shared decision making.* Paper presented at the annual meeting of the American Educational Research Association, Atlanta.

Index

About the Authors

Dianna L. Newman is an Associate Professor at the University of Albany/ State University of New York where she teaches program evaluation and directs the Evaluation Consortium. She has applied evaluation experience as an internal evaluator for a public school system and a public utility and is currently directing evaluation projects in the fields of health and mental health as well as education. She is author or coauthor of over 50 articles related to the field of program evaluation and has presented over 100 papers at regional and national conferences on the practice and theories of evaluation. Her research on the utilization of evaluation is widely published, and she is currently working on a contextual model of use for program evaluation. Theoretical and empirical works have appeared in numerous journals, including *Educational Evaluation and Policy Analysis, Evaluation Review,* and *Evaluation and the Health Professions.* She is active in both the American Evaluation Association and the American Educational Research Association through presentations, committee service, and work with students and new professionals entering the field of evaluation. She has served on the Board of Directors of the American Evaluation Association, was a member of the task force that drafted the Guiding Principles for Evaluators, and chaired AEA's Ethics Committee. She is a member of the Joint Committee on Standards for Educational Evaluation. She has served on the editorial board of *New Directions in Program Evaluation*, chaired the AERA Special Interest Group Research on Evaluation, and is on the editorial board of *Applied Measurement in Education.*

Robert D. Brown is the Carl A. Happold Distinguished Professor Emeritus of Educational Psychology at the University of Nebraska-Lincoln and Senior Associate with Aspen Professional Development Associates. He has served in administrative, research, and student affairs positions including Director of the Counseling Center, Director of Student Affairs Research, Assistant Vice President for the University of Nebraska, and Assistant Dean of Teachers College. He was president of the American College Personnel Association and editor of the *Journal of College Student Development* (1983-1988) and serves on several editorial boards. He taught graduate classes in educational research, college student development, and program evaluation. He has published over 150 articles and chapters, which include empirical research articles on college student life and information use by educational decision makers, and has written or edited six books, including *Utilization of Evaluation Information* with Larry Braskamp, *Applied Ethics in Student Services* with Harry Canon, and *Performance Appraisal as a Tool for Staff Development in Student Services.* He is a recipient of the University of Nebraska Distinguished Teaching Award in 1978 and again in 1992, the Burlington-Northern Outstanding Teacher-Scholar Award in 1986, and the American College Personnel Association Outstanding Contribution to Knowledge Award in 1979 and Senior Scholar award in 1984. He was awarded the 1993 Robert H. Shaffer Award for Academic Excellence as a Graduate Faculty Member by the National Association of Student Personnel Administrators.